DESIGN & THE DECORATIVE ARTS

GEORGIAN BRITAIN 1714-1837

DESIGN & THE DECORATIVE ARTS

GEORGIAN BRITAIN 1714-1837

Michael Snodin and John Styles

V&A Publications
Distributed by Harry N. Abrams, Inc., Publishers

First published by V&A Publications, 2004

V&A Publications
160 Brompton Road
London SW3 1HW

Originally published as part of
Design and the Decorative Arts: Britain 1500–1900, 2001

Distributed in North America by Harry N. Abrams, Incorporated, New York

ISBN 0-8109-6618-2 (Harry N. Abrams, Inc)

Library of Congress Control Number 2003110743

Designed by Janet James

Front cover illustration: Teapot with London hallmarks for 1774–5. Marks of James Young and Orlando Jackson. VAM M.24c–1974.
Back cover illustration: Pattern book with worsted wool samples mounted on paper, 1763. VAM 67–1885.
Frontispiece: Snuff box, about 1765–75. VAM C.470–1914.
Contents page: Crayfish salt cellar, 1752–6. VAM C.73–1938.

Printed in Italy

HARRY N. ABRAMS, Inc
100 Fifth Avenue
New York, N.Y. 10011
www.abramsbooks.com

Contents

Acknowledgements

Planning, writing and editing this book and its companion volumes was an integral part of the wider British Galleries project at the V&A. As the book's editors and principal authors, we owe a great debt of gratitude to Christopher Wilk, who led the British Galleries project, Alan Borg, former Director of the V&A, Gwyn Miles, Director of Projects & Estate, and to all the staff of the project, in particular to Leela Meinertas, the Hanoverian Gallery Team Co-ordinator.

For ideas, references and advice on illustrations we are grateful to Cathy Arbuthnot, Richard Edgcumbe, Werner Freundel, Hazel Forsyth, Eileen Harris, Anthony Kersting, Julia Muir, Sarah Medlam, Christopher Nicholson, Michael Sonenscher, Alex Werner, the late Clive Wainwright and James Yorke, as well as to all our fellow contributors to the book. Thanks are also due to the many students on the V&A/RCA M.A. Course in the History of Design who have written relevant essays and dissertations, from which we learned much. We are grateful to Anthony Burton, Maurice Howard, Joanna Innes and Amanda Vickery for reading sections of the text and commenting on them.

We would like to thank the following people for their hard work and support: Mary Butler at V&A Publications and the team she assembled, especially project manager Geoff Barlow, copy-editor Mandy Greenfield, designer Janet James and indexer John Noble; the V&A's photographers and the staff of the V&A Picture Library; Kim Smith; Alicia Weisberg-Roberts; Paul Greenhalgh and Carolyn Sargentson.

Finally we must register our gratitude to our colleagues in the Department of Prints, Drawings and Paintings at the V&A and on the V&A/RCA M.A. Course in the History of Design, and most importantly, to our families. Thank you.

The book is dedicated to our fathers.

Michael Snodin and John Styles

Notes for Readers

For books and prints, the place of publication is London unless otherwise stated. For objects, the country of manufacture is Great Britain unless otherwise stated. Illustrations are numbered by chapter. Cross-references to illustrations take the form 3:12, the first number indicating the chapter, the second the illustration number. In the captions, h. indicates height, w. width, l. length and diam. diameter. Dimensions are provided only in those cases where the size of an object is unclear or is discussed in the text.

Foreword

This book originally appeared as the middle section of *Design and the Decorative Arts: Britain 1500–1900*, the book published to complement and contextualize the Victoria & Albert Museum's new British Galleries 1500–1900, opened in November 2001. *Design and the Decorative Arts: Georgian Britain 1714–1837* now appears as a separate paperback, alongside its Tudor and Stuart and Victorian counterparts, to make the subject accessible to a wider audience.

Like the V&A's British Galleries, this book is primarily concerned with those apparently functional, but often deliberately aesthetically pleasing objects which fall between the traditional concerns of the fine arts and architecture. They include furniture, ceramics, metalwares, textiles and clothing, graphic works of various kinds, as well as the immensely varied products of manufacturing we associate with the phrase 'industrial design'. These are the objects which have come to constitute the territory of design in its most familiar modern usage.

The question of design is central to this book. The earliest meaning of the word in Britain was close to the Italian term *disegno* and was intimately linked to the activity of drawing. Thus a design was a drawing or print, and the activity of designing was to make a drawing which would enable a two- or three-dimensional object to be made, whether by hand, machine, or a combination of the two. More recently, the term design has often been used to refer exclusively to modern objects, especially those whose appearance was shaped by architects, industrial or product designers, by the tenets of twentieth-century Modernism, or the imperatives of industrial mass production. In this context the focus is on the final look of the object – its design. By contrast, historic objects like those in the V&A have been described as decorative, or applied, art. These are nineteenth-century terms which aimed to associate decorative, practical or utilitarian objects with the status of the fine arts, whilst continuing to differentiate them from it. The term decorative art, unlike applied art, still has popular currency and is therefore used in the title of this book.

Yet even before the nineteenth century, the word design could have the broader meaning of an intention, a plan, or a conception. Today it is this meaning which prevails when we use the word design in relation to objects. When we speak of an object's design we mean its overall characteristics and the processes that have taken place in order to create it. It is in this sense that the word design is employed in this book. The book identifies design as a complex and multi-layered process, including research, experimentation, manufacture, marketing and use, rather than concerning itself solely with the history of drawn or printed designs, or with the appearance of the finished object.

The V&A is Britain's National Museum of Art and Design. Its collections represent what people at various periods in the past – patrons, consumers, collectors, curators – have considered to be the best of their kind in aesthetic terms. This book, rooted as it is in the V&A's collections, reflects this history of institutional collecting. As a consequence, it deals principally with what are referred to as high-design objects. These were objects that embodied a deliberate striving after the most prized aesthetic effects of their era. They were made to be used by the economically and socially privileged whose tastes dictated what was considered beautiful and fashionable at any time. It was they who commanded the resources necessary to procure the most expensive materials and to enjoy the fruits of the most skilled techniques of manufacture. The book acknowledges that these high-design objects were only one element in the wider visual culture that prevailed in Georgian Britain, a visual culture which in many of its more everyday aspects remains poorly understood. It is able to address a wider range of objects than the British Galleries and place them in a deeper historical context. Where possible, it makes reference to everyday objects and to the people for whom and by whom they were made.

The book is organized around four distinct but complementary questions: What were the formal aesthetics of different styles? Which people and institutions led taste? How did new modes of living lead to the design of new types of objects or the increased consumption of existing ones? What was new, in terms of products, materials and techniques of manufacture? Different questions might have been asked, but these four themes would inevitably form the core of them. It is not a book about the history of Georgian Britain, although its introduction links design to that broader history. Nor is it a history of British designers, although many of them grace its pages. Rather it is a book about design in Georgian Britain. It considers what was distinctively British about British design, but it also explores the ways that 'Britishness' was constructed, more often than not, by the creative adaptation of objects and visual ideas that originated elsewhere. Britain is taken to mean the territory of Great Britain, in other words England, Scotland and Wales.

CHAPTER 1

Introduction

JOHN STYLES

1. Georgian preoccupations

In 1715 the Scottish lawyer and architect Colen Campbell published a book of architectural prints entitled *Vitruvius Britannicus*. Its title points to two of its most important features. The mention of Vitruvius, the architectural author whose writings had survived from ancient Rome, demonstrates Campbell's obsession with classical accuracy. The reference to Britain testifies to the book's patriotic rejection of French influence on architecture, which, Campbell believed, had been excessive under the later Stuart monarchs. Against the French, Campbell held up two men as models of classical purity in architectural design – the seventeenth-century English court architect Inigo Jones and the sixteenth-century Italian architect, Andrea Palladio, who inspired much of Jones's work.

Prominent among the prints in *Vitruvius Britannicus* was an engraving of Campbell's own design for Wanstead House, a palatial mansion then being built in the neo-Palladian style in the Essex countryside, close to the outskirts of London (*see 2:8*). Campbell designed Wanstead for Sir Richard Child, the heir to an East India Company fortune, but it was the young nobleman, the third Earl of Burlington, who was to become Campbell's principal patron. Burlington promoted Campbell's ideas and developed them, giving Campbell's new approach to architecture a cachet that was both intellectual and social, and which could not have been supplied by Campbell himself.

Vitruvius Britannicus was to become the single most influential work of architecture published in the Georgian era; and Wanstead its single most influential building. Emerging together, in the immediate aftermath of George I's coronation in 1714, the book and the house embody a number of the Georgian period's deepest cultural preoccupations. Between them they exemplify many of the imperatives that were to shape design and architecture in Georgian Britain – the hunger for authentic classical precedent; the cultural

1 Detail of *Wanstead House*, about 1780. By George Robertson. The house designed by Colen Campbell. Built 1715–20 for Sir Richard Child. Pen, ink and wash. VAM E.2517-1938.

leadership of the nobility and professional designers, rather than of royalty; the power of the printed image; the influence of urban, mercantile wealth; and the spur of international competition, particularly vis-à-vis the French. Fittingly, therefore, Wanstead was not to outlast the Georgian era. It was demolished in 1822, precisely at the time when a very different set of preoccupations was coming to dominate design and architecture, preoccupations that we now regard as characteristically Victorian.

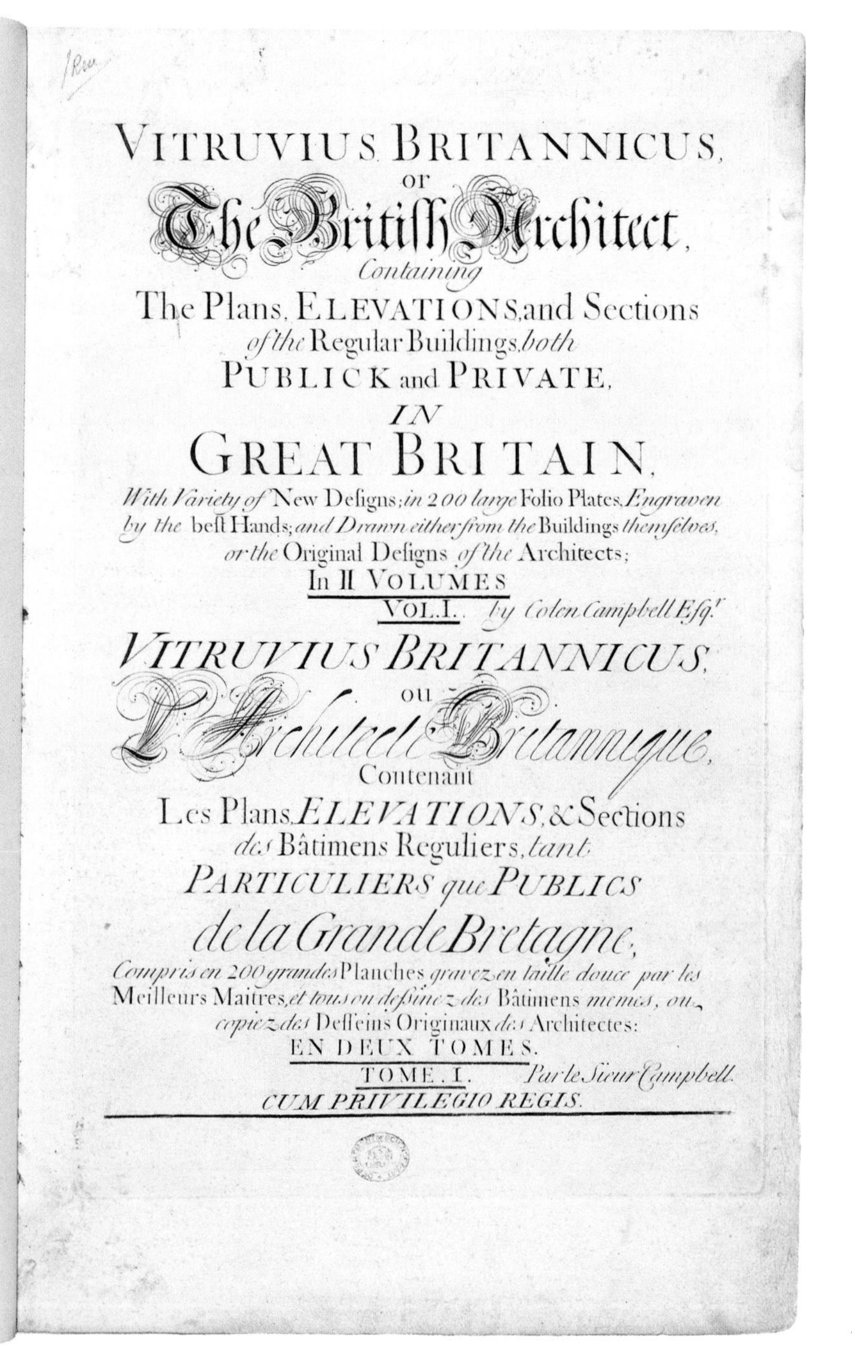

VITRUVIUS BRITANNICUS,
or
The British Architect,
Containing
The Plans, ELEVATIONS, and Sections
of the Regular Buildings, both
PUBLICK and PRIVATE,
IN
GREAT BRITAIN,
With Variety of New Designs; in 200 large Folio Plates, Engraven
by the best Hands; and Drawn either from the Buildings themselves,
or the Original Designs of the Architects;
In II VOLUMES
VOL. I. by Colen Campbell Esq.r
VITRUVIUS BRITANNICUS,
ou
L'Architecte Britannique,
Contenant
Les Plans, ELEVATIONS, & Sections
des Bâtimens Reguliers, tant
PARTICULIERS que PUBLICS
de la Grande Bretagne,
Compris en 200 grandes Planches gravez en taille douce par les
Meilleurs Maitres, et tous ou desinez des Bâtimens memes, ou
copiez des Desseins Originaux des Architectes:
EN DEUX TOMES.
TOME. I. Par le Sieur Campbell.
CUM PRIVILEGIO REGIS.

2

2 Title-page from *Vitruvius Britannicus* by Colen Campbell, vol. 1, second edition, 1725. A reprint of the title-page of the first edition. Engraving. VAM 64.H.93.

2. The political regime

George I, the Elector of the German state of Hanover, became King of Great Britain and Ireland in 1714, not because he was the direct hereditary heir to the throne, but because he fulfilled religious conditions laid down by his new subjects. To be more precise, he fulfilled conditions laid down by a parliament elected by the small minority of his subjects who were entitled to vote – roughly the wealthiest quarter of the adult male population. Undemocratic this electorate may have been, but the control it exercised over the monarchy was in marked contrast to the experience of most of George's fellow monarchs across the English Channel. The vast majority of European states at the start of the eighteenth century were monarchies, ruled by princes, kings or emperors, but most of the monarchs in continental Europe claimed to rule by God's will, as revealed through the direct hereditary succession. The most renowned exponent of this view of monarchy was Louis XIV of France (reigned 1643–1715), who styled himself the Sun King, because just as all light and warmth radiated across the solar system from the sun, so in France all authority was said to derive from the King. With a few exceptions, continental monarchs did not have to worry about troublesome constraints on their authority imposed by parliaments representing the views of their subjects. In principle, at least, they ruled alone.

The peculiar circumstances of George I's accession to the British throne tell us a great deal about the country over which he was to reign. Great Britain at the beginning of the eighteenth century was one of the most aggressively Protestant countries in Europe. For the majority of the English, at least, national identity was inextricably tied up with belief in the Protestant religion and violent hostility to the Roman Catholicism promoted by the country's principal foreign rival, France. Such was this hostility that a large proportion of the ruling élite was prepared to override the hereditary principle and endorse the enthronement of a non-English-speaking king from one of the less prominent German states; a king who had only a tenuous genealogical claim to the British throne. 'A Protestant country can never have stable times under a Popish Prince,' wrote one bishop in justification of the succession of the new German king, 'any more than a flock of sheep can have quiet when a wolf is their shepherd.' The Protestant succession was achieved by an Act of Parliament, an indication that, in contrast to countries like France and Spain, Britain enjoyed a mixed constitution. It was far from being a democracy, but Parliament – an institution that represented at least some of the people – was a more important source of authority than the monarch. Yet this was a country where political divisions over religion, the monarchy and the constitution ran deep, as the Jacobite rebellions of 1715 and 1745 indicate. These divisions found expression in an intense rivalry between the two main political parties, the Tories and the Whigs. It was the Whigs, militantly anti-Catholic and anti-Jacobite, who were to monopolize government between 1714 and the 1750s.

3. Britain in Europe

The intensity of these political divisions should not surprise us, because they were rooted in a history of repeated political upheavals in the previous century, upheavals that had resulted in one king losing his head and another being forced into permanent exile. Yet Britain's long-standing reputation for political division and instability was not sufficient to deter the ruler of a middle-sized European principality from leaving his native Germany for Britain in order to become its king.

Early eighteenth-century Britain had a number of attractions for its new monarch. It was certainly wealthy, although for some continentals its wealth did not always compensate for its shortcomings. 'A cold, dark, dull, dirty country, where there is nothing but money' was how the poet James Thompson summed up prevailing French attitudes to England in 1732. But it was not just money that excited French resentment. Britain was also newly powerful on the international stage. The Peace of Utrecht in 1713 had brought to an end the long period of warfare between the major European powers dating from 1689. These wars had arisen out of Louis XIV's ambitions for French dominance in Europe. Britain emerged from the conflict immensely strengthened. Within the British Isles, the Act of Union between England and Scotland in 1707 brought about the political integration of the British mainland. Protestant dominance in Ireland, initially established by Oliver Cromwell in the 1650s, had been reinforced in the 1690s. In Europe, Britain's leadership of the coalitions that had contained France made the country a major military and political power for the first time since the Middle Ages. In the extra-European world, Britain's colonies in North America and the West Indies had been safeguarded and extended and its trading links with India and China reinforced. Moreover, Britain was on the point of usurping the position of the Dutch as the leading European commercial power. This, too, prompted French resentment. 'The French were jealous of England,' one visitor to Paris reported on his return in 1727, 'they said that we were for engrossing the whole commerce of the world.'

In 1714, therefore, Britain enjoyed a new respect among the states of Europe for its achievements in the spheres of war, diplomacy and commerce. That respect did not, however, extend to design and the decorative arts. In these spheres it was France that dominated the rest of Europe in the first half of the eighteenth century. As the French visitor Marie-Anne du Bocage remarked in 1750, 'though there is great luxury in England, it does not come up to ours, which the people of the country imitate nevertheless, as all other nations of Europe do'. Britain's neighbours saw little that was admirable or even worthy of comment, while its natives complained about the country's subservience to French taste: 'we Englishmen are justly styled apes of the French,' protested the Buckinghamshire gentleman Edmund Verney at the end of the seventeenth century. In the course of the Georgian period this state of affairs was to be transformed. By the second half of the eighteenth century British design and decorative arts had become the subject of esteem and imitation throughout continental Europe and beyond. In the 1760s even a Frenchman like Jean-Paul Grosley could extol 'the perfection of all English manufactures, whether of steel or needlework'.

3 Jug, mid-18th century. Made in Staffordshire. The portrait shows Prince Charles Edward Stuart, the Young Pretender, son and heir of the Stuart claimant to the British throne. He led the Jacobite rebellion of 1745. Salt-glazed earthenware. VAM 414:929-1885.

4 *Taste in High Life*, 1746. By William Hogarth. Hogarth ridicules the subservience of wealthy Britons to French fashions in dress and food. The man is wearing his Parisian finery, while the monkey reads a menu listing French dishes. Engraving. VAM F.118:129.

GEORGIAN MONARCHS, 1714–1837

John Styles

Despite 18 pregnancies and five children who survived birth, Queen Anne (1702–14), the last Stuart monarch, had no direct heirs. None of her children lived to adulthood. She was succeeded by George, ruler of the Electorate of Hanover, one of a patchwork of kingdoms, electorates, principalities and statelets that made up Germany in the eighteenth century. He ascended the throne of Great Britain and Ireland as George I (1714–27), and at the same time continued to rule Hanover. His direct male descendants – his son George II (1727–60), his great-grandson George III (1760–1820) and his great-great-grandsons George IV (1820–30) and William IV (1830–7) – were to reign in Britain, Ireland and Hanover until William's death in 1837. William was succeeded by his niece Victoria (1837–1901). Women were not, however, permitted to rule in Hanover, so there he was succeeded by Victoria's uncle, Ernest, Duke of Cumberland, and the direct British royal link with Hanover was severed.

British kings from George I to William IV are collectively known as the Hanoverian dynasty, although the 123 years of their rule are more familiar as the Georgian period. The family had a weakness for the name George and, for all but the last seven of those years, it was a George who occupied the throne.

In 1714 George I had never been to Britain and spoke hardly any English. Indeed, by birth he was only 59th in line to the British throne, but those with a stronger genealogical claim were Catholics and therefore excluded by the Act of Settlement passed by Parliament in 1701. George was eligible to become King because he was a Protestant. The Act of Settlement was intended to bar from the throne the remaining Catholic members of the Stuart family, who in strictly genealogical terms constituted the legitimate royal family. This branch of the royal line was descended from the militantly Catholic James II (1685–8), who had been removed from the throne and exiled in what his victorious Protestant enemies termed the 'Glorious Revolution' of 1688. In 1714 his exiled son, also a committed Catholic, continued to claim the English throne as James III. The following year he led his supporters, known as Jacobites, in an unsuccessful attempt to seize back the throne by means of a military campaign in Scotland and northern England. His son Charles, now best known as Bonnie Prince Charlie, was to attempt the same thing in 1745, with no greater success. On his father's death in 1766, he too claimed the British throne as Charles III.

6. *George II*, 1760. By John Michael Rysbrack. Marble. VAM A.10-1932.

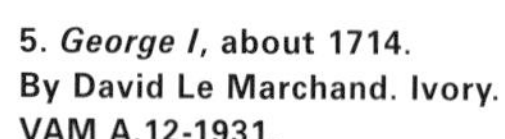

5. *George I*, about 1714. By David Le Marchand. Ivory. VAM A.12-1931.

7. *George III*, 1776–7. By John Nost the Younger. Marble. VAM A.3-1957.

8. *George IV*, 1831. Reigned as Regent 1811–20 during his father's illness, and as King 1820–30. By Samuel Joseph. Marble. VAM A.12-1956.

9. *William IV*, 1835. By Sir Francis Chantrey. Marble. © The Worshipful Company of Goldsmiths.

10. Jacobite fan, 1714–30. The images portrayed are, from left to right: Charles II in the Boscobel Oak; Queen Anne being raised to heaven with a single ostrich feather symbolizing the monarchy; a woman in mourning, probably representing the state; the Stuart arms; and a white rose with two buds, the symbol of the Stuarts. Gouache on paper with plain ivory sticks. VAM T.160-1970.

The reasons for French mastery of European design and decorative arts at the start of the eighteenth century were many, but two in particular stand out. Firstly, the sheer size of the country and its resources, from which an opulent ruling élite benefited disproportionately. In terms of population, France in 1700 was the largest western European country, with about 20 million people. Great Britain, by contrast, had little more than six million. Despite the poverty of much of the French peasantry, the country's ruling élite was large and immensely wealthy, constituting a sizeable market for expensive, luxury goods. The second reason for French supremacy lay in the success of Louis XIV's deliberate policy of cultural domination. European monarchs in the baroque age were well accustomed to competing by means of elaborate displays of splendour and magnificence. Louis XIV raised such theatricality to new levels of sophistication. Not only did his royal palace at Versailles dwarf the architectural achievements of other European monarchs, but it served as a showcase for the products of French high-design industries, like Gobelin tapestries and Lyons silk textiles. These industries were themselves in several cases the creations of the French state and benefited from state subsidies. In addition, the state provided specialist training for designers.

Rivalry with France was a crucial element in Georgian Britain's rise to international prominence in design and the decorative arts. As in many such rivalries, the British copied a great deal from the French, despite their virulent Francophobia. The British imported both French stylistic ideas, such as rococo and aspects of neo-classicism, and French workers, most prominently the Protestant Huguenots. But they did not borrow the French policy of systematic royal promotion of the visual arts. In a constitutional monarchy of the British eighteenth-century type it was hardly possible to do so. The third Earl of Shaftesbury argued in his *Letter concerning the Art, or Science of Design*, written on the eve of the accession of George I, that under a free constitution it was undesirable, inappropriate and futile for the monarch to dictate taste. Anyway, most of the kings descended from the royal house of Hanover were unsuited to the task, both in their personalities and their interests. Royal palaces continued to be refurnished and rebuilt; foreign ambassadors and the British nobility continued to attend at court. Yet neither George I's court nor those of his two successors (his son, George II, and his great-grandson, George III) were crucial sites of national cultural display, in the manner of Versailles. Indeed, the only Hanoverian king who exhibited a special interest in design and the decorative arts was George IV. His trend-setting activities as Prince of Wales, Prince Regent and ultimately King included the building or rebuilding of Carlton House, London, and the Pavilion at Brighton. But by this stage his was only one influence among many. By the end of the eighteenth century cultural leadership had become dispersed among a multiplicity of designers and craftspeople, manufacturers and shopkeepers, noble patrons and Grub Street critics.

4. Commerce

To understand Britain's increasing international reputation in design and the decorative arts in the Georgian period we need, therefore, to look beyond the royal court. The sources of Britain's success in this sphere lay ultimately in the economy, in particular in the achievements of British commerce and manufacture. Already regarded as a wealthy country at the start of the eighteenth century, Britain was to be the most successful European economy of the eighteenth and early nineteenth centuries. On almost every front British output outpaced that of its major rivals.

Take agriculture, which was still, at the beginning of the Georgian period, the largest single sector of the economy. Between the start of the eighteenth century and the 1830s the output of British agriculture grew rapidly enough to go on feeding the population without much recourse to imports, even though the number of people nearly tripled, from little more than six million to well over 16 million. Yet agriculture was not the most consistently dynamic area of the economy. It was commerce and manufacturing that grew most rapidly.

The best evidence for this lies in the spectacular expansion of towns, the key centres for trade and industry, and communications. London was already, in 1700, the largest city in western Europe, with about 575,000 people, approximately one-tenth of the country's population. Paris was the second-largest western European city, with 510,000 people. Among the rest of the cities of western Europe, only Amsterdam and Naples had populations over 200,000. London's size reflected its triple role as the capital city, the leading port and the country's largest industrial centre. It was the arbiter of fashionable taste, the natural habitat of the *beau monde* and its seductively designed shops

11

12

11 Trade card of Martha Cole and Martha Houghton, at the Sun in St Paul's Churchyard, London, about 1720–30. Engraved by B. Cole. At the start of the Georgian period fashionable London shops were already using carefully designed interiors to lure customers. This trade card depicts a shop fitted out with a mirror and a glazed partition, where well-dressed female customers enjoy the comforts of an open fire and an elegant stool. Engraving. VAM E.2299-1987.

12 *The Thames and the City of London from Richmond House*, about 1747. By Antonio Canaletto for the second Duke of Richmond. Oil on canvas. By courtesy of the Trustees of the Goodwood Collection.

13

dominated the retailing of high-design goods. It enjoyed these same advantages 130 years later, when its population had more than tripled to well over one and a half million people, some of them accommodated in the spacious houses that surrounded the new streets and squares laid out in the classical style, with many more living in mean one- or two-room lodgings.

However, this figure still represented only about one-tenth of the country's (by then) much larger population. It was not in London, but elsewhere in Britain – in the English provinces, in Wales and in Scotland – that the most dramatic urban growth took place during the Georgian era. There towns grew far more rapidly than London, although none of them came close to rivalling London in terms of sheer size. In 1831 London was still eight times larger than Glasgow or Liverpool, the country's next largest towns.

14

13 *Messrs Harding, Howell & Co. of Pall Mall*, 1809. Plate from Rudolph Ackermann's *Repository of Arts*, vol. 1, no. 3, March 1809. Harding, Howell & Co.'s Grand Fashionable Magazine opened in Schomberg House, Pall Mall, London, in 1796. An early precursor of the department store, its spacious and elegant ground floor, shown here, was divided into four departments separated by glazed partitions. The first sold furs and fans, the second haberdashery, the third jewellery, clocks and perfumery, and the fourth millinery and dresses. Upstairs was a refreshment room. Etching and aquatint. VAM 11.RC.R.1.

14 *Bloomsbury Square, London*, about 1787. By Edward Dayes. Etching and aquatint. The Museum of London.

15

15 *The Distressed Poet*, 1736. By William Hogarth. The sparsely furnished London garret lodging of an impoverished poet and his family. The arrival of a truculent milkmaid demanding to be paid underscores his distressed circumstances. Oil on canvas. Birmingham Museums and Art Gallery.

The towns that grew most quickly were ports like Bristol and Liverpool, Whitehaven and Glasgow, centres of industry like Manchester, Leeds and Merthyr Tydfil, and leisure resorts like Bath, Brighton and Scarborough. It was as a consequence of their growth, not of the growth of London, that by 1851 more than half the population of Britain lived in towns. In 1700 less than one-fifth had done so.

The growth of towns was encouraged by the rapid improvement of the means of communication between them. In contrast to many continental European states, Britain had no internal customs duties or other barriers to internal trade. The country formed one large, uninterrupted market, ringed by a fence of customs duties, designed to defend British manufactures from foreign competition. Within the customs ring, trade was facilitated by a succession of transport innovations, almost all based on commercial rather than

17

16

16 *Leeds*, 1816. By J. M. W. Turner. Watercolour. Yale Center for British Art, Paul Mellon Collection.

17 *Prospect of Whitehaven from Brackenthwaite*, 1736. By Matthias Read. Oil on canvas. The Beacon, Whitehaven.

18

government investment. Rivers were made navigable and, from the 1760s, a new network of canals was built. Roads were improved by establishing turnpike trusts, which charged tolls to pay for the cost of rebuilding. In 1750 there were barely more than 3,000 miles (4,827km) of turnpike road; by the 1830s 20,000 miles (32,180km) of road had been turnpiked. The consequences were dramatic. In 1700 it took 90 hours to get from Manchester to London; in 1800 it took just 33. Some, of course, disapproved. 'I wish with all my heart,' moaned the conservative John Byng at the end of the eighteenth century, 'that half the turnpike roads of the kingdom were ploughed up, which have imported London manners and depopulated the country.' For men like Byng, worse was soon to come. The first passenger railway, from Stockton to Darlington in County Durham, was opened in 1825; by 1838, 743 miles (1,195km) of track had been laid.

19

18 *North Parade, Bath*, about 1777. By Thomas Malton junior. The second and third buildings from the left were Assembly Rooms. Watercolour. VAM 1723-1871.

19 *Greenwich Railway. View from the Surrey Canal*, 1836. By G. F. Bragg. The new London–Greenwich railway on its continuous viaduct as it crosses the Surrey Canal. Lithograph. Ironbridge Gorge Museum Trust.

20

Improvements in communication were not simply a matter of the physical movement of goods and people. Just as significant was the development of new media for the circulation of information. The most important of these were the newspaper and the periodical, although we should not ignore the poster, the handbill and the trade card. For much of the half century before 1695, only one newspaper had been allowed to circulate. This was the weekly *London Gazette*, which had a semi-official status. After restrictions were lifted in 1695, newspapers began to be published as purely commercial enterprises in greater and greater numbers. The first daily paper, *The Daily Courant*, appeared in London in 1702; by 1792 there were 16 London dailies. London newspapers and periodicals were widely read in the provinces, but local newspapers also sprang up in almost every major provincial town. Both newspapers and periodicals played a significant role in the development of design and the decorative arts. In addition to political news, they carried advertising for a wide range of goods and also articles that commented on almost every aspect of cultural life. Indeed, by the later Georgian period, journals such as Rudolph Ackermann's *Repository of Arts, Literature, Commerce, Manufactures, Fashion and the Politics* (1806–29) were almost entirely devoted to high-design goods.

The growth of population in the port towns, especially those on the western seaboard that faced the Atlantic and the world beyond Europe, reflected the importance of international trade and colonies to Britain's economy. Throughout the Georgian period, no other major European economy was more heavily committed to international trade than the British, with the single exception of the Netherlands, a country in economic decline. Britain's self-image was that of a trading nation. 'Our trade,' announced Lord Carteret in 1739, 'is our chief support.' Indeed, so dedicated were Britons to the cult of trade that Thomas Mortimer, the historian, could describe commerce in 1762 as 'the great idol of this nation, and to which she sacrifices every other consideration'. The common seaman, notoriously truculent and uncouth, was fêted as the epitome of British courage and the mainstay of Britain's prosperity. The Royal Navy, which secured the trade routes, was the focus of national pride. Victorious admirals like Vernon, Rodney and Nelson were national heroes.

21

22

20 Poster advertising the programme at Astley's circus, 1833. Philip Astley founded his circus in London in 1768. It became a leading British innovator in advertising, pioneering large posters printed in an arresting variety of display typefaces, with different-coloured inks and woodcut and wood-engraved illustrations. Woodcut and letter-press. [h. 74cm]. VAM S.2-1983.

23

21 *A Flagship Shortening Sail*, 1736. By Samuel Scott. A view from the starboard of a British three-deck naval vessel firing a gun. The Union Flag denotes the presence of an Admiral of the Fleet. Oil on canvas. © National Maritime Museum, London.

22 Plate showing Emma Hamilton as Britannia unveiling a bust of Admiral Nelson, 1806. Made at the Coalport porcelain factory, Shropshire, and painted by Thomas Baxter junior in the London workshop of Thomas Baxter senior. Hard-paste porcelain, painted in enamel colours. VAM C.67-1984.

23 *A Thames-side Quay*, about 1757. By Samuel Scott. The mark 'UEIC' on the bale in the foreground is for the United East India Company. Oil on canvas. VAM FA.249.

THE BRITISH EMPIRE, 1715 AND 1815

John Styles

In 1715, in the aftermath of its successes in the War of Spanish Succession, Britain had emerged as one of the most formidable European powers. Nevertheless, the extent of British possessions in the extra-European world remained strictly limited. A string of British colonies stretched along the eastern seaboard of North America, from Newfoundland in the north to the Carolinas in the south, but the territory subject to effective British control and settlement did not extend very far inland. Britain also controlled a number of West Indian islands, most prominently the sugar colonies of Barbados and Jamaica. In Asia, the East India Company had little more than a toehold on the Indian subcontinent, with trading posts on the coast, including those at Bombay, Madras and Calcutta. It had secured a semi-permanent trading presence in China at Canton only in 1713. A century later, at the end of the Napoleonic Wars in 1815, Britain was the leading world power. Although most of its North American colonies had been lost in the American War of Independence of 1776–83, the later Georgian years saw the continued expansion of the British Empire in Canada, India, Australia and Africa, accompanied by the imposition of much more direct imperial controls from London.

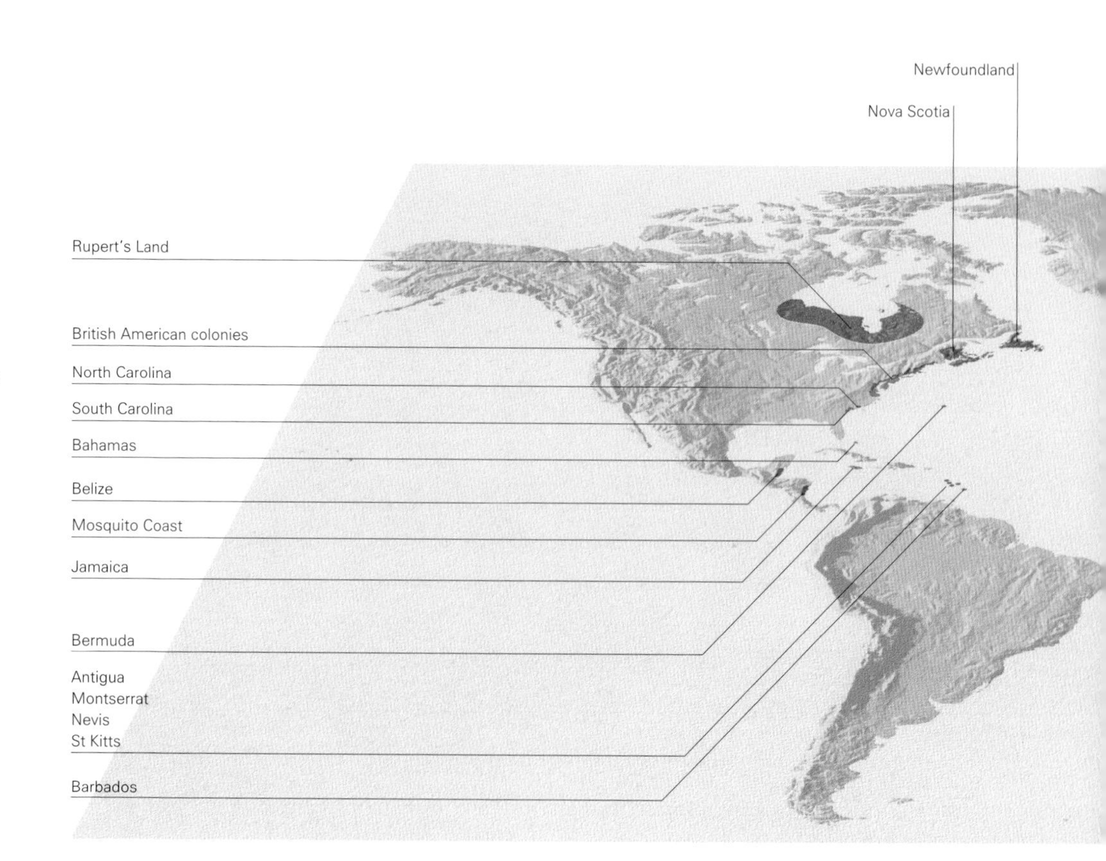

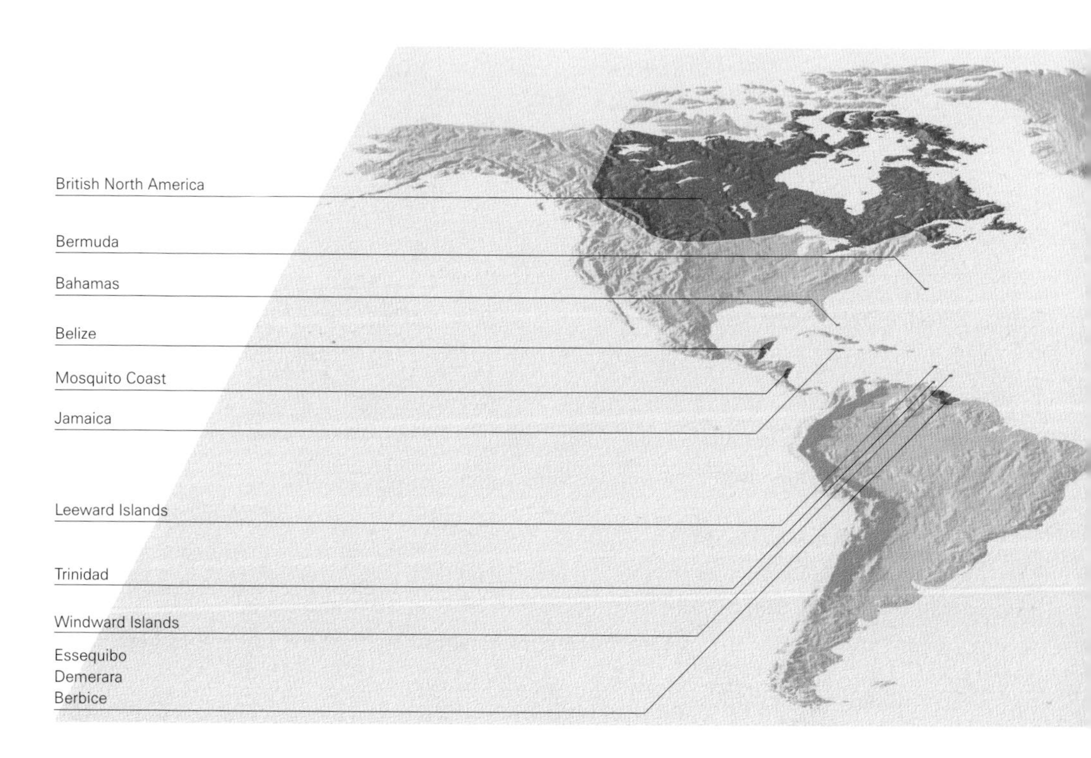

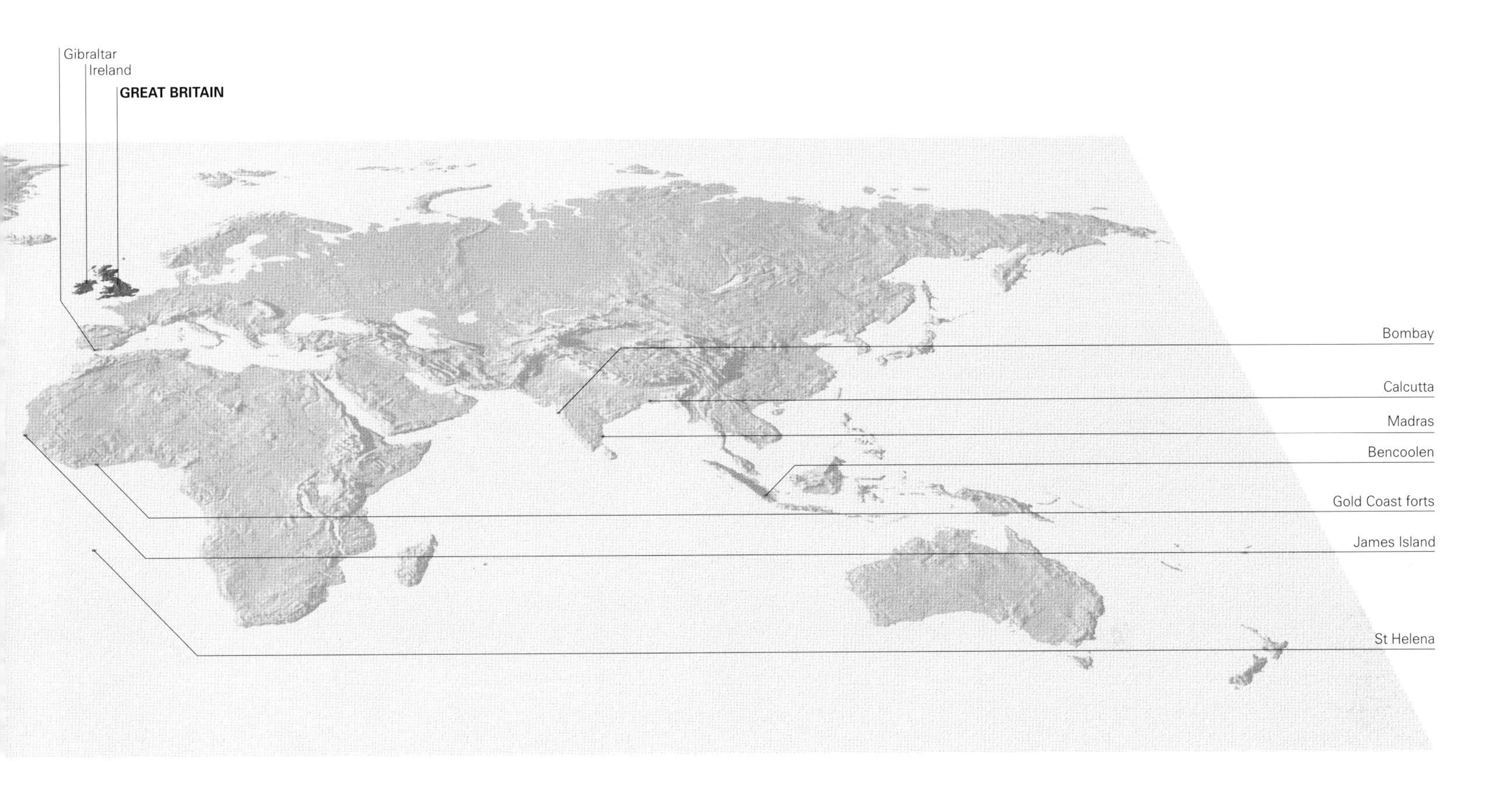

Gibraltar
Ireland
GREAT BRITAIN
Bombay
Calcutta
Madras
Bencoolen
Gold Coast forts
James Island
St Helena

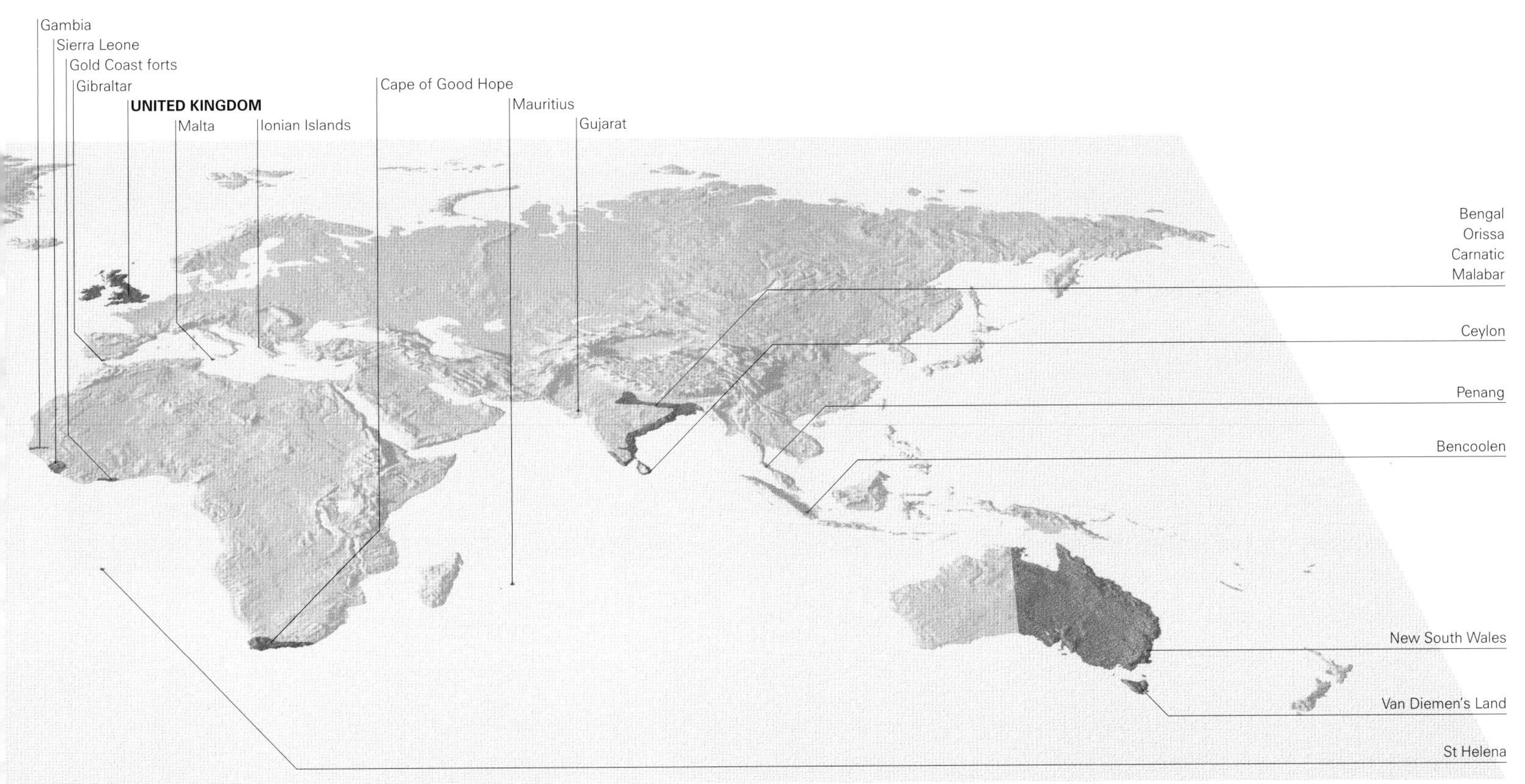

Gambia
Sierra Leone
Gold Coast forts
Gibraltar
UNITED KINGDOM
Malta
Ionian Islands
Cape of Good Hope
Mauritius
Gujarat
Bengal
Orissa
Carnatic
Malabar
Ceylon
Penang
Bencoolen
New South Wales
Van Diemen's Land
St Helena

Trade followed the flag. Britain was at war for more than one-third of the period from 1714 to 1837, and was largely victorious, with the notable exception of the American War of Independence (1776–83). In all these wars France was the principal enemy, while trade and colonies figured prominently among the causes of conflict. In the eighteenth century, especially, colonies offered unrivalled opportunities for the expansion of trade. They might serve as exclusive markets for manufactured exports, like Britain's North American territories with their fast-growing populations of European and African descent. They might serve as sources of exotic manufactures, like muslins and ivory wares from India; or as suppliers of tropical foodstuffs, like the West Indian sugar islands. Indeed, it was the West Indies that were the jewels in the imperial crown in the eighteenth century and the object of the most intense colonial rivalry among the European powers. Throughout the Caribbean, on islands owned by the British, the French, the Spanish, the Dutch and

24 *A View of Charles Town*, 1774. By Thomas Leitch. At this period Charleston in South Carolina was one of the most prosperous ports in the British North American colonies. Oil on canvas. Courtesy of the Museum of Early Southern Decorative Arts, Winston-Salem.

25 Work box in the shape of a cottage, 1790–1800. Made in Vizagapatam, India, for the English market. The country cottage symbolized rustic simplicity and uncorrupted Englishness, yet this example was made in India. Wood veneered with ivory. [h. 15.5cm]. VAM W.20-1951.

26 *Elija Boardman*, 1789. By Ralph Earl. Boardman, depicted in his shop, was a dry-goods merchant in New Milford, Connecticut. His large stock of patterned textiles would have been mainly imported from Britain. Oil on canvas. © 2003. The Metropolitan Museum of Art, New York.

27

28

other European powers, huge numbers of slaves from Africa toiled on sugar plantations. They laboured to satisfy the insatiable appetite for sweetness among European consumers and to generate spectacular wealth for their European owners. It was only towards the end of the Georgian era, in 1833, that slavery was abolished in the British territories, at a time when the significance of the West Indian colonies for the British economy was reduced. Nevertheless, the colonies as a whole continued to make an important contribution to the success of British commerce through the later Georgian years. The United States of America may have been lost in 1783, but thereafter Britain went on to conquer new territories – in India, Africa and Australia.

British trade grew enormously between the start of the eighteenth century and the middle of the nineteenth. Not only did the volume of trade expand perhaps thirtyfold, but the geographical extent of British commerce and the variety of goods traded also increased. All this contributed to the huge growth in national wealth that took place during the Georgian era. Changing patterns of trade register the growing international status of British manufactures. They also register a growing international respect for British design and decorative arts. Between the sixteenth and nineteenth centuries Britain underwent a long drawn-out transformation that saw a peripheral and relatively unsophisticated economy transformed into the manufacturing workshop of the world. A country that had exported mainly raw materials and semi-finished goods now became one whose exports consisted principally of high-quality, finished manufactures. It was the Georgian period that witnessed the decisive shift from one pattern of trade to the other.

27 Medallion for the Society for the Abolition of the Slave Trade, about 1787. Modelled by William Hackwood. Made at Josiah Wedgwood's factory, Etruria, Staffordshire. The design was taken from the Society's seal and bears the words 'AM I NOT A MAN AND A BROTHER'. The medallions were given to the society's members. Wedgwood was a keen supporter of the campaign to abolish the slave trade. White jasper ware, with black relief, mounted in gilt-metal. [h. 3cm]. VAM 414:1304-1885.

28 *Francis Williams,* about 1745. By an unknown artist. Williams was a mathematician and poet. Educated in England, he returned to Jamaica to set up a school in Spanish Town. He is shown in his study, with a Jamaican landscape in the background. The population of Jamaica in the 18th century consisted overwhelmingly of people of African descent, almost all of them slaves. Williams was a member of a tiny minority of free blacks. Oil on canvas. VAM P.83-1928.

29

Imports displayed equally dynamic changes. At the start of the eighteenth century about one-third of all imports consisted of manufactured goods – silk and cotton textiles from India, porcelain from China, lacquered wares from Japan, linen cloth from Germany and bar iron from Sweden. But as British manufacturing flourished and a government policy of high tariffs restricted manufactured imports, they became less and less important. By the eve of Victoria's reign manufactured goods constituted only a tiny proportion of British imports, which increasingly comprised foodstuffs and raw materials. Britain remained largely self-sufficient in the foods produced in a temperate climate, so it was exotic foodstuffs from beyond Europe that were imported – tea from China and sugar from the slave plantations of the British West Indies. Raw materials to feed Britain's growing workshops were initially imported mainly from Europe – timber and flax from the Baltic, raw silk and dyestuffs from the Mediterranean. As the Georgian era progressed, however, more and more raw materials came from further afield – mahogany for fine furniture from the Caribbean, raw cotton for the Lancashire mills from the slave plantations in the newly independent United States, raw silk from China and, by the 1830s, wool from the new British colonies in Australia.

30

We can observe one element of this shift in the destinations of manufactured exports. In 1700 the principal market was Europe, and woollen cloth remained by far the most important product exported, just as it had been for more than two centuries. By the early 1770s, on the eve of the American Revolution, there had been striking changes. Europe had been overtaken as a market by Britain's colonies on the American mainland and in the West Indies. Woollen textiles remained important, but the range of products exported had widened to include Spitalfields silks, Lancashire printed cottons, Staffordshire pots, Bristol glasswares and a huge diversity of small metal goods, from humble nails to fine silverware. By the 1830s the destinations and the mix of exports had changed again. Now approximately one-third of exports went to Europe, one-third to the United States, Canada and the West Indies, and one-third to the rest of the non-European world. As for the mix of goods, cotton was now king, with cotton cloth and yarn accounting for just under half of all exports, although the remainder included almost every kind of manufactured product imaginable at the time, such was Britain's manufacturing prowess.

29 Commemorative jug, about 1825. Probably made by J. & R. Clews in Cobridge, Staffordshire, for export to the United States. The scene on the jug is entitled 'Landing of Gen. Lafayette at Castle Garden New York 16 August 1824'. Lead-glazed earthenware, transfer-printed. VAM C.38-1974.

30 Armorial plate, about 1772. Made at the Jingdezhen kilns, China, and decorated either there or in Canton, for export to Britain. It bears the arms of Pitt, Earl of Chatham, impaling those of Grenville, copied from an English pattern. Porcelain, decorated in overglaze enamels and gilt. VAM C.71-1932.

31 *Paul Crespin*, about 1730. By an unknown artist. Crespin was born in London in 1694, the son of a Huguenot immigrant, and became one of the capital's leading goldsmiths. Oil on canvas. VAM P.29-1985.

5. Manufacturing

The key to these shifts in patterns of trade was a progressive increase in the output, range and sophistication of British manufactures that continued through the Georgian period. The innovations associated with the Industrial Revolution after 1760 – innovations principally in steam power and textile machinery – made a critical contribution to this process of improvement. But it is important to emphasize that it was a process that was already well advanced by the mid-eighteenth century and one that extended to a far wider range of industries than those conventionally associated with the Industrial Revolution.

1

Consider the experience of the high-design industries during the first half of the eighteenth century. Already, at the start of the century, the range and the quality of skills that were available in Britain had grown significantly by comparison with the early seventeenth century. By the accession of George I in 1714, Britain was manufacturing virtually the whole range of high-design products that the country had previously imported, from stoneware jugs to decorated cotton textiles, from engraved prints to lacquered cabinets, although notable exceptions, such as porcelain, remained. Yet British high-design manufactures displayed important weaknesses at this stage. Often British producers could not match the quality of their European equivalents, so high-design manufactures remained heavily dependent on immigrant designers and makers from all over Europe – from France, the Low Countries, Germany, Switzerland, Italy and Sweden. Most prominent were the Huguenots – exiled French Protestants and their immediate descendants – like the silversmith Paul Crespin and the silk designer and manufacturer James Leman. What most of these foreigners shared, irrespective of their trade or country of origin, was the freehand drawing skills that were the key to eighteenth-century design, skills that were in lamentably short supply among native Britons. Also a weakness was the narrowness of indigenous innovation. It was in only a handful of fields that Britain enjoyed a reputation as a leading innovator at the start of the eighteenth century, most notably in the manufacture of clocks, watches and scientific instruments. During the second half of the eighteenth century, most of these weaknesses were successfully addressed. Britain became widely admired across Europe for the quality of products such as ceramics, decorative metalwares and prints. It was regarded as a leading innovator in fields like coach building, printed textiles and men's fashion. The country's reliance on foreign designers and makers was much reduced.

The Industrial Revolution of 1760–1850 was, therefore, part of a wider process of improvement in British manufacturing that continued through the Georgian period, and not its cause. The Industrial Revolution is usually associated with two sets of inventions – James Watt's rotary steam engine and the cotton-spinning machines developed by James Hargreaves, Richard Arkwright and Samuel Crompton – which were brought together in a new kind of productive unit: the factory. The impact of these inventions was immense. Cotton became the largest single British manufacturing industry by

32

32 *Sir Richard Arkwright*, 1789–90. By Joseph Wright. Prominently displayed on the table beside Arkwright is a set of cotton-spinning rollers, a crucial part of the spinning machine that he patented in 1769, which earned him an immense fortune. Oil on canvas. Private collection.

33

33 *Morning View of Coalbrookdale*, 1777. By William Williams. Smelting iron by means of coke was invented by Abraham Darby at Coalbrookdale, Shropshire, in 1709, but the major expansion of iron making with coke began there only after 1750. In the last quarter of the 18th century the furnaces belching smoke and flame and the new iron bridge across the gorge of the River Severn became wonders of the age, much visited and depicted in paintings and prints. Oil on canvas. Clive House Museum, Shrewsbury.

the early nineteenth century. Steam engines were used not just to drive many new factories, but to pump water out of mines, to provide the blast in iron works and to power ships and railway locomotives. It is, however, important to stress just how limited was the direct impact of the new steam-powered technologies on the making of high-design goods. Outside of cotton and woollen textiles, most high-design artefacts continued to be made at the start of Victoria's reign largely by hand tools and hand-driven machines (stamps, presses, lathes and the like). The workshop remained much more characteristic of these trades than the factory reverberating to the din of steam-powered machinery.

34 *Carding, Drawing and Roving*, 1835. By Thomas Allom. Engraved by J. Carter. Plate from *History of the Cotton Manufacture in Great Britain* by Edward Baines, 1835. Engraving. VAM 43.D.88.

35 *The Collier*, 1814. By George Walker. Etched by R. and D. Havell. Plate from *The Costume of Yorkshire* by George Walker, 1814. Steam power is used here both at the mine and to move coal on the wagonway. Etching and aquatint. VAM 11.RC.F.19.

Ceramics, glasswares, small decorative metalwares, furniture: in 1837, and indeed well into the final decades of the nineteenth century, their manufacture remained overwhelmingly a hand trade. But this is not to say that such industries were unaffected by technical change. Hand making was itself transformed by innovations in technique, such as transfer printing on ceramics and glass pressing, and by new materials, such as mahogany, Sheffield plate and steel furniture springs. Innovations of these kinds in what remained fundamentally hand trades could make high-design goods cheaper and encourage the proliferation of new varieties of object.

37

36

6. People

Who provided the market for the surge of artefacts that poured forth from workshop and factory alike? Overseas markets may have grown faster, but it was British consumers who bought the bulk of British manufactured goods throughout the Georgian period. Not only did the number of these consumers more than treble as population growth took off from the mid-eighteenth century, but they became better off, at almost every social level. Nevertheless, this remained a profoundly unequal society. At the top were the nobility, whose wealth came from their ownership of a considerable proportion of the nation's land. There were very few of them. In England and Wales the 160 peers of 1688 had risen to some 350 by 1832 – a mere handful compared with the 120,000 nobles in France on the eve of the Revolution in the 1780s or the half million in Spain. On the continent, where nobles were numerous, it was far from unusual for them to be impoverished. In Britain, where nobles were few, almost all were fabulously wealthy, and becoming more so. The nobility benefited not only from growing agricultural profitability after 1760, but indirectly, through their ownership of urban and industrial property, from the expansion of trade and manufacturing. Consequently they had a huge impact on the aesthetic life of the nation. Nobles could afford to travel throughout their country and the continent, collecting art works and antiquities as they went. They built, rebuilt and refurnished enormous houses in London and the countryside, which were often the equal of royal palaces in the smaller European states. They patronized artists and artisans, shopkeepers and showmen. But, however wealthy and influential the nobility was, their numbers were far too small to soak up all the high-design consumer goods that British manufacturers produced in ever greater quantities. This role fell principally to their immediate inferiors, the burgeoning middling ranks in the British social hierarchy.

36 *John Cuff*, 1772. By Johann Zoffany. Cuff was master of the Worshipful Company of Spectacle Makers in 1748. He is depicted in his workshop with an assistant, at his bench, surrounded by his tools, polishing a lens. Oil on canvas. © The Royal Collection.

37 *Sheffield Cutler*, 1814. By George Walker. Etched by R. and D. Havell. Plate from *The Costume of Yorkshire* by George Walker, 1814. Etching and aquatint. VAM 11.RC.F.19.

38

38 *Marriage à la Mode. The Tête à Tête*, 1745. By William Hogarth. In his second painting from the *Marriage à la Mode* series, Hogarth ridicules the excesses of noble splendour, in particular the style of William Kent in interior decoration, the rococo, and the cult of Old Masters and the antique. Oil on canvas. © Tate, London, 2003.

39

40

Immediately below the nobility on the social ladder lay the massed ranks of the moderately wealthy. By the early nineteenth century they were numbered in hundreds of thousands and were growing faster than the rest of the population. In some respects they were not a homogeneous group. Their wealth came from a number of different and sometimes antagonistic sources – from land, trade, manufacturing, the professions. These differences were the occasion of myriad petty snobberies, as were differences in the sheer scale of their wealth. The middling group in British society embraced a huge range of incomes, from merchants, bankers, industrialists and landed gentry, whose wealth occasionally matched that of the nobility, to shopkeepers, farmers, workshop masters and country curates, whose incomes might not be very much greater than that of a skilled workman. It was also deeply divided in matters of religion between Anglicans and Nonconformists.

Nevertheless, the various elements that made up the middling group in Georgian Britain did have a number of things in common. They formed a much larger proportion of the British population than was the case in the rest of Europe – in France, unlike Britain, noted one British traveller in the 1780s, 'you go at once from beggary to profusion'. They were also becoming increasingly urban. They enjoyed more than their fair share of the fruits of Britain's economic success when compared with their inferiors among the labouring classes. And, most importantly for design and the decorative arts, they shared an aspiration to a genteel way of life that found much of its expression in owning, using and displaying the right goods. It was they, above all, who sustained that growing multitude of manufacturers producing the high-design objects that comprised the essential props of gentility – porcelain tea sets, mahogany dining tables, wine decanters, patterned floor carpets, creamware dining services. English manufactured products, it was pointed out by the writer on economics Josiah Tucker in the mid-eighteenth century:

> are more adapted for the demands of peasants and mechanics, in order to appear in warm circumstances, for farmers, freeholders, tradesmen and manufacturers in middling life; and for wholesale dealers, merchants, and for all persons of landed estates to appear in genteel life; than for the magnificence of palaces or the cabinets of princes. Thus it is . . . that the English of those several denominations have better conveniences in their houses, and affect to have more in quantity of clean, neat furniture, and a greater variety, such as carpets, screens, window curtains, chamber bells, polished brass locks, fenders etc . . . than are to be found in any other country of Europe.

41

39 *The Duet*, 1749. By Arthur Devis. Devis was famous for portraits like this showing genteel families in polite poses. Although the detailed settings did not always represent real interiors, they reflected the social rank and aspirations of his sitters, who were usually wealthy landed gentry, professionals or merchants. Oil on canvas. VAM P.31-1955.

Those in the middle ranks of British society may have enjoyed a disproportionate share of the fruits of Georgian economic success, but that does not mean we should ignore the significance as a market for consumer goods of those beneath them in the social ladder – those frequently described in the eighteenth century as the 'labouring poor'. After all, the working classes comprised a large majority of the population. Their experience of the Georgian years was a mixed one. At some periods (especially before the 1780s) and in some regions (especially in the industrial areas of the north and west) they enjoyed periods of modest prosperity. At other times and in other places they suffered terrible hardships, as a result of impossibly high prices for basic foodstuffs, falling wages and mass unemployment. Especially hard were the long years of war with France from 1793 to 1815 and their aftermath. The

42

40 *Grace before a Meal*, about 1725. By Joseph Van Aken. A moderately prosperous middle-ranking family prepares to eat. The sparsely furnished interior is typical of the possessions of small shopkeepers, craftspeople and farmers at the start of the Georgian period. Oil on canvas. Ashmolean Museum.

41 Detail of a bill advertising Packer's Royal Furniture Gloss, 1793. Two well-dressed women are depicted sitting in a genteel, but not opulent, interior. Their polite conversation turns on the merits of the furniture, but quickly transmutes into an advertising pitch for Packer's polish. Engraving. The British Museum.

42 *A Cottage Interior*, 1793. By William Redmore Bigg. The teapot, tea bowl and saucer, the side-table, chair and clock suggest a modest degree of material comfort. By the end of the 18th century it was not uncommon for the labouring poor to own possessions of this sort. Oil on canvas. VAM 199-1885.

worst privations were endured by the farm workers of eastern and southern England. Nevertheless, as the prices of manufactured goods fell, even the labouring poor were able to indulge in some of the aesthetic and social pleasures of decorative goods, albeit of an inexpensive kind. At the end of the eighteenth century, in contrast to its beginning, printed cotton gowns were commonly owned by working women and silver watches by many labouring men. Clocks and earthenware teapots were familiar adornments of their living rooms. Indeed, the labouring poor could aspire to a certain plebeian gentility, even if those aspirations were often dashed by unemployment, unforeseen price hikes or ill health. 'I made shift,' remembered one old man, looking back to 1741 when he was a poor, 17-year-old apprentice stocking maker at Nottingham, 'with a little over-work, and a little credit, to raise a genteel suit of clothes, fully adequate to the sphere in which I moved.'

43 *Plucking a Turkey*, 1770s. By Henry Walton. A young woman, probably a servant, at work. She wears a cotton or linen bedgown printed in lilac with white spots and a fashionable cap with a silk ribbon. Oil on canvas. © Tate, London, 2003.

7. Culture

Georgian Britons often prided themselves on being a distinctively commercial people. This is not surprising, because in Britain so many goods and services were subject to commercialized forms of supply. This was particularly striking in the arts. In continental Europe, facilities from the academies that trained artists to the factories that manufactured porcelain were often creations of the state. In Britain, they were all overwhelmingly commercial in character. Nevertheless, the kind of successful commercial society that the British had made caused its creators great unease. At the heart of that unease lay the conviction that increasing wealth – what they called luxury – would lead to political corruption, military enfeeblement, debauched morals and ultimately national decline. Among the educated, who idolized the civilizations of ancient Greece and Rome, the decline and fall of the Roman empire presented a terrible warning of where luxury could lead. For many, the growing consumption of high-design goods offered prime evidence of luxury's inexorable advance. This was certainly the critic John Dennis's opinion in his *Vice and Luxury Public Mischiefs* of 1724:

> When the plague of luxury is once become epidemical and has thoroughly infected a nation, when there is a general contention who shall out do and outshine his neighbour in the pomp and splendour of it; in the pomp and splendour of buildings, furniture, gardens, apparel, equipage, and sumptuous tables, when that respect is paid to vice and folly, which to wisdom and virtue is only due; then riches, the food and support of luxury, are fraught with insatiable avarice, and to obtain them, the most solemn obligations are infringed, the most sacred trusts are violated.

This view exercised a powerful grip on the public imagination throughout the eighteenth century, though it did little to inhibit the growth of national wealth. It fuelled intense British suspicion of French design, which epitomized luxury in its most enticing but most corrupting form. It promoted widespread admiration for the virtues of the simple, rustic life. Later in the eighteenth century it also encouraged a deep, moralizing suspicion of aristocratic excess. It did not go uncontested, however. It was argued, most powerfully by the Scottish philosophers David Hume and Adam Smith, that commerce, far from

44 *The Imports of Great Britain from France*, 1757. Drawn and engraved by Louis-Philippe Boitard. Inscribed 'Humbly Address'd to the Laudable Associations of Anti-Gallicans, and the generous promoters of the British Arts and Manufactories'. A Thames-side quay, upstream from the Tower of London: dancing masters, hairdressers, milliners and other purveyors of effeminacy disembark, while on the quay are imported French wines, cheeses and luxury goods. Etching and engraving. The British Museum.

undermining public morality, political freedom and national advancement, could promote all of them, and in addition polish public taste where matters of artistic judgement were concerned. Increasingly, it was this view that prevailed among the powerful and the wealthy in the later Georgian years. Nevertheless, a deep suspicion of the corrupting potential of wealth and commerce persisted among those who advocated a more democratic polity and society.

In the everyday lives of the upper and middling groups in British society many of these anxieties were worked out through the code of manners known as politeness. Just as Georgian Britons frequently chose to characterize themselves as a commercial people, so too they often described themselves as a polite people. Politeness in the eighteenth century meant much more than mere etiquette. It was an all-embracing philosophy of manners, a model of how people should behave to one another. It promoted openness and accessibility in social behaviour, but at the same time set demanding standards as to precisely how people should behave. Politeness demanded that people should make themselves agreeable to others. This was one of its great attractions, because it offered an alternative to the uncompromising religious fanaticism that seemed to many to have been responsible for the disastrous civil strife of the seventeenth century. Politeness did not deny the legitimacy of social rank, but it required the different ranks to mix with each other in an agreeable manner. Hence the rule made early in the eighteenth century by Beau Nash, the Master of Ceremonies at the resort city of Bath, that nobles should treat lesser visitors with the same courtesy they usually reserved for each other. 'That ease and open access,' wrote the poet Oliver Goldsmith of Nash's rule, 'our gentry brought back to the metropolis, and thus the whole kingdom by degrees became more refined by lessons originally derived from him.'

Ease and open access were principles that lay at the heart of politeness and explain why it touched so many aspects of eighteenth-century life. 'Polite science' was science that was accessible to a wide public through lectures and demonstrations, not hidden away in the laboratory. 'Polite literature' could be read with understanding and enjoyment by a broad, educated public, in contrast to the obscure, impenetrable writings of pedants. 'Polite entertainments' were those that encouraged polite forms of social mixing and were accessible to anyone who could pay the entry charge. Typical examples were assemblies, concerts and pleasure gardens, like those at Vauxhall and Ranelagh in London. They were run sometimes as commercial enterprises, sometimes by individuals who clubbed together to raise a subscription. The club or association was one of the characteristic Georgian institutions, and many, though not all, were dedicated to polite purposes.

45 *A Perspective View of the inside of the Grand Assembly Room in Blake Street, York*, 1759. Drawn and engraved by William Lindley. The interior of the magnificent assembly room at York designed by the Earl of Burlington and opened in 1732. Rococo carved work and mouldings were added in the 1750s. Engraving. York City Art Gallery.

46 *The Court of Equity or Convivial City Meeting*, 1779. By Robert Dighton. Engraved by Robert Laurie. This print depicts a room at the Globe Tavern, Fleet Street, London, where a club is meeting. Those present include a printer, a printseller, a silversmith, an auctioneer and (at the far right at the back) the artist Robert Dighton himself. Mezzotint. VAM E.540-1976.

47

Much of the appeal of politeness lay, therefore, in its inclusivity. It had a particular appeal for women, because its stress 'on the art of pleasing in conversation' set limits on male boorishness. But for all its inclusivity, politeness was far from being a democratic code of manners. It defined itself against plebeian vulgarity and provincial grossness. It aimed to create people of decorum, taste and refinement who could be agreeable in the correct way. Politeness did not require its followers to be genteel by birth, merely that when in company they behave in a genteel manner. For many, such performances had to be learned. Instruction was widely available, though at a price, from the growing numbers of dancing masters, music teachers and drawing tutors, as well as from a host of advice books. Politeness also required the purchase of equipment. Many of the high-design goods that British manufacturers made so readily accessible to a broad group of consumers – upholstered sofas and knives and forks, tea services and snuff boxes – were indispensable props in the genteel performances that constituted politeness, whether in the dining room or the assembly room. Your gentility was judged by whether you owned the right items, whether they were sufficiently genteel in their design and whether you were capable of using them in the correct way.

Politeness did not carry all before it. Many felt that its stress on performance led to artificiality, insincerity and dishonesty. From the mid-eighteenth century it was opposed by the cult of sensibility, which stressed authenticity rather than display, sincerity of emotion rather than performance, rustic simplicity rather than metropolitan polish. Sensibility had important consequences for the arts. It focused artistic interest on wild and authentic nature – the Cumbrian mountains, the Welsh hills, the Scottish Highlands – and, in the process, came to redefine what was quintessentially British. It promoted the idea that people's responses to works of art should rely less on intellectual discrimination and more on overwhelming, spontaneous inner feeling. Here lay the roots of the full-blown Romantic view of art that achieved such a widespread currency by the early nineteenth century. In practice, however, sensibility and politeness managed to coexist as cultural ideals for most of the Georgian period.

49

48

47 *The Complement RETIRING*, 1737. By Bartholomew Dandridge. Engraved by Louis-Philippe Boitard. Plate from *The Rudiments of Genteel Behaviour: An Introduction to the Methods of attaining a graceful Attitude, an agreeable Motion, an easy Air and a genteel behaviour* by François Nivelon, 1737. Engraving. VAM L.766-1876.

48 *Conway Castle, North Wales, by Moonlight*, 1794. By Julius Caesar Ibbetson the Elder. By the late 18th century the Welsh landscape was becoming popular with tourists, who appreciated its wild and sublime grandeur. Artists such as Ibbetson took advantage of this taste, capitalizing on the growing interest in native landscape. Oil on panel. VAM 377-1888.

8. Towards Victoria: the later Georgian years

By the time Victoria ascended the throne in 1837 Britain was the dominant world power. It owed this status to the continuing vitality of the British economy and to the country's victory in the long wars with revolutionary and later Napoleonic France, between 1793 and 1815. It still basked in the glory of admiration for all things British – the veritable anglomania – that had swept Europe in the second half of the eighteenth century. Yet economic, military and cultural success was accompanied by a new political and moral unease that was to have immensely important consequences for design and the decorative arts. Among the educated classes, confidence in Britain's achievement was tempered by fears that the nation was in the grip of a soulless, inhuman materialism, productive of undreamt riches for the few, but physical squalor and moral degradation for the many. Foreign visitors, too, began to express the view that Britain's success had been bought at too high a price. Heinrich Heine, the German poet, caught the pessimistic note in 1827. 'The perfection of machines, which are everywhere in use here and have taken over so many human functions, has for me something uncanny,' he wrote. 'The certainty, the exactness, the madness, the precision of life in England fills me with not less anxiety; for just as the machines in England seem like human beings, so the human beings there seem like machines.' Eight years later the French historian Alexis de Tocqueville visited Manchester. 'From this foul drain the greatest stream of human industry flows out to fertilize the whole world,' he observed with dismay, 'from this filthy sewer pure gold flows. Here humanity attains its most complete development and its most brutish; here civilization works its miracles, and civilized man is turned back almost into a savage.'

Among the British, such doubts reflected the rise of a new moral earnestness from the 1780s, encouraged by the spread of evangelical religious belief at every social level. They also reflected dismay at the conditions of life in many of the new industrial towns and a growing fear among the prosperous of the urban working classes. The prosperous responded by electing mainly Tory governments, opposed to reform, from the 1780s to the 1820s. The threat posed by the lower classes of the rapidly growing towns was both a political and an economic one. It had its origins in demands for the extension of political rights that were encouraged, in the later eighteenth century, by the American and French Revolutions. The threat intensified after the defeat of Napoleon at the Battle of Waterloo in 1815. Resentment mounted among the working classes at their failure to secure an adequate share of the fruits of economic growth and at the refusal of governments to alleviate the distress of those suffering the consequences of technological change. It was reinforced by the fact that when political reform did at last arrive, in the guise of the Great Reform Act of 1832, the working classes were excluded. The Great Reform Act extended the vote only to sections of the middle classes.

Educated men and women at the end of the Georgian era responded in a variety of ways to these doubts about the world they had created. Many retained a degree of confidence in the capacity of a commercial society, well administered, to improve the lives of the population. Some advocated much more radical moves towards democratic politics and social equality. Others rejected modern society and sought refuge in a vision of a medieval past untainted by commerce. There was wide agreement, however, that society's ills required a response that was self-consciously moral in character. This powerful sense of a moral agenda was to be a defining characteristic of British life during Victoria's reign – one that was to have an especially powerful impact on the development of design and the decorative arts.

50

49 *The Gough Family*, 1741. By William Verelst. This painting shows Captain Harry Gough of the East India Company with his family. The Goughs were a wealthy merchant family who had built their fortune on trade with India and China and were consolidating their position through the gradual acquisition of land. They are shown taking tea, displaying their taste and wealth. The painter has taken care to show that the silver tea kettle has a coat of arms on the side. Oil on canvas. VAM Anonymous Loan.

50 *Cotton Factories, Union Street, Manchester*, 1831. By Samuel Austin. Engraved by McGahey. Plate from *Lancashire Illustrated* by S. Austin, J. Harwood and G. and C. Pyne, 1831. The plate depicts the factories of Messrs McConnel and Co. Engraving. VAM 233.A.6.

CHAPTER 2

Style

MICHAEL SNODIN

1. A matter of choice

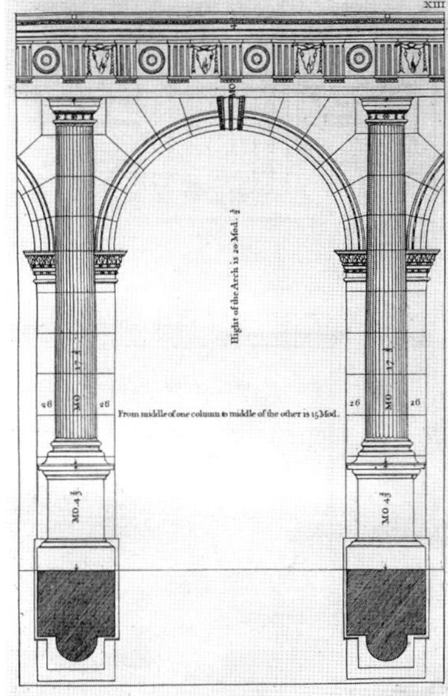

The story of style from 1714 to 1837 is one of complexity and rapid change. To an extent this is deceptive, for the dizzying range of Georgian styles can be grouped broadly into two distinct tendencies. The dominant trend was based on ancient Roman and Greek architecture and decoration, and its Renaissance interpretations. It included the baroque, neo-Palladian and neo-classical styles. From time to time it was matched by anti-classical styles, including the rococo, neo-Gothic and chinoiserie. The mere possibility of such choice was a sign of profound changes in attitudes to style, for it allowed style and ornament to carry the kinds of meanings and feelings that mark our experience of them today. As far as we know, this was something new, for earlier viewers and consumers had tended to 'read' the meaning of a piece of decoration or design principally through its heraldry and symbolic content, rather than its ornamental forms. With style now being 'read' in formal terms, it became an indicator of other areas, including taste, social position, religious affiliation, political allegiance and national pride. The expansion in available styles was greatly encouraged by the opening up of the market for manufactured goods to the growing middle classes. This became especially evident from the 1770s onwards, as styled goods became increasingly available through improved marketing and labour-saving means of production, which reduced the reliance on craft skills.

The Georgian period also saw the establishment of nationwide styles. The growing sense of nationhood, and Britain's increasing power in the world, was matched by a conscious desire to create national styles, normally set by trends in London. Although continental Europe, and especially France, continued to be a touchstone for taste and style, some of the new national styles, like the neo-classicism of Robert Adam, were both admired and imitated abroad.

1 *A Common Council man of Candlestick Ward and his wife on a visit to Mr Deputy – at his Modern Built villa near Clapham*, 1771. By an unknown artist. The social pretensions and flawed taste of City of London merchants is here satirized. To Mr Deputy's suburban house, a plain clapboard cottage, have been added disparate neo-Palladian, Gothic and chinoiserie elements. Hand-coloured engraving. Courtesy of the Lewis Walpole Library, Yale University.

2 *The Tuscan Order*. Plate from *The four books of Andrea Palladio's Architecture*, translated and published by Isaac Ware, 1738. Engraving. VAM 62.B.19.

2. British baroque

A new monarch seldom means a new style, and the accession of George I in 1714 was no exception. The baroque style, which from the 1680s was being employed across architecture, interiors and movable objects, continued into the 1730s. Its greatest architectural expressions, Castle Howard and Blenheim Palace, had already been built or were under construction. At Blenheim, Sir John Vanbrugh put up the only British palace to rival in scale Louis XIV's Versailles, a composition of immense spatial drama intended to express the nation's pride in the Duke of Marlborough's victories in the War of the Spanish Succession. At a more modest level, from about 1700, many new houses were baroque in their varied sense of scale, elaborate skylines, occasional breaking of the classical rules or the addition of a few Italian details taken from a book. They shared a growing taste for the imposing and monumental, assisted by the increasing use on façades of classical pediments and a preference for giant orders of columns, rising from the ground to the roof.

In the background was a growing interest in classical architecture and the buildings and ideas of the Italian Renaissance architect Andrea Palladio, whose work (and publications) had inspired the buildings of Inigo Jones 75 years before. Eventually this trend resulted in the triumph of the neo-Palladian style, but up to the 1730s it was a mixed story, with nominally baroque architects increasingly taking on Palladian ideas. Chief among these was James Gibbs, who had, unusually, trained in Italy, under the baroque architect Carlo Fontana. In Britain, in such characteristic buildings as St Martin-in-the-Fields in London and the Radcliffe Camera in Oxford, Gibbs developed a modest baroque style based on a Palladian framework. The publication in 1728 of his *Book of Architecture*, packed with ornamental details as well as designs for buildings, brought his style to thousands of ordinary builders in Britain and the colonies, setting a notion of 'Georgian' style that is still with us today.

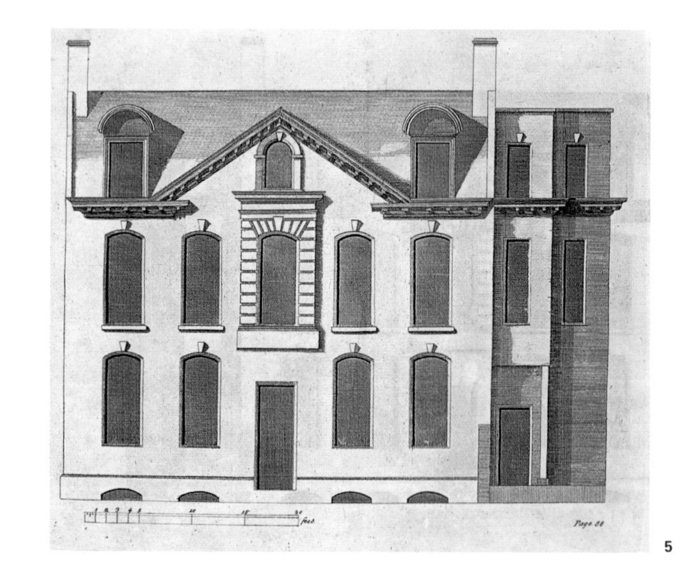

3 *The South-West Prospect of St Martins-in-the-Fields, London*, 1738. Engraved by William Henry Toms after Robert West. James Gibbs's church, built 1722–6, became a model for new churches in Britain and the colonies. Engraving. VAM E.1688-1888.

4 Wine cooler, with London hallmarks for 1719–20. Mark of Anthony Nelme. Magnificent equipment like this was the focal point of the baroque dining room. Made for Thomas Parker, later first Earl Macclesfield, for Shirburn Castle, Oxfordshire. Parker was made Lord Chancellor in 1718. Silver. VAM M.27-1998.

5 *A baroque-style house*. Plate from *An Essay in Defence of Ancient Architecture* by Robert Morris, 1728. Engraving. VAM 33.B.1.

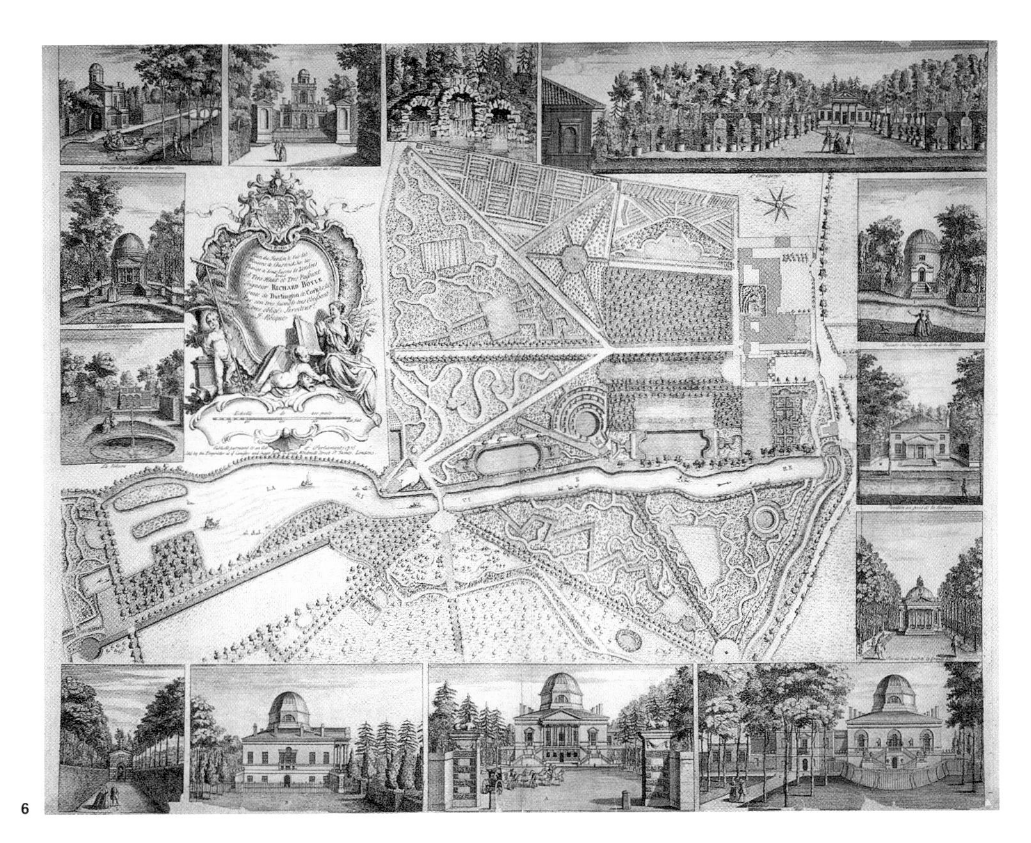

Neo-Palladian buildings were intimately linked to the gardens that surrounded them. At first such gardens (like that at Lord Burlington's villa at Chiswick), filled with small classical buildings and complicated paths, were designed to recall the gardens described in the great literary works of classical antiquity. As no such ancient gardens survived, the models used were often taken from more modern Italian examples. Although they now seem rather artificial, the asymmetry of these gardens was in marked contrast to the grand symmetrical gardens of the baroque, making them part of a trend towards the natural in British gardening, which began about 1700. In a more simplified form such neo-Palladian gardens, like that at Stourhead, were designed as a circuit, with temples and other buildings set in relationship to a lake (*see 3:11*). Stourhead is an evocation of a classical arcadia, a vision of harmony and order. But its likeness to an Italian landscape painting is no accident, for such paintings, by the seventeenth-century artist Claude Lorraine and others, lay at the heart of the true 'natural' gardening promoted from the 1750s by Lancelot 'Capability' Brown. The natural or 'open' style of gardening, so perfectly suited to setting off the clarity of neo-Palladian architecture, was a genuine innovation, involving nothing less than the creation of an ideal landscape. In that sense it was just as artificial as the earlier style, since it always involved the introduction of water and sometimes extensive topographical remodelling.

3. Neo-Palladianism

In 1728 the neo-Palladian architect Robert Morris delivered a withering attack on a baroque house built four years earlier:

> There is not a single object in the whole execution, but is in a direct opposition to the rules of ancient architecture: for instance, look on the pediment what a false bearing, or rather what bearing at all has it? How irregular is it in the disposition, how contrary even to the most common notions in the pitch of it, the roof; with the windows, how disproportionate are they with their ill dispos'd pediments, the returns of the cornice in every part, the irregular breaks, and likewise the disagreeable affinity they have to each other?

Morris's attack, published in his *Essay in Defence of Ancient Architecture*, not only reveals his humble background, but also shows the power of the neo-Palladian revolution, with its captivating mantra of classical rules, first clearly demonstrated by Colen Campbell and later taken up to huge effect by Lord Burlington. The composition of Campbell's design for the great country house of Wanstead was indebted to Castle Howard, but its detail made it Palladian rather than baroque (*see 2:8*). The great pedimented entrance portico, the alternately arched and pedimented windows, the rusticated basement in rough blocks and the end pavilions lit by three-part Venetian windows were all to become key neo-Palladian features. Above all, the composition relied for its effect on the careful balance between the blank, untextured wall surface and the window openings, giving it a sense of combined grandeur and repose.

6 *Plan du Jardin & Vüe des Maisons de Chiswick*, 1736. Designed and engraved by Jean Rocque. Etching and engraving. VAM E.352-1944.

7 *Croome Court, Worcestershire*, 1758–9. By Richard Wilson. George, sixth Earl of Coventry, employed Lancelot 'Capability' Brown to landscape the grounds around his neo-Palladian house, also designed by Brown and created from an earlier building, 1751–2. Oil on canvas. Croome Estate Trustees.

NEO-PALLADIANISM

Michael Snodin

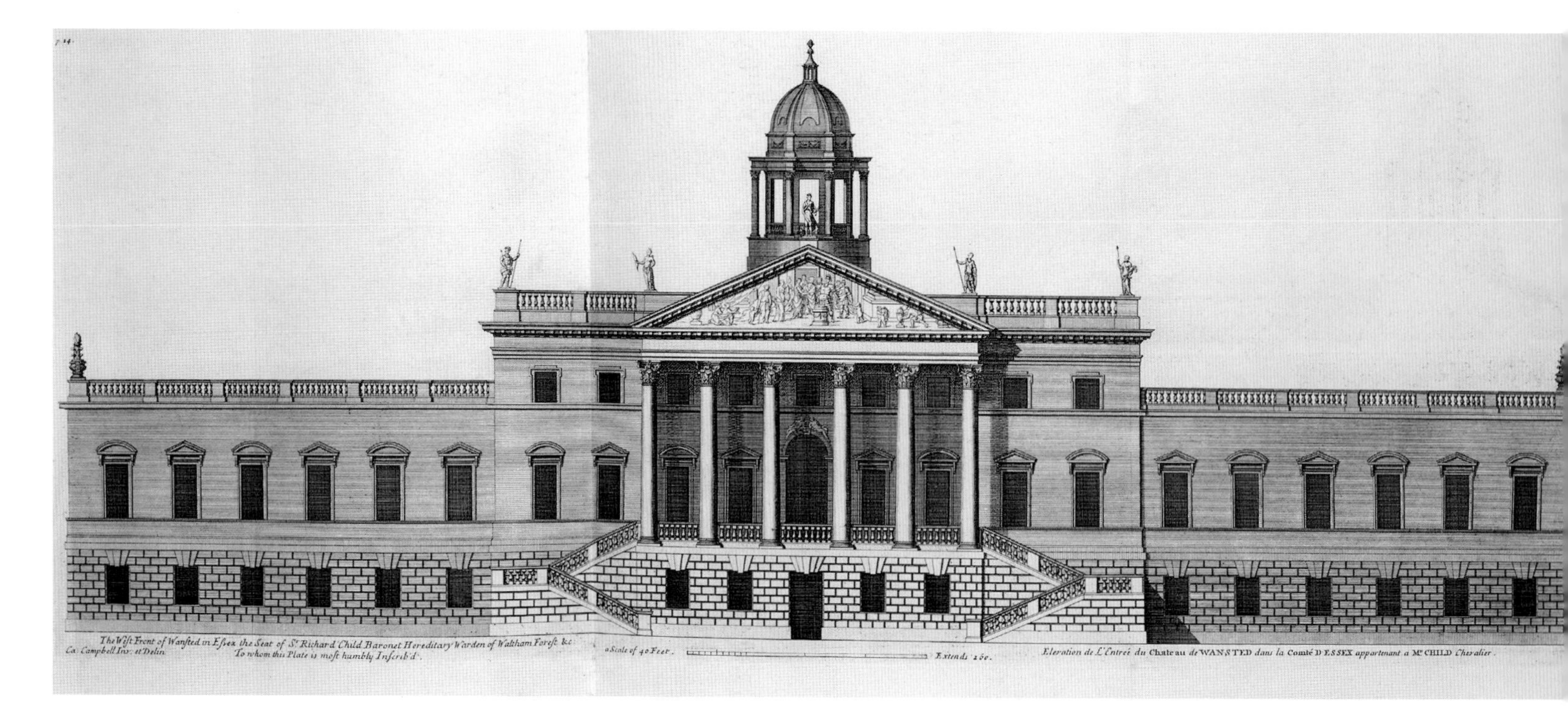

8. Wanstead House, London, built about 1714–20. Designed by Colen Campbell for Sir Richard Child. Plate from *Vitruvius Britannicus* by Colen Campbell, Vol. 1, 1715 (this plate from the 1731 edition), published by the author. Engraving. VAM 34.G.182.

Neo-Palladianism was a classical style used in architecture and interiors, which emerged fully in about 1715 and was in use up to about 1800. It was based on the forms and ornament of ancient Roman buildings, the work of Andrea Palladio and other Italian Renaissance architects, and the seventeenth-century architecture of Inigo Jones, who also admired Palladio. It first emerged in the work of the Scottish architect Colen Campbell. His book *Vitruvius Britannicus* (1715) featured his pioneering house at Wanstead, but similar great neo-Palladian houses were not to appear for another 15 years. In that time neo-Palladianism acquired a much more persuasive champion, the architect Lord Burlington, who, first in the company of Campbell and later with others, set the character of the neo-Palladian style. From a scholarly amalgam of Italian and Jonesian sources, Burlington formed a classically correct style that was uniquely British. It was as applicable to the smallest terraced house as it was to the grandest mansion, setting the pattern for British architecture for the next 100 years. For Burlington's followers, neo-Palladianism also had a special meaning, signalling a link between the virtues and power of ancient Rome and the culture of Italy and the culture, political systems and power of the burgeoning British nation.

Burlington's own designs were mainly for small buildings, the most characteristic being an extension to his own house at Chiswick. Begun in 1725, it was based partly on Palladio's Villa Rotonda at Vicenza. It established the idea of the small independent villa, a house type that came to invade every suburb some 100 years later. As with many neo-Palladian buildings, the plain exterior contrasted with richly decorated interiors. These were not based on Palladio's own designs, but on details from ancient Roman buildings, combined with fireplaces, ceilings and other details taken from Inigo Jones.

9. Console table, 1727–32. Designed by William Kent for the gallery at Chiswick House and perhaps made in London by John Boson. Carved and gilded pine and Siena marble. [h. 88.9cm]. VAM W.14-1971.

10. The entrance front of Chiswick House, London, 1725–9. Designed by Richard Boyle, third Earl of Burlington.

While the walls of most of the rooms were hung with woven textiles, the central saloon was plastered and painted, and enlivened with sober sculptural ornament, a pioneering and highly influential concept. The interiors were designed by Burlington's assistant and protégé, William Kent, who was also responsible for designing furniture and other movable items for subsequent neo-Palladian interiors. Again there was no accessible precedent in Palladio, so Kent, who was trained as a painter but had a brilliant and poetic imagination in a number of design fields, devised new models derived equally from Italian baroque examples and ancient Roman sculptural ideas.

11. Design for a chimneypiece at Oatlands Palace, Surrey, 1636. By Inigo Jones. Pen and brown ink over black chalk. RIBA Library Drawings Collection.

12. The Gallery, Chiswick House, London, 1725–9. Designed by Richard Boyle, third Earl of Burlington, and William Kent.

4. The neo-Palladian interior

In their interiors, Lord Burlington and his interior designer William Kent aimed to depart from current baroque fashions: tall, vertically panelled rooms, often in wood, or the more expensive, dramatically painted interiors rich with Italian plasterwork and extravagantly 'incorrect' mouldings. It is interesting to compare the interiors of Burlington's villa at Chiswick with a room designed by James Gibbs at about the same date. While the Chiswick ceilings are beamed in the Inigo Jones manner, Gibbs employs a baroque ceiling of curved mouldings made by Italian plasterworkers and enclosing Italian paintings. While Burlington's chimneypieces and other details are faithfully copied from Jones and Palladio, Gibbs employs his own repertoire of forms related to – but developing – Jonesian ideas.

The same opposition can be seen in furniture and other movable items. William Kent's blocky designs were very different in style from the leading luxury furniture style of the day, still indebted to the ideas of Daniel Marot from the 1690s, or the more modest pieces reflecting the broken pediments, pilasters and other architectural elements of the baroque interior. Neither furniture nor interiors in Kent's heavy style were to remain fashionable much beyond 1750. The main reason was the arrival in the 1730s of a new anti-classical style, the rococo.

14

13

5. The rococo

Rococo was a style without rules. In France it was known as the *genre pittoresque* (picturesque manner) and in Britain simply as 'modern', clearly signalling its break with the ancient classical norms. While classicism was based on the architectural orders, with their measured proportions and fixed hierarchy of ornamentation, rococo had only the asymmetrical pictorial composition known as the *morceau de fantaisie*, an infinitely variable exercise in illogicality. The nearest the rococo ever came to a theoretical justification was William Hogarth's *Analysis of Beauty* (1753), which isolated the serpentine 'line of beauty and grace' as the essence of aesthetic beauty: 'there is scarce a room in any house whatever, where one does not see a waving line employed in some way or other'. It was no accident that the same line was linked to drawing exercises for the essential element of British rococo design, the curled acanthus or 'raffle leaf' (*see 3:17*).

The anti-classical nature of rococo and its perceived origins in the craft workshop were by the 1730s provoking counterattacks by French academic critics. In 1755 the miniaturist (and friend of Hogarth) André Rouquet was attacking 'the taste called *contrast* . . . which men of indifferent taste adopt without feeling, and apply without judgement'. A year later the neo-Palladian architect Isaac Ware was deploring rococo as the product of the French, 'a frivolous people we are too apt to imitate . . . It consists of crooked lines like

13 Ceiling from the drawing room of No. 11 Henrietta Place, London, about 1727–30. Designed by James Gibbs, with plasterwork by Giuseppe Artari and Giovanni Bagutti. As re-installed in the Victoria and Albert Museum. VAM W.5-1960.

14 Design for a rococo-style interior, about 1755. By John Linnell. Pen, ink and watercolour. VAM E.263-1929.

C's and ƆC's, the Gothick is hardly more contemptible'. The rococo style joined such undesirable French imports as dancing masters, smelly cheeses and effete manners, all offensive to robust Englishmen. But the opposition could only be beaten by emulation, especially in the field of luxury goods. Although anti-French groups like the Anti-Gallican Society, founded in 1745, sought to oppose the 'insidious arts of the French Nation', their keenest supporters, like the carver and drawing master Thomas Johnson, were among the most enthusiastic exponents of the rococo style.

15

6. Gothic and chinoiserie

Rococo was a natural partner for two other styles, Gothic and chinoiserie. To critics like Isaac Ware all three were 'unmeaning' – that is, confused and without system. This did nothing to halt their popularity, which reached a peak in the years around 1750. They could be used either separately or together. At Claydon House, Buckinghamshire, there were adjacent Gothic, Chinese and French (or rococo) rooms, while all three styles were frequently combined in a single piece of furniture. In architecture, the medieval forms of the Gothic style had occasionally been revived earlier, even by such distinguished classicists as Sir Christopher Wren, and it had never entirely disappeared from certain traditional environments, such as the Oxford and Cambridge colleges. What happened in the 1730s was new, for Gothic began to be treated as a historical style with a meaning, both playful and deeply serious. Early Gothic buildings in gardens and pioneering domestic projects, such as Horace Walpole's house of Strawberry Hill, were intended both to be decorative and to suggest through their style a link with a specifically British history. From such serious beginnings, however, Gothic was quickly adopted as a popular style, abetted by the publishers of architectural books, who even attempted to impose upon it the rule of classical orders. It was not until the 1770s that an increasingly serious antiquarian study of medieval architecture led to neo-Gothic buildings accurate in their details, if not in their overall design.

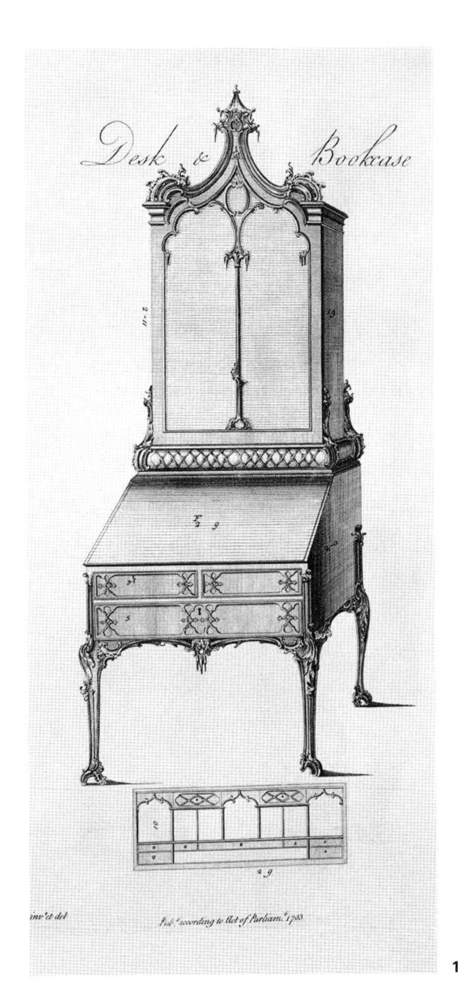

16

The years around 1750, which saw the height of the rage for Gothic and rococo, also witnessed the peak of popular interest in chinoiserie. A style evoking an imaginary China had been popular since the 1690s. At that time it chiefly involved the display and use of items from China, India and Japan in sympathetic and evocative surroundings, sometimes created by covering walls with lacquer, paint or paper. While the enthusiasm for East Asian and Indian things increased over the next 50 years, the forms of consumption changed, and a new style emerged that was based on scenes and motifs on lacquer and porcelain, but which was purely European and could be applied to objects outside those traditional materials.

15 *Fontaine Glacée*, 1736. Plate from the set *Livre nouveau de Douze Morceaux de Fantaisie*, 1736, engraved by Jean-Baptiste Guelard after Jacques de Lajoue. Etching and engraving. VAM 229678.3.

16 *Bureau bookcase*, 1754. Engraved by Matthias Darly after Thomas Chippendale the Elder. Plate from *The Gentleman and Cabinet Maker's Director* by Thomas Chippendale, 1754. While the upper part is Gothic – vaguely recalling medieval window tracery – the legs are rococo and the finial Chinese. Engraving. VAM RC.CC.11.

Rococo Style

Hilary Young

The rococo was an ornamental style that had a long genesis, but which emerged as a distinct style in France during the 1720s and 1730s. Key elements were C- and S-scrolls, and an amorphous, organic, shell-like substance known as rocaille. These were frequently used in combination with fish, shells and other marine motifs. Compositions were often markedly asymmetric and featured illogical combinations of scale. Naturalistic fruit and flowers were introduced, notably in ceramics and on silks, and the style was used in combination with Chinese and Gothic motifs.

The style flourished in English design between about 1740 and 1770, but was rarely taken up for architecture. Its chief promoters in Britain were artists, craftspeople and entrepreneurs from the middle ranks of society, rather than architects and their noble patrons. Rococo was used for both luxury and utilitarian goods – it appears in grand furnishings and silver, for example, but also on inexpensive pottery and ephemeral prints.

The rococo first appeared in England in silver and engravings of ornament of the 1730s. Immigrant artists and craftspeople, including Huguenot refugees from France, played a key role in its dissemination. Its seedbed was the St Martin's Lane Academy, with which the book illustrator Hubert-François Gravelot and the painters Andien de Clermont and William Hogarth were all associated.

17. Inkstand, with London hallmarks for 1738–9. Mark of Paul de Lamerie. Silver-gilt. Duke of Marlborough.

18. Design for a brocaded silk tobine, 1749. By Anna Maria Garthwaite for the London weaver Daniel Vautier. Watercolour on paper. VAM 5987.1.

19. Two-handled cup, with London hallmarks for 1759–60. Mark of Thomas Heming. Silver-gilt. [h. 39.5cm]. VAM M.41-1959.

20. Trade card of Henry Patten, razor maker and cutler, about 1750. Engraved by Edward Warner after Henry Copland, London. VAM E.571-1976.

21. Chimneypiece, about 1750. From Winchester House, Putney, London. Carved pine with marble and glass. [h. 321.9cm]. VAM 738-1897.

22. Plate, about 1756. Transfer-printed with a scene from *The Aeneid*, after a drawing by Hubert-François Bourguignon, called Gravelot. Made at the Bow factory, London. Soft-paste porcelain with transfer-printed decoration and enamelled border. [diam. 19.7cm]. VAM C.217-1940.

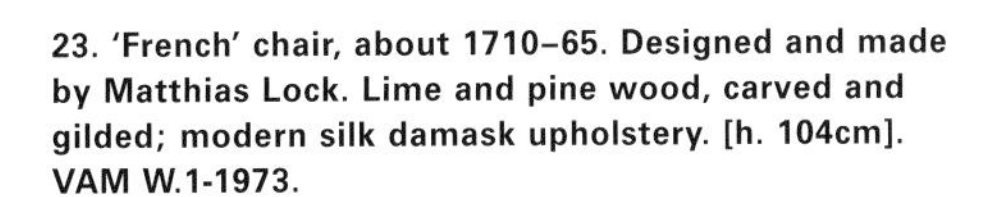

23. 'French' chair, about 1710–65. Designed and made by Matthias Lock. Lime and pine wood, carved and gilded; modern silk damask upholstery. [h. 104cm]. VAM W.1-1973.

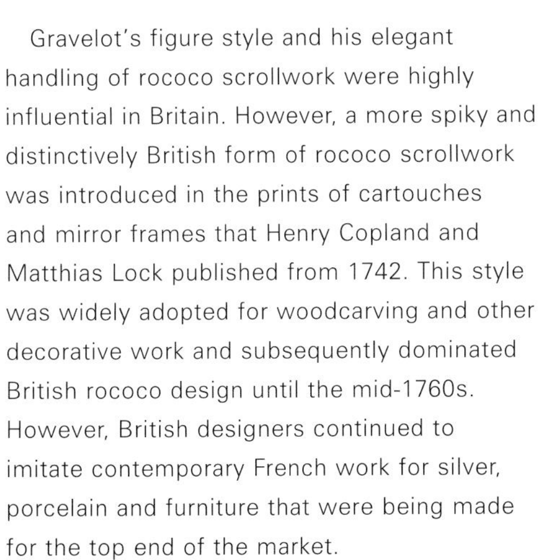

Gravelot's figure style and his elegant handling of rococo scrollwork were highly influential in Britain. However, a more spiky and distinctively British form of rococo scrollwork was introduced in the prints of cartouches and mirror frames that Henry Copland and Matthias Lock published from 1742. This style was widely adopted for woodcarving and other decorative work and subsequently dominated British rococo design until the mid-1760s. However, British designers continued to imitate contemporary French work for silver, porcelain and furniture that were being made for the top end of the market.

Many pattern books of rococo ornament of the type issued by Lock and Copland were published in England in the 1740s and 1750s. These were largely intended for craftspeople and designers and were hugely influential in disseminating rococo idioms. Their popularity stemmed from the complexity of the style, which placed great demands on the design and modelling skills of British craftspeople. Many felt that the nation lacked the design skills necessary to compete with imported French goods, which led to initiatives to improve design standards during the years when the rococo was current in Britain.

This formal interest was signalled as early as 1683 when Sir William Temple recognized asymmetry and 'beauty without order' (which he called by an apparently Chinese word, 'Sharawagdi') as a characteristic of the design of lacquer screens, porcelain and 'Indian Gowns', as well as of Chinese gardens. It was not, however, until the 1730s that true chinoiserie was born, a child of the rococo style, with which it shared similar fantastic and asymmetrical elements. It was only to be expected that such style plurality, especially when it was so eagerly taken up by the nouveaux riches, should be satirized in books and newspapers. In fact the Chinese style was thought to be particularly appropriate for bedrooms at the highest social level, hung with Chinese wallpaper, decorated with ceramics and housing a chinoiserie bed. This was attested by Sir William Chambers, whose *Designs of Chinese Buildings, Furniture, Dresses, Machines, and Utensils* (1757) attempted to regulate the Chinese mania by supplying the reading public with examples taken from his own observations in China.

Chambers put theory into practice in 1761 by designing for Princess Augusta at Kew Gardens the first pagoda built in Europe and the most permanent of many garden buildings in the Chinese style. At Kew the pagoda joined an 'Alhambra', a 'Mosque', a Gothic 'cathedral' and a range of classical temples, turning the gardens into a demonstration of world architectural styles. While such stylistic mixes in other contexts drew snobbish ridicule, they were all expressions of a generally more relaxed attitude towards rule-breaking in style, easing the arrival of neo-classicism in the late 1750s.

24 *A view of the wilderness, with the Alhambra, the Pagoda and the Mosque in the Royal Gardens at Kew*, 1763. All of these were built between 1758 and 1762. Anonymous engraver after William Marlow. Hand-coloured engraving. VAM 29428.A.

25 Pier glass in the chinoiserie style, about 1758–60. Similar to designs by the carver and gilder Thomas Johnson. Carved gilded wood. [h. 329cm]. VAM W.23-1949.

7. Neo-classicism

Neo-classicism was known to contemporaries as the 'antique manner'. As a European style it had complex roots linked to Italy and Greece and the archaeological rediscovery of antiquity, combined with a reassessment of Renaissance design. A return to the antique had, of course, been part of art and design since the fifteenth century, but now it was directed at creating an eternally valid 'true style'. It was not simply a matter of motifs, but also of a search for the ideal, characterized in its purest form by a high moral seriousness in stark opposition to the frivolous, hedonistic nature of the rococo. Nor was it a matter of strict architectural rules and proportions, but of reactions to the antique on the level of emotion and imaginative aesthetic enquiry. This not only gave neo-classicism the freedom to develop beyond the models that inspired it, towards forms and treatments that the ancients would hardly have recognized, but allowed the parallel use of other, seemingly diametrically opposed styles, such as Gothic.

Neo-classicism was as much about the rediscovery and reassessment of ancient painting and sculpture as it was about architecture and design. The result was a style of remarkable homogeneity, in which two- and three-dimensional classical figures, used in a more or less scholarly manner, became an integral part of the vocabulary of architecture, interior decoration and the applied arts, matching the actual ancient (or not so ancient) sculpture that was sent home following the Italian Grand Tour of many an English milord. The archaeological tendency also meant that neo-classicism became a total style, extending beyond architecture and interiors to fixed and movable objects of all types, from furniture to silver.

26 Chimneypiece, about 1775. Designed by Sir William Chambers and probably made by Joseph Wilton. Commissioned by Granville Leveson Gower, second Earl Gower, for the great drawing room at Gower House, Whitehall, London. Carrara marble. [h. 190cm]. VAM A.1-1998.

8. British neo-classicism

Robert Adam, James Stuart and Sir William Chambers, the architect founders of British neo-classicism, had all been in Rome during the exciting years around 1750, when French students and others were laying the ground for the style. The British approach nevertheless turned out to be very different from neo-classical developments on the continent, for Britain – unlike the rest of Europe – already possessed in its neo-Palladian architecture and interior decoration a controlled and simple classical style. Indeed, some examples of neo-Palladianism, like Lord Burlington's Assembly Rooms at York (a re-creation of Vitruvius's Egyptian Hall as envisaged by Palladio), can be described as neo-classical in the true sense (*see 1:45*) . Thus, while neo-classical ideas transformed the ornament, and even the forms, of objects both large and small, architecture and interiors at first tended to take only the decorative devices, adding them to fundamentally neo-Palladian structures.

Robert Adam claimed, in 1773, to have effected in buildings 'a remarkable improvement in the form, convenience, and relief of apartments; a greater movement and variety in the outside composition, and in the decoration of the inside an almost total change'. The last was certainly true, for Adam's version of neo-classicism set off a revolution in style. His distinctive decorative system used a limited range of ornament, brilliantly distilled from ancient and Renaissance sources, chiefly wall paintings and room decorations. By the very early 1760s Adam had developed a form of interior decoration that sought to suggest the rooms of the ancients, but adapted to modern uses. Ceilings and walls, and often floors (in the form of inlays or carpet), were covered with continuous areas of small-scale ornament, which played down architectural definition and were frequently based on the antique form of decoration known as the grotesque. A genre of ancient Roman painted wall decoration, the grotesque had been codified into a usable form by Raphael in the sixteenth century and had continued in use with gradual changes. Neo-classical designers sought to purify the form by re-establishing the link with ancient Roman painting through the earliest systematic excavations of ancient domestic sites, including (from 1748) the buried cities of Pompeii and Herculaneum, as well as by going back to Raphael. The use of colour in ancient interiors inspired Adam, in a radical departure from neo-Palladian precedent, to introduce strong colours into his own designs.

Adam's own theory of design was based on the principle of 'movement', the rise and fall and advancement and recession of forms, ultimately derived from the buildings of Burlington and Kent, but clothed in columns, decorated pilasters and other ancient devices. The idea was matched in his interiors by their manner of arranging sequences of rooms that were different in plan, often punctuated by three-dimensional effects in the form of detached columns (*see 3:36*). The concentration on visual and scenic effects, at the expense of stately logic, matched the growing engagement with the idea of the Picturesque, which by the end of the century was to dominate all fields of design.

27

27 View of the gallery, or library, at Syon House, London, 1763–73. By an unknown artist for Robert Adam. The Syon gallery was created by Adam for the Duke and Duchess of Northumberland. Pen, ink and wash. VAM E.1063-1940.

9. Coordinated design

Although notions of coordinated design had occurred before the neo-classical period, most notably in the furniture and interiors of Daniel Marot in about 1700 and in those of William Kent, they had never before been so widespread in British design. The process was encouraged by the relative ease with which repetitious and regular neo-classical ornament (and Adam ornament in particular) could be produced in flat pattern or low relief, and standardized simple shapes could be fitted together in interestingly different combinations. Ideally, modern objects, both practical and decorative, would imitate antique prototypes. When these could not be found, as was frequently the case, a few key antique forms were adapted. The most important were the vase and the tripod, both powerful and appealing signals of antiquity.

Among the first neo-classical objects to be made in Britain were an ormolu vase and tripod, both designed by James Stuart before 1760. The vase, characteristically, concealed its function as a plate warmer, and was an original composition. The tripod was a perfume burner, its design taken from the finial of the choragic monument of Lysicrates in Athens (*see 2:35*). Stuart had seen the monument in 1751 and illustrated it in his book (written with Nicholas Revett), *The Antiquities of Athens*, published in 1762, the first accurate survey of classical Greek remains. In 1762 Robert Adam incorporated both objects in his scheme for the dining room at Kedleston Hall (a project he took over from Stuart), a characteristically unified neo-classical scheme incorporating furniture, utensils and decoration. Tripods continued to be a rich source of design ideas in many fields.

Vases became an acknowledged mania. They were especially exploited by manufacturers like Josiah Wedgwood and Matthew Boulton, who vigorously plundered sources ranging from Renaissance prints to excavated Greek pottery in order to satisfy an insatiable market for vases as ornaments. Among their chief sources were the illustrated volumes published in 1766–7 by Sir William Hamilton on his collection of antiquities in Naples, *Catalogue of Etruscan, Greek, and Roman Antiquities* by Baron d'Hancarville. This was aimed at instructing craftspeople and artists, and was immediately taken up by Wedgwood, who not only named his factory Etruria, but celebrated its opening in 1769 by making a set of vases after d'Hancarville's illustrations.

Neo-classicism took some 10 years to spread beyond the fashionable élite. Even Adam was content to add a neo-classical spin to sofas of rococo form and chair types devised by William Kent, although his fixed furniture, such as pier tables and glasses, was more often strictly architectural in design. By the early 1770s full-blown neo-classical furniture had penetrated the general market, and in 1774 the architect John Carter could describe a pair of Adam-style grotesque panels shown in *The Builder's Magazine* as being 'in the present reigning taste'. Such characteristic ornament was translated into inlay and paint on furniture and as sparkling 'bright-cut' engraving on silver, while figures in cameo were found on all sorts of objects, from chimneypieces to jewellery.

28 Detail of a design for the dining-room alcove, Kedleston Hall, Derbyshire, drawn 1762. Designed by Robert Adam. Pen, ink and watercolour. The National Trust, Kedleston Hall.

29 Left: vase, about 1773–5. Made at Josiah Wedgwood's factory, Etruria, Staffordshire. White 'terracotta stoneware', with applied reliefs and 'pebble' glaze. Right: vase, about 1770–80. Probably made by Humphrey Palmer or his successor James Neale at the Church Works, Hanley, Staffordshire. Creamware, with applied medallion and 'porphyry' glaze. [h. 25.08cm]. VAM 2386-1901 and 304-1869.

NEO-CLASSICISM

Hilary Young

Neo-classicism was a style that emerged in Britain and France in the 1750s; it affected all the visual arts and flourished into the early years of the nineteenth century. Its birth and rapid spread were the result of a renewed passion for the remains of the classical past and a dissatisfaction with the rococo style. Initially confined to a small circle of collectors and patrons, this interest in antiquity was fuelled by a number of publications championing ancient art, publicizing archaeological discoveries at Herculaneum in Italy, Palmyra in Syria and elsewhere. They also illustrated major collections of antique engraved gems, vases and sculpture.

Architects pioneered the style in Britain, and in its earliest, most vigorous phase the decorative vocabulary of neo-classicism was architectural. The pioneering neo-classical artists and designers were consciously creating an emphatically modern style based on the remains of the classical past.

The architects who introduced the style in Britain were James 'Athenian' Stuart, Sir William Chambers and Robert Adam, all of whom had studied in Rome and travelled widely. Chambers's and Adam's designs were disseminated by their folio publications of 1759 and 1773 respectively. By the 1770s Adam's early robust, archaeologically inspired manner had given way to a more delicate and attenuated style, which was taken up and further developed by James Wyatt. All these men designed coordinated interior schemes, sometimes with furniture and silver to match.

30. *Design for a dining room*, about 1770–5. By James Wyatt. Pencil, pen, ink and watercolour on paper. VAM 7231.35.

31. Table, 1769. Designed by Sir William Chambers for his own use and made in London by Georg Haupt. Oak and pine carcase veneered with satinwood; the top inlaid with ebony veneer and samples of jasper, onyx, lapis lazuli, quartz and serpentine. VAM W.38-1977.

32. *Thetis and Her Nymphs Rising from the Sea to console Achilles for the loss of Patroclus*, about 1778. Carved in Rome by Thomas Banks. Marble. [h. 91.4cm]. VAM A.15-1984.

33. Armchair, about 1790. Supplied by the firm of Seddon and Shackleton to Daniel Tupper of Hauteville House, St Peter Port, Guernsey. Painted satinwood. VAM W.2-1968.

34. Armchair, 1764–5. Designed by Robert Adam and made in London in the workshop of Thomas Chippendale for 19 Arlington Street, London, the house of Sir Lawrence Dundas. Gilded beechwood and walnut; replacement upholstery. VAM W.1-1937.

The designs and decorative language of the leading architects were imitated and freely adapted by craftspeople and manufacturers, effecting a revolution in English design around 1770. In silver of the 1770s, for example, rococo ornament was replaced by plain areas of silver set against narrow bands of classical motifs. Some designers, however, combined rococo and neo-classical elements, creating an elegant hybrid style. Wedgwood and other manufacturers took up the 'antique' vase as a fashionable sign of the new style. Changes in manufacturing technologies encouraged the taste for plainness during the final decades of the century, as seen in Sheffield plate. What had begun life as a learned and exclusive style confined to a small social élite was enjoying a wide market by the 1780s, when Birmingham and Sheffield metalwork and Staffordshire pottery in neo-classical styles were being made for nationwide markets and for export.

36. Water jug, about 1785. Probably made in Sheffield. Copper plated with silver (Sheffield plate). VAM M.207-1920.

35. Perfume burner, about 1760. Designed by James Stuart and made by Diederich Nicolaus Anderson. Cut and chased ormolu; marble stand. [h. 53.97cm]. VAM M.46-1948.

10. After Adam

In architecture, the Adam style was quickly taken up and developed by others. It was refined in the hands of architects like James Wyatt, while acute observers like Horace Walpole began to tire of the Adam brothers' 'gingerbread and sippets of embroidery'.

A bolder approach had already been proposed by Adam's great rival, the royal architect Sir William Chambers, who designed in a stately amalgam of neo-Palladianism and ideas learned in Rome and Paris. Chambers's biggest project, Somerset House, housing the new Royal Academy as well as civil servants, conspicuously brought the style before the public. Its deep masonry basements were a built demonstration of the ideas of the architect Giovanni

38

37

37 The Bank Stock Office, Bank of England, London, built 1792–4. Designed by Sir John Soane. Drawn by Joseph Michael Gandy, 1798. Pen, ink and watercolour. Trustees of the Sir John Soane Museum.

38 Detail of *The Strand, London*, about 1796. By Thomas Malton. On the right is Somerset House, designed by Sir William Chambers and built 1776–96. The comparatively narrow street front of the building opens into a huge courtyard, giving onto the Thames. In the middle distance of this view is James Gibbs's Church of St Mary-le-Strand, built 1714–17. Watercolour. VAM 1725-1871.

Battista Piranesi, at whose feet both Chambers and Adam had sat when in Rome. Piranesi's sensationalist prints of huge Roman structures and ponderous neo-classical inventions led architects all over Europe to use simpler, more dramatic forms, which became increasingly separate from strict classical precedent.

Britain was not exempt from this tendency, and in the buildings of George Dance junior from the mid-1760s, and of his brilliant pupil Sir John Soane from the 1780s, a new type of poetic architecture developed, employing elemental geometric forms. The same trend towards simplification showed itself in other forms of design from the 1780s onwards. At the highest level neo-classical styles were imported from France, marking a return to the historical tendency for Britain to follow the French lead in matters of design.

At Carlton House, designed by Henry Holland for the Prince of Wales from 1783 onwards, a French-style exterior enclosed a French interior, ornamented and supplied with furniture by French decorators and craftspeople. By 1785 Horace Walpole was admiring its 'august simplicity . . . it is the taste and propriety that strike. Every ornament is at a proper distance, and not one too large, but all delicate and new, with more freedom and variety than Greek [i.e. Adam-style] ornaments; and although probably borrowed from the Hôtel de Condé and other new Palaces, not one that is rather classic than French.' A similar 'august simplicity' showed itself in a wide range of more modest applications in furniture (for instance, the designs shown by George Hepplewhite and Thomas Sheraton), and in ceramics and metalwork. Often these designs were admirably suited to production by means of the new, mainly hand-powered machines that proliferated in the Georgian era.

39

40

39 *The hall, Carlton House, London*, about 1819. By Charles Wild. Part of the alterations to Carlton House, designed for the Prince of Wales by Henry Holland, carried out 1785–9. Watercolour. © The Royal Collection.

40 Kettle and stand, about 1795. Made in Sheffield. Copper plated with silver (Sheffield plate). [h. 33cm]. VAM M.637-1936.

11. Style plurality

The 1790s marked a turning point in the way styles were viewed and used. For the first time a whole group of historical and non-European styles, including Gothic, Chinese and two newcomers, Indian and Egyptian, became legitimate alternatives to classicism, opening the door to a wave of style plurality that continued to the end of the nineteenth century. This development was condemned by many contemporary commentators as a frenetic striving for novelty (fed as it was by the first style and fashion magazines), but was nevertheless very different from the superficially similar style plurality of 40 years before, for now all styles, both classical and non-classical, were treated with a new seriousness, both in their application and their accuracy.

The application of style came increasingly to be based on the notion of association – the idea that a certain style might conjure up certain thoughts or feelings. This led naturally to a code of appropriateness. A learned institution might, for instance, be housed in the sober and majestic style of the Greek Revival but never in Chinese, while the Prince Regent's summer palace at Brighton was an exercise in extravagant exoticism. Patriotism during the Napoleonic Wars also played its part; Egyptian motifs were reminders of British victories, while the Gothic style recalled ancient British values and virtues during the years of international insecurity.

At the same time, the treatment of style became ever more accurate in its detail. Classical styles were spurred on by new archaeology. Non-European styles were promoted by illustrated accounts of foreign travels, like Baron Denon's *Voyage dans la Basse et la Haute Egypte*, published in London in 1802. In 1817 Thomas Rickman's *An Attempt to Discriminate the Styles of English Architecture from the Conquest to the Reformation* established the stylistic nomenclature of medieval architecture that is still in use today. The new stylistic accuracy encouraged the idea of coordinated design, pushing it from architecture and decoration to movables of all sorts, including furniture and even clothes.

41 *Early English*. Plate from *An Attempt to Discriminate the Styles of English Architecture from the Conquest to the Reformation* by Thomas Rickman, 1817. Published by Longman, Hurst, Rees, Orme and Brown. Engraving. VAM 34.E.66.

42 The Royal Institution, Edinburgh, built in the Greek Revival style, 1822–6. Designed by William Henry Playfair.

12. The Picturesque

Central to the whole approach to style and design from about 1790 was the notion of the Picturesque, which combined a heightened sense of history with a tendency to see things in specifically pictorial terms. Picturesque theory – as expounded, for instance, in Sir Uvedale Price's *Essay on the Picturesque as Compared with the Sublime and the Beautiful* (1794) – was heir to various investigations into aesthetics that had begun to appear from the 1720s onwards, most especially in Edmund Burke's writing on the sublime in the 1750s. Burke had explored the idea of extreme emotional reactions to nature and works of art derived from purely visual criteria. In Picturesque theory, irregular ancient buildings combined with agreeably rough natural landscapes to produce an emotional reaction, partly through their forms and partly through historical associations.

43

43 *Ludlow Castle, Shropshire*, 1778. By William Hodges. Oil on canvas. VAM 43-1880.

Translated into real terms, the Picturesque meant Humphry Repton's landscape gardens. They depended on a single viewpoint and were demonstrated by pictures from that viewpoint, both before and after construction. Equally Picturesque were John Nash's plans for London, with the great curve of Regent's Street (*see 3:59*) leading up to the Repton-like Regent's Park, surrounded by 'villages' of small houses in varied styles (including rustic Italian and Gothic), as well as palace-like classical terraced houses peering enticingly through the trees. The scenic effect of the Regent's Park architecture was symptomatic of the whole Picturesque movement, which was about appearances rather than solid substance; a similar insubstantial approach was found in other areas of design, including furniture and interiors, which were deeply concerned with imitation materials and heightened optical effects.

Greater historical and archaeological knowledge, and the visual emphasis of the Picturesque, encouraged the idea that architecture and the fine and applied arts were intimately linked. In creating his house-museum, filled with sculpture and paintings in dramatically lit interiors, Sir John Soane was aiming to demonstrate 'the unity of the arts'. The house-museum of the banker and collector Thomas Hope in Duchess Street, London, aimed at a visual totality based on the use of a symbolic programme. Of the room centred on John Flaxman's statue of Aurora and Cephalus, Hope wrote:

> the whole surrounding decoration has been rendered, in some degree, analogous to these personages, and to the face of nature at the moment when . . . the goddess of the morn is supposed to announce the approaching day . . . The sides of the room display, in satin curtains, draped in ample folds over panels of looking-glass, and edged with black velvet, the fiery hue which fringes the clouds just before sunrise: and in a ceiling of cooler sky blue are sown, amidst a few still unextinguished luminaries of the night, the roses which the harbinger of the day . . . spreads on every side about her.

The furniture was decorated with appropriate symbolic motifs, including emblems of the night, medallions of the god of sleep, owls and stars.

44

45

44 *The Aurora room, at the house of Thomas Hope, Duchess Street, London*. Plate from *Household Furniture and Interior Decoration executed from Designs by Thomas Hope*, 1807. Engraving. VAM FW.10D/2.

45 *Cumberland Terrace, Regent's Park, London*, 1827. Planned by John Nash, executed by James Thompson, built 1826. Engraved by James Tingle after Thomas Hosmer Shepherd. Plate from *Metropolitan Improvements* by James Elmes, 1827. Engraving. VAM 237.F.44.

46

47

13. The growth of the medieval

The enhanced status of medieval styles as alternatives to the classical was most clearly shown by the new Commissioners' churches, built with one million pounds from the government from 1818 onwards. Planned as simple preaching boxes, they could be either Greek or Gothic; that most were the latter was due more to the cheapness of Gothic than to any aesthetic preference. The symmetrical plans of the Commissioners' churches ran counter to the most complete handling of Gothic style, for anti-classical irregularity had become a key characteristic of the Gothic from the much-publicized Strawberry Hill onwards. At Downton Castle, in 1772, Richard Payne Knight, a major theorist of the Picturesque, built the first irregular castle, set in a naturally wild landscape. Downton had classical interiors, but James Wyatt's Lee Priory of 1783–90, which had never been a medieval religious site, was Gothic both inside and out.

From the 1790s large, irregularly planned Gothic country houses were built in considerable numbers, the most spectacular being Fonthill Abbey, designed by James Wyatt for the collector and West Indian plantation-owner William Beckford. The message of such houses was one of ancient lineage (in Beckford's case invented), feudal land ownership and the romance of Old England. According to the purpose, several styles were on offer: Humphry Repton listed Castle Gothic (as at Downton), Abbey Gothic (used at Fonthill) and Manor House. It was the last, a revival of the Tudor late-Gothic style of the early sixteenth century, that came to be the most popular and expanded to

46 *St Nicholas's Church, Lower Tooting, London*, 1832. By C. Rosenberg after Thomas William Atkinson. The church, designed by Atkinson, replaced a medieval church behind it, which had become too small for a rapidly growing congregation. Hand-coloured aquatint. Wandsworth Museum.

47 *Fonthill Abbey, Wiltshire*, 1822. By J. Barnett after John Chessell Buckler. The Abbey was designed by James Wyatt and built 1796–1818. The tower, 273ft (83 metres) high, fell down in 1825. Etching. VAM 29635.415.

embrace furniture and fittings as well as architecture, eventually being adopted as a suitably national style for the huge project of the Palace of Westminster, built from 1840. The biggest Gothic project before Westminster was the comprehensive restoration and enhancement of the castle at Windsor under Sir Jeffry Wyatville, a nephew of James Wyatt. Its rich interiors, completed in 1828, showed an entirely characteristic combination of gilt Gothic detail and luxurious modern textile furnishings. At a less exalted level, Gothic styles became especially popular in the cheaper forms of metalwork.

From about 1810 the medieval repertoire expanded chronologically in both directions. At one end it grew to encompass pre-Gothic Norman styles and at the other Elizabethan, Jacobean and even the Restoration styles of the later seventeenth century. The second group was especially associated with 'antiquarian interiors' of the type first promoted by Horace Walpole at Strawberry Hill from the 1750s onwards. At Fonthill Abbey, filled with a dazzling array of art objects of the highest quality, chiefly from the continent, the great Gothic galleries were furnished with new pieces in a variant of the Jacobean style, while among Beckford's collections of precious objects were the earliest examples of the revived continental Renaissance style. By the later 1830s the Elizabethan and Jacobean styles had become conflated into a 'Jacobethan' style, which eventually ousted Tudor-Gothic as the chief indicator of the 'Olden Days', a position it still holds today.

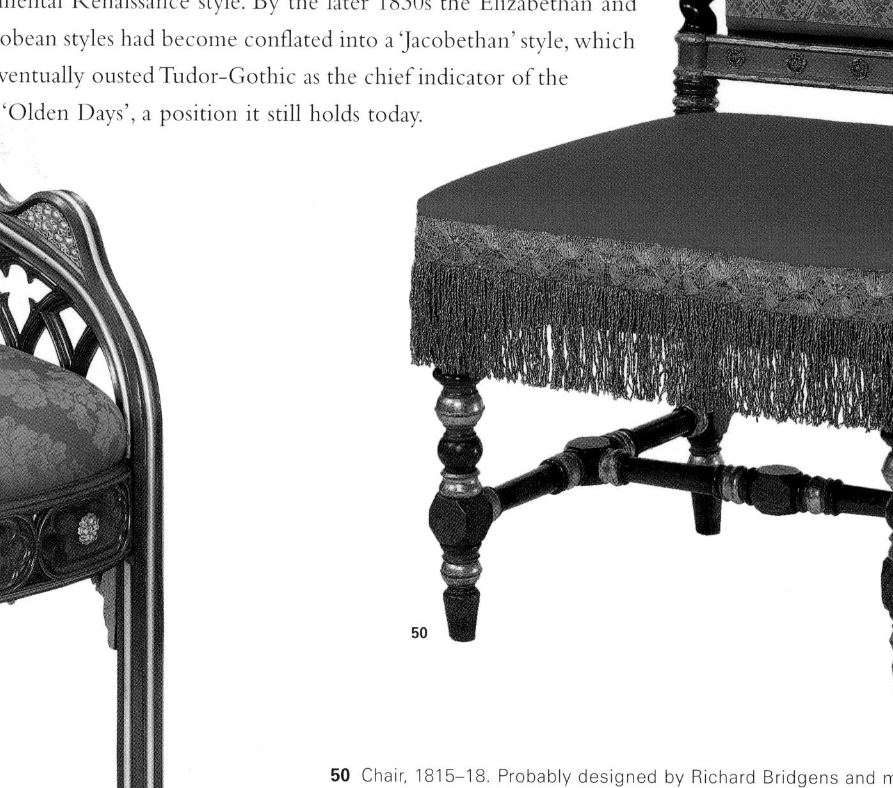

50 Chair, 1815–18. Probably designed by Richard Bridgens and made in the workshop of George Bullock. Commissioned by Sir Godfrey Vassal Webster for Battle Abbey, Sussex. The chair was intended to recall Jacobean and Restoration examples. Oak, painted and gilded, with gilt-brass mounts; the replacement upholstery based on the original. [h. 101cm]. VAM W.53-1980.

48 Standing cup and cover, in the Renaissance style, with London hallmarks for 1815–16. Mark of James Aldridge. Commissioned by William Beckford. Probably designed by Beckford and Gregorio Franchi. The bowl and cover mounted in London. Agate, with chalcedony knops set with rubies, mounted in Persia, the whole set in silver-gilt mounts. [h. 24.13cm]. VAM 428-1882.

49 Armchair, about 1823. Probably designed by Augustus Charles Pugin and possibly made by Gillow & Co. Made for the drawing room at Eaton Hall, Cheshire, designed for the second Earl Grosvenor. The huge Gothic house at Eaton was extravagantly furnished in much the same manner as Windsor Castle. Mahogany, gilded; modern upholstery. [h. 94cm]. VAM W.22-1959.

51

52

14. Exotic styles

Non-European styles were used in two ways. The first was as part of a popular and generalized exoticism, of the type that had long been part of public spectacle and the theatre. Transfer-printed plates and printed textiles, for instance, combined vaguely Indian, Chinese and even Italian scenes and motifs. Ceramics were also the context for the most popular chinoiserie design of this period, the decoration known as the Willow Pattern. Loosely derived from painted Chinese porcelain of the late eighteenth century, it had no precise Chinese origin, while the famous 'Chinese tale' that still accompanies it was invented as a marketing tool by a ceramic manufacturer in the 1830s.

The second, purer approach to exoticism was marked by the move to greater stylistic accuracy. As with Gothic, the various styles were adapted to certain characteristic uses. Chinese was a domestic style and, except for garden buildings, was not used on external architecture. Significantly, rococo-derived chinoiserie furniture was replaced by furniture that incorporated Chinese motifs into classical forms, or by pieces that were really Chinese or imitations of them. The first approach was adopted in the famous Chinese rooms at the Prince of Wales's Carlton House, which were decorated by imported French artists and filled with French furniture. The second type of furniture was found in the Prince's pavilion at Brighton, which appears as a Chinese fantasy without parallel, but in fact employs on a huge and extravagant scale many of the decorative techniques used on Chinese export goods and real Chinese buildings. The extraordinary Mogul-inspired exterior of the Pavilion had relatively few parallels, and they, significantly, were usually made for nabobs: men who had returned to Britain with fortunes made in India.

The Egyptian style, unlike the Chinese and Indian, was a Europe-wide craze. While isolated examples of Egyptian motifs had been part of earlier neo-classicism, archaeological surveys linked to Napoleon's campaigns in Egypt produced evidence of an ancient and mysterious civilization, raising it to the status of a historical style. Egyptian gods and hieroglyphs provided a whole new range of useful symbols to give meaning to objects and buildings. In architecture, the massive dignity and pure lines of Egyptian remains, and their predominantly sepulchral and solemn nature, made the style especially useful for public structures, from cemetery gateways to suspension bridges. At a more popular level, the striking Egyptian façade of William Bullock's Museum in Piccadilly, London, signalled the history and wonders within, as well as spawning several direct imitations and a rash of novel shop fronts.

53

51 *The Banqueting Room, Royal Pavilion, Brighton*, created 1815–17. Designed by Robert Jones. Plate from *The Royal Pavilion at Brighton* by John Nash, 1826. Etching and aquatint, hand coloured. VAM 100.B.32.

52 Willow Pattern plate, dated 1818. Possibly made at the Spode factory, Stoke-on-Trent, Staffordshire. Earthenware, cobalt-blue printed under a lead glaze. [diam. 22.54cm]. VAM C.231-1934.

53 Mantel clock, about 1807–8. Made by Benjamin Lewis Vulliamy. The design of the clock, except for the sphinxes, taken from plates in *Voyage dans la Basse et la Haute Egypte* by Baron Dominique Vivant Denon, published in Paris and London, 1802. Black marble, with mounts of ormolu and patinated bronze, gilt dial. [h. 22.86cm]. VAM M.119-1966.

EXOTICISM AND HISTORICISM

Frances Collard

Designs influenced by exotic and historical sources were very fashionable between 1714 and 1837 in Britain. Artists, architects, designers, makers and manufacturers produced an extensive range of motifs, forms and patterns to satisfy a sophisticated and eager market. This interest intensified at the end of the eighteenth century, establishing exotic and historical styles on an equal footing with the leading style of neo-classicism.

54. Furnishing chintz, possibly for a window blind, about 1830–5. Printed cotton. VAM T.354-1972.

The range of exotic styles included Chinese, Egyptian, Moorish and Hindu, but the most popular style throughout the Georgian period was the Chinese; Egyptian and Indian designs became fashionable only in about 1800. Historicism, or the interest in and reinterpretation of British historical styles, included Gothic, Norman, Tudor and Elizabethan styles, with Gothic being the most prominent.

The Chinese style was used right across the applied arts, as well as in interior decoration and garden buildings and furniture. John Linnell's chairs for Badminton House are starkly original and innovative, with panels of painted lattice replacing the usual carved back and arms.

Designers or architects often combined elements from more than one style. The most elaborate example is the Royal Pavilion at Brighton, built in a mixture of Indian, Moorish and Chinese architectural styles. Originally designed in the neo-classical style in 1787 by Henry Holland for the Prince of Wales, the building was transformed in 1815–23 by the architect John Nash. For Indian architectural details, he borrowed William and Thomas Daniell's book, *Oriental Scenery*, from the Prince's library. Nash incorporated tent-roofs, Mogul domes, Islamic arches and perforated screens, based on Indian *jalis*, into the east front of the Pavilion. The interiors underwent several phases of chinoiserie decoration, designed by Frederick Crace and Robert Jones.

55. Design for a chair for the bedroom at Badminton House, Gloucestershire, about 1754. By John Linnell. Watercolour. VAM E.71-1929.

56. Bureau bookcase in the Gothic, classical and Egyptian styles, 1808–10. Probably designed and made by George Oakley of Oakley and Evans, Old Bond Street, London. The doors contain watercolour views of the River Clyde, dated 1808, by James Baynes. Mahogany, veneered with zebrawood and satinwood, inlaid with box; mahogany mouldings, ormolu mounts. [h. 158.5cm]. VAM W.15-1930.

57. Wallpaper border in the Egyptian style, about 1806. From the drawing room at Crawley House, Bedfordshire. Coloured print from woodblocks and flock. VAM E.2498&A-1966.

58. The Royal Pavilion, Brighton. Remodelled by John Nash, 1815–23.

Historical styles, particularly the Gothic Revival, were also plundered for ideas. Forms and motifs borrowed from architectural sources included arches, ruins, fan vaulting, stained glass and columns. Furniture designers and makers incorporated Gothic or Norman arches into the backs of chairs; more appropriately, chintz for blinds was printed with designs of stained-glass windows.

Designers and manufacturers sometimes combined both exotic and historical motifs in the same design. Furnishing textiles were printed with Chinese pagodas and medieval ruins. Exotic motifs were used as decorative details. Gothic glazing bars and pilasters with Egyptian heads decorated a bookcase made of zebrawood, an imported exotic timber.

59. *Design for a Gothic Saloon*, 1810. Designed by Gaetano Landi. Plate from *Architectural Decorations* by Gaetano Landi, 1810. Published in London. Hand-coloured aquatint. VAM 57.K.9.

60. *Parlor chairs fronts & profiles*, in the Norman style, 1807. Designed by George Smith. Plate from *A Collection of Designs for Household Furniture and Interior Decoration* by George Smith, 1808. Published in London by J. Taylor. Hand-coloured etching and aquatint. VAM II.RC.S.2.

15. Classical varieties

Two broadly defined varieties of classicism emerged in about 1800: Greek and Roman. Both marked a shift from what were seen as the light, insignificant forms of earlier neo-classicism and benefited from a greater archaeological correctness. James Stuart had built the first European Greek Revival buildings in the 1750s, but it was not until 1800 that a Greek architectural style appeared employing simple elements like the baseless Doric order and adopting the forms of peripteral temples. In Britain it became widely popular after about 1810, eventually replacing neo-Palladianism in most official architecture. Greek-style interiors, in parallel with the contemporary Empire style in France, employed ideas derived from a wide range of sources – Greek, Roman and even, on occasion, Egyptian. All were marked by an attention to archaeology, precision of detail and purity of line. This last, which had long been a key element in neo-classicism, was emphasized by the practice of showing designs in outline only, even in the case of brightly coloured interiors like those of Thomas Hope. The archaeological drive led to furniture, vessels and even clothes being copied and adapted from ancient models, or being formed, either in whole or in part, in the shape of classical motifs. By the 1830s a restrained Greek style had become the norm for modest furniture and furnishings.

61

61 *The Library-Drawing Room at Bromley Hill House, Kent*, 1816. By John Chessell Buckler. Bromley Hill, with its Greek-style Library-Drawing Room, was the country house of the politician and connoisseur Sir Charles Long, later Lord Farnborough. Corporation of London.

62 Chair, about 1805. Probably designed and made by James Newton, for Soho House, Birmingham, the home of Matthew Boulton. A direct copy of the ancient Greek Klismos chair. Mahogany with a cane seat. [h. 89cm]. VAM W.2-1988.

Like the Greek Revival, the Roman style had equivalents in the rest of Europe. Characterized by a magnificent heaviness and attention to sculptural detail, it was especially suitable for the grandest interiors. The sources of the style lay in a re-examination of Roman imperial architecture and sculptural fragments. Silver and metalwork, adopting the forms of ancient stone vases, were often taken from those illustrated in Piranesi's *Vasi, Candelabri, Cippi* of 1778, giving it a suitable sculptural drama, while furniture borrowed ideas from ancient stone seats and table legs.

63 Plate from *A Series of twenty-nine designs of Modern Costume Drawn and Engraved by Henry Moses, Esq.*, 1823 (first published in 1812). The dresses are adapted from ancient Greek models, the pole screen from an ancient shield. *Designs of Modern Costume* closely reflected Thomas Hope's ideas on the Greek style. VAM 24.B.189.

64 Ice pail, 1809–10. Mark of Paul Storr. Retailed by the royal goldsmiths, Rundell, Bridge and Rundell. The form is taken from the famous Medici vase (a stone vase of the first century AD) in the Uffizi Gallery, Florence. Silver-gilt. [h. 34.7cm]. VAM M.48C-1982.

65 Stool, about 1800. Designed by Charles Heathcote Tatham and possibly made by Marsh and Tatham. The stool imitates an ancient marble seat seen by Tatham in Italy, and recorded in his *Etchings of Ancient Ornamental Architecture*, 1799. Beechwood, painted white and gold to imitate marble. VAM W.2-1975.

16. Pluralism absorbed

The 1820s saw the start of a synthesis of historical styles into new wholes. In the hands of Charles Robert Cockerell, a great scholar of Greek architecture, a classical style emerged that incorporated ideas from Italian sixteenth-century architects and Sir Christopher Wren. Italian vernacular styles, which had been part of irregular Picturesque architecture since John Nash's villas of about 1800, grew up at Hope's The Deepdene. Sir Charles Barry's Travellers' Club in London's Pall Mall of 1829 reintroduced Italian sixteenth-century *palazzo* forms and the same style achieved truly palatial proportions in his Trentham Hall, Staffordshire, begun in 1838.

This eclecticism was paralleled by developments in interior decoration. A fashion for collecting baroque objects, including French late-seventeenth-century furniture, German ivories and English silver, had been boosted by the quantities of material coming from the continent after the French Revolution. This fashion probably helped to prepare the ground for the gradual reappearance of the rococo style in objects and interiors from the 1820s onwards. The most admired models were French: one of the first examples of the revived style, a silver tureen of 1812, copied a French example of the 1730s. Ceramics and textiles were profoundly affected. Although there were few examples of complete rococo interiors, baroque and rococo elements were frequently added to a Roman framework. The French rococo furniture style, confusingly described as either Louis XIV or Louis XV, began the climb that was to make it the preferred British style from the 1840s to 1900. However, its story belongs in that period.

66

67

66 The Deepdene, Surrey. *View from the Hall: entrance towards turret etc*, 1825–6. By William Henry Bartlett. The Deepdene, designed by Thomas Hope and William Atkinson, was built in 1818–19 and 1823. Watercolour. London Borough of Lambeth Archives Department.

68 The Elizabeth saloon, Belvoir Castle, Rutland, decorated in the rococo style 1824–8. Designed for Elizabeth, Duchess of Rutland, by Benjamin Dean Wyatt and Matthew Cotes Wyatt. Some of the panelling was taken from a French château. The ceiling painting by Matthew Cotes Wyatt.

67 Vase, about 1826. Designed in a rococo style by Thomas Brameld, painted by Edwin Steele. Made at the Rockingham pottery, Yorkshire. Porcelain, painted and gilded. VAM 47-1869.

68

CHAPTER 3

Who led taste?

MICHAEL SNODIN

1. The development of taste

The Georgian years witnessed a fundamental transformation in the ways that taste in design and the decorative arts was created and transmitted. For centuries high design existed to serve and reinforce a social system with the monarch at its head, and its consumption – at least in its most expensive form – was limited largely to those at the top. Below that level, consumption and display were expected to reflect social rank. By 1714 this was changing. Shifts in political power from the Crown to Parliament and the nobility meant that the personal tastes of the monarch counted far less. In place of a court focused on the monarch, a range of centres of taste formation emerged. Important elements in this process were a steady increase in manufactured goods and of the number of people able to consume them, as well as the arrival of new cultural ideas. These included the identification of a group of activities as 'fine arts', also called 'the elegant arts' or 'arts of taste'. They included music and poetry, painting and sculpture, architecture and garden design, which were thought to involve the emotions. At a lower level, although not in terms of consumption, stood the 'useful' or 'mechanical arts', among which were what we now call the applied or decorative arts. Both the fine and the useful arts played a key role, as arenas for the exercise of taste, in the creation of a distinctive 'polite' culture. As this spread, so did the arts, taking high design to vastly greater numbers of people. A variety of taste makers participated in this process, but they naturally included the nobility and gentry. Their consumption of fashion goods was often eagerly emulated further down the social scale, with sometimes confusing results: 'In a few years we shall have no common folk at all.' The process was also geographical, for while London remained the centre of style, new design ideas passed rapidly to provincial centres, aided by better roads, newspapers and prints, and by shopkeepers visiting London.

By the end of the Georgian period, recognizably modern forces of taste formation were well in place. On the one hand, there was the commercial tendency, dedicated to maximizing selling and promoting the cycle of fashion. On the other, official and unofficial bodies worked to control a national taste that they considered to be corrupted by the forces of commerce. The positions taken by these two groups had emerged early in the eighteenth century. Commentators had begun to argue that the increase of goods – of 'luxury' – across society could have moral consequences. Only by the exercise of taste through 'politeness' could consumption be controlled. One critical voice was the Whig philosopher Anthony Ashley Cooper, the third Earl of Shaftesbury. In his *Letter concerning the Art, or Science of Design* of 1712 he deplored the courtly taste of 'the long reign of luxury under King Charles II', suggesting that the free spirit of the nation, and more particularly of its nobility, would most effectively promote the arts and foster national taste.

1 The hall at Holkham Hall, Norfolk, begun 1734. Designed by William Kent. One of the major neo-Palladian houses, Holkham was built for Thomas Coke, Earl of Leicester, a great collector of antique sculpture.

The Duke and Duchess of Northumberland, Aristocratic Patrons

Rachel Kennedy

The Duke and Duchess of Northumberland were one of the wealthiest couples in mid-eighteenth-century Britain: Elizabeth Seymour Percy was heir in her own right to six of England's oldest baronies, while her husband Sir Hugh Smithson owned estates in Yorkshire and Middlesex, as well as Northumberland House in London.

Like many other wealthy landed families in Britain, they divided their time between their estates in Northumberland and London, where the Duke was a Member of Parliament and later a member of the House of Lords. Like other members of the nobility, both the Duke and Duchess held royal appointments at the courts of George II and George III, but it was in their shared role as patrons of the fine and decorative arts that they are chiefly remembered today.

The Duke's interest in art began in his youth on the Grand Tour when he first started to collect antique sculpture and Old Master paintings. In addition, he commissioned works of art from artists whom he met in Italy and was one of Antonio Canaletto's first patrons on his arrival in England in 1746. The Duchess preferred northern European art and travelled abroad to buy paintings. In 1771 she acquired what she described as her 'best Teniers' and observed of a private collection of ivories, enamels and miniatures, 'I really think my own Collection of Ivorys at least equal to any which I saw there.' She chose the Gothic style when making architectural improvements to her family seat, Alnwick Castle in Northumberland, where a medieval rather than a neo-classical interior was thought to better reflect her historical Percy lineage.

One of the Duke and Duchess's most prestigious projects was the refurbishment of Northumberland House in London, for which Robert Adam designed a magnificent drawing room and picture gallery. He also designed neo-classical interiors and furnishings for Syon House in London, where the Great Hall contains a copy of the antique sculpture *The Dying Gaul*, commissioned by the Duchess.

The Northumberlands became leaders of taste through their patronage of fashionable architects and artists like Adam, Canaletto and Reynolds. However, the couple's deliberately ostentatious displays of wealth, frequently exhibited at the social events they hosted in London and at Alnwick, sometimes attracted criticism. Even the Duchess's Gothic-loving friend, Horace Walpole, declared that her excessive love of entertainment and jewellery made her 'coarse' and 'junketaceous'.

2. Left: *Hugh, 1st Duke of Northumberland*. By James Barry. Oil on canvas. Far left: *Elizabeth, 1st Duchess of Northumberland*. By Sir Joshua Reynolds. Oil on canvas. Collection of the Duke of Northumberland.

3. The Glass Drawing Room at Northumberland House, London, 1870s. By an anonymous artist. The drawing room designed by Robert Adam, 1770–5, enlarged about 1820. Watercolour. Collection of the Duke of Northumberland.

4. The Great Hall, Syon House, London, 1762–9. Designed by Robert Adam.

5. *Alnwick Castle, Northumberland*, 1752. By Antonio Canaletto. Oil on canvas. Collection of the Duke of Northumberland.

2. Lord Burlington and neo-Palladianism

Shaftesbury's ideas were reflected in the work of Richard Boyle, the third Earl of Burlington and the chief promoter of neo-Palladian architectural style. Burlington's architectural success derived from his position as a general leader of taste and was closely linked to contemporary politics. Although some recent commentators have suggested that he was a Jacobite, many of his connections were with the ruling Whig group of grandees, who supported the Hanoverian succession and monopolized political power. His supreme reputation as the 'Apollo of the Arts' derived from twice having made the Grand Tour and from his active promotion of Italian ideas in music, painting, literature and architecture. By the mid-1720s his own style was established among his friends and relatives. His associated position at court, meanwhile, meant that he could place his protégés in key positions on the Board of Works, which dealt with all government building. These included his main assistant, William Kent, as well as Henry Flitcroft (nicknamed Burlington Harry), John Vardy and Isaac Ware.

Neo-Palladianism's domination of ordinary urban architecture began with Burlington's own building schemes on the fields behind his house in London. It was finally achieved through the activities of hundreds of small builders using the pocket handbooks that began to come out in large numbers from the mid-1720s. While Burlington himself played no part in their publication, they frequently took their illustrations from more expensive publications that he sponsored. The most important of these was Isaac Ware's translation of Palladio's *Four Books of Architecture*, published in 1738 (*see 2:2*).

7

6

6 The Horse Guards, London, built 1751–9. Designed by William Kent and built under the direction of the Board of Works.

7 *Richard Boyle, 3rd Earl of Burlington and 4th Earl of Cork*, 1717–19. By Jonathan Richardson. In the background is Burlington's first building, the Bagnio or Casina, in the gardens of Chiswick House, London. Oil on canvas. National Portrait Gallery, London.

8 Frontispiece to *The chimney piece Maker's Daily Assistant* by John Crunden, Thomas Milton and Placido Columbani, 1766. Designed by Isaac Taylor, engraved by R. Pranker. In this pattern-book frontispiece, a client and his architect discuss a design while a carpenter puts up a neo-Palladian chimneypiece. A bust of Inigo Jones presides over the scene. Engraving. VAM 34.B.62.

The work and influence of the architect James Gibbs revealingly demonstrate the strengths and weaknesses of the Burlingtonian revolution. Gibbs was a covert Catholic and politically suspect, as both a Tory and a Scot. In the reign of Queen Anne, the influence of the Catholic Earl of Mar had briefly gained Gibbs a place as one of the surveyors for the scheme to build fifty new London churches, leading to his St Mary-le-Strand and St Martin-in-the-Fields. His unusual Italian training and a customer base of Tory magnates led to a career as a successful independent architect, while his flexible baroque style allowed him to absorb neo-Palladian elements. In 1728 he published his *Book of Architecture*, the first book to be devoted to the work of a single British architect. It was immensely influential in Britain and the British colonies, not only for its designs for whole buildings but for its decorative and other useful details, especially in interiors, a field not well covered in publications by the Burlington group.

9

8

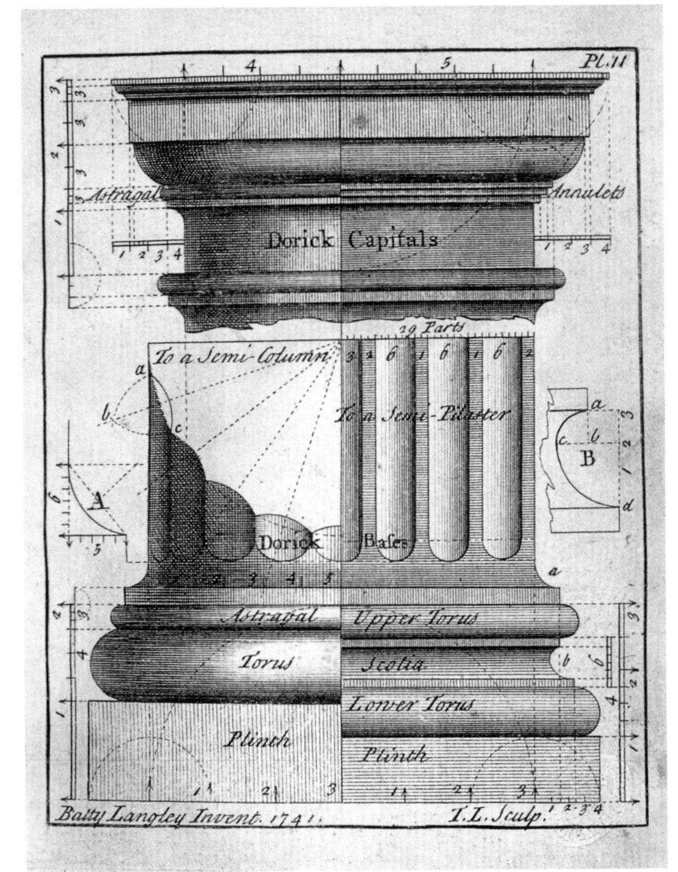

10

9 *James Gibbs*, signed and dated 1726. By John Michael Rysbrack. Marble. VAM A.6-1988.

10 *The Doric Order*. Plate from *The Builder's Jewel, or, The Youth's Instructor, & workman's remembrancer* by Batty Langley and Thomas Langley, 1741. Engraving. VAM L.1146-1981.

The importance of Italy in the careers of Gibbs and Burlington shows how the Grand Tour had become the key experience in the acquisition of taste. While such tours always took in Paris and often Germany, the most prized destination was Italy. The power of Italy for generations of young men brought up on classical literature is hard to imagine today. There, at the actual sites of classical mystery and myth, they absorbed the glories of classical culture and the virtue associated with the contemplation of ancient art, as well as the knowledge of works of art that made them virtuosi. Returning laden with paintings, sculpture, books, Italian silks, exotic furniture and ideas about architecture, culture and luxurious living, they became the leading taste makers. Their Italian spoils filled their new neo-Palladian houses. Their grounds, modelled on contemporary Italy, ancient Rome and the paintings of Claude Lorraine, were dotted with temples symbolic of classical ideals and filled with portraits of the owner, his friends and political supporters. In this setting, ideas of ancient virtue could be linked to notions of British history and British liberty, free of the shackles of an oppressive monarchy. By such means Burlington's modern classical style turned into something quintessentially British.

The dominating taste of Lord Burlington and his circle was not without its critics. They included William Hogarth, who, in his popular print *Masquerades and Operas*, satirized the Italianate nature of Burlington's patronage and promotion of

11 *The gardens at Stourhead, Wiltshire, from the West*, about 1770. By Copplestone Warre Bamfylde. The gardens were created 1741–72. Watercolour. VAM E.360-1949.

12 *The Painter and his Pug*, 1745. By William Hogarth. On the palette is Hogarth's 'line of beauty and grace'. Oil on canvas. © Tate, London, 2003.

the arts. In the foreground he attacks the Italian opera promoted by Burlington, while English plays are being carted off in a wheelbarrow as waste paper. In the background is the gate of Burlington House, inscribed 'Accademy of Arts'. It is surmounted by the figure of William Kent, palette in hand, at whom figures of Raphael and Michelangelo gaze up in admiration. While Hogarth may have had a personal motive in attacking Burlington (his future father-in-law, the mural painter Sir James Thornhill, was competing for commissions with Kent), he had a continuing interest in drawing British taste away from foreign influences and especially from a love of foreign artists. His most effective initiative was the revival in 1735 of the private academy of painting and sculpture at St Martin's Lane, originally founded in 1720.

Until the foundation of the Royal Academy in 1768, the Academy in St Martin's Lane, London, was the chief school for British artists. It taught principally drawing and included working from a living model. But these exercises were aimed at the useful, as well as the fine, arts. In 1745 the instructors included not only the history painter Francis Hayman and the French sculptor Louis François Roubiliac, but also the Swiss gold chaser George Michael Moser, the medallist Richard Yeo and the French illustrator and draughtsman Hubert Gravelot. In stylistic terms, the most important was certainly Gravelot, whose ornamental style and elegant figure draughtsmanship were taken up by the other members, making the academy one of the principal engines for the introduction of the rococo style in the 1740s. But this loose-knit group of taste makers operated in a very different way from the rather remote, if single-minded, operations of Lord Burlington. They were part of a network of artists and craftspeople working in London's West End and congregating in its coffee houses, especially Slaughter's (also in St Martin's Lane). Many academy pupils must have come from the workshops of the surrounding furniture makers, goldsmiths and other trades as well as neighbouring artists' studios. Its known pupils included the famous furniture designer and maker John Linnell and the architect James Paine, both of whom designed in the rococo style.

13

14

13 *Masquerades and Operas* or *'The Bad taste of the Town'*, 1724. By William Hogarth. Etching and engraving. VAM F.188:152.

14 Detail of a design for a candlestick, with a figure of Daphne, about 1740. By George Michael Moser. The candlestick was matched by another with the stem formed as a figure of Apollo. Key elements in this candlestick are taken from prints by Gilles-Marie Oppenord and the goldsmith Juste-Aurèle Meissonnier. Pen, ink and wash. VAM E.4895-1968.

3. Rococo and the printed pattern book

The complex and irregular three-dimensional forms of the rococo style, and its emphasis on variety and invention, made great demands on the drawing and design skills of craftspeople. It was therefore no accident that from the mid-1730s the previously thin and hesitant stream of English engraved ornament rapidly grew to a flood that did not abate until the 1770s. For the first time in Britain most of the prints were original designs rather than copies of continental productions, acknowledging a specifically English variant of the rococo style then emerging from the craft workshops. They were primarily made by craftspeople, especially woodcarvers, a number of whom – like Matthias Lock and Thomas Johnson – were also drawing masters. Rather than copying such prints entire, carvers mined them for ideas, cutting them up and adding their own notions. The rococo style also arrived in the form of engraved trade cards, at that time reaching an unprecedented size and elaboration. As trade-card motifs can be found on tablets and gravestones, porcelain, maps, metal tickets and many other types of object, they probably transmitted rococo design ideas more effectively than any other type of printed ornament.

The most influential single set of pattern prints, however, was put out as a book of furniture designs. *The Gentleman and Cabinet Maker's Director* by Thomas Chippendale the Elder (his son, also a furniture designer, was also called Thomas) was published first in parts and then as a collected edition in 1754, with the full apparatus of dedication (to the Earl of Northumberland), frontispiece and text, followed by 106 engraved plates drawn by Chippendale. The *Director* broke new ground in being both a source of design ideas and a pattern book for his potential customers. Its 308 subscribers, who sponsored its publication, included noblemen and architects as well as major furniture makers. They would have appreciated its large, impressive format, which mimicked that of expensive architectural books. It was, however, among smaller furniture makers, mostly outside London, that the patterns had their greatest effect.

16

15

4. Promoting design, and a national crisis

By the mid-eighteenth century design and aesthetic theory had become a subject of intense debate. The ideas in Hogarth's *Analysis of Beauty* (1755) were developed in Edmund Burke's *Philosophical Inquiry into the Origin of our Ideas of the Sublime and Beautiful* (1756). Theory was joined to practice in Mayhew and Ince's *The Universal System of Household Furniture* (1759), which was prefaced by an exercise 'for young practitioners in drawing', showing 'a Systematical Order of Raffle Leaf from the Line of Beauty', from the fundamental design principle set forth in Hogarth's *Analysis*. But most concern was shown for the consequences of poor national taste in international competitiveness. As an Irish commentator on the silk trade in Dublin commented in the middle of the century, 'as we depend upon England for matters of fashion, so England for the like matters depends upon France, where many schools and academies are established, at the public expence, for carrying those manufactures to their highest perfection.' The deficiency was made up by foreign immigrants from all over Europe – from France, the Low Countries, Germany, Switzerland, Italy and Sweden. In Birmingham alone in 1759, '30 or 40 Frenchmen and Germans are constantly employed in drawing and designing'.

15 Trade card of Peter Griffin, map and print seller, London, 1746–9. Among the large range of prints (both political and satirical) and a drawing book is Matthias Lock's *A Book of Ornaments*, 1745, shown at the bottom right. Engraving. The British Museum.

16 *Design for a mirror*. Plate from *Six Sconces* by Matthias Lock, 1744. Etching. VAM 27811:6.

A common solution was the establishment of societies for the encouragement of the arts and manufacture and to promote design training, often through prizes. The aim was to improve drawing and, by that means, invention in design. As the commentator R. Campbell observed in 1747, 'he who first hits upon any new Whim is sure to make by the Invention before it becomes common in the Trade; but he that must always wait for a new Fashion till it comes from *Paris*, or is hit upon by his Neighbour, is never likely to grow rich or eminent in his Way'. The first example in the British Isles was set up in Dublin in 1731, with similar societies in Glasgow and Edinburgh in 1753. In London the Anti-Gallican Society gave premiums, while the Society for the Encouragement of Arts, Manufactures and Commerce, still in existence as the Royal Society of Arts, was founded in 1754. William Shipley, its principal promoter, sought to exclude fine arts from the society's concerns, aiming instead to encourage 'ingenious mechanics, such as carvers, joiners, upholsterers, cabinet makers', in the belief that an improvement in taste would lead to general refinement, as well as usefully relieving unemployment. The society gave prizes for design exercises in specific fields. The competition entrants were chiefly teenagers from private drawing schools, who covered both textile and three-dimensional design.

The establishment of such societies was matched by calls for the founding of a national academy of the visual arts. In 1755 a group of leading artists, headed by Francis Hayman, unsuccessfully proposed to the Society of Arts and the Society of Dilettanti an academy 'for the improvement of the arts in general' and the 'refining of taste'. It would cover architecture (both internal and external), painting and sculpture, engraving and chasing, and planting and gardening, but would also recognize the 'Subordinate branches of design: namely utensils of all sorts, plate [silver] and cabinet-work, patterns of skills [silk design], jewelling, garniture, carriage-building and equipage, down even to toys and trinkets'. In the event, when a Royal Academy was eventually founded, in 1768, architecture was in, but the applied arts were out. A state-supported system of schools of design was not to appear for another 60 years, the training of designers lying meanwhile in the hands of private drawing masters and enlightened manufacturers.

17

18

17 *A Systematical Order of Raffle Leaf from the Line of Beauty*. Plate from *The Universal System of Household Furniture* by William Ince and John Mayhew, 1759. Engraved by Matthias Darley. Engraving. VAM RC.CC.14.

18 *Design for a clock*, 1759. By William Herbert. This drawing for a competition run by the Society for the Encouragement of Arts, Manufactures and Commerce won the second prize in its class: 'For the best drawing or compositions of ornaments, being original designs, fit for Weavers, Callico Printers, or any Art or manufacture, by Youths under the age of twenty'. Herbert was a pupil of Francis Vivares. Pen, ink and wash. Royal Society of Arts.

Thomas Chippendale and the London Furniture Makers

Tessa Murdoch

By 1754, when Thomas Chippendale the Elder (1718–79) had settled in St Martin's Lane and had published the first edition of his *Gentleman and Cabinet Maker's Director*, the West End of London was the centre of the London furniture trade. Many of the workshops were large, and as a German visitor to London noted in 1767, 'the master himself no longer touches a tool. Instead he oversees the work of his forty journeymen.' Established close to the royal court, the seat of government and a fashionable residential area, the leading cabinet makers, carvers and upholsterers were well placed to make furniture of new and fashionable design for the nobility, gentry and the growing merchant classes.

Chippendale's design ideas reached a much wider audience through the *Director*, which came out in parts that were eagerly awaited by regional and metropolitan cabinet makers. In 1760 Richard Gillow of Lancaster urged his cousin James in London to send 'Chippindale's additional Number as soon as possible'. Such published designs could then be adapted to suit an individual. Gillow wrote to a client in 1765 about some library bookcases: 'if any of Chippindales designs be more agreeable, I have his Book and can execute 'em & adapt them to the places they are for'.

Chippendale's neighbours in St Martin's Lane included John Channon, an Exeter-trained maker, whose bookcases of 1740 for Sir William Courtenay's library at Powderham Castle in Devon were decorated with brass inlay inspired by continental practice. William Vile and John Cobb specialized in quality carcase furniture, embellished with exquisite carving – then regarded as the highest skill associated with the furniture trade. They supplied King George III and Queen Charlotte with cabinets for their collections of medals and jewellery.

Carved woodwork or composite substitutes such as papier mâché lent themselves to both spirited rococo and disciplined neo-classical ornament. The demand for flat decoration to harmonize with neo-classical interiors led to a revival of marquetry techniques, as used on Chippendale's desk for Edwin Lascelles of Harewood House in Yorkshire, his most important patron. A complex decorative effect could be achieved more cheaply with painted furniture. Painted chairs were appropriate for occasional use in bedrooms and drawing rooms. A decorator's sample – a rare survival – demonstrates how patterns for colour and form were shared.

19. Panel showing alternative schemes for decorating a painted shield-back chair, about 1790. Painted oak. [h. 53cm]. VAM W.11-1993.

20. Bookcase, 1740. Made at the workshop of John Channon in St Martin's Lane, London, for the library of Sir William Courtenay at Powderham Castle, Devon. Veneered in padouk wood with carved and gilt decoration. VAM W.1-1987.

21. *A cabinet maker's office,* about 1770. By an unknown artist. Oil on canvas. VAM P.1-1961.

22. *A Variety of New-Pattern Chairs*, 1754. Plate xii in *The Gentleman and Cabinet Maker's Director* by Thomas Chippendale the Elder, 1754. By Matthias Darly after Chippendale. Engraving. VAM RC.CC.11.

23. Medal cabinet, 1760–1. Made by the firm of William Vile and John Cobb for George III. Mahogany. [h. 200.5cm]. VAM W.11-1963.

24. Chair, about 1754. Inscription beneath the splat reads '6 pedistals for Chipendel's backs'. Splat taken from Plate xii in Chippendale's *Director*. Mahogany, carved; modern upholstery. VAM W.67-1940.

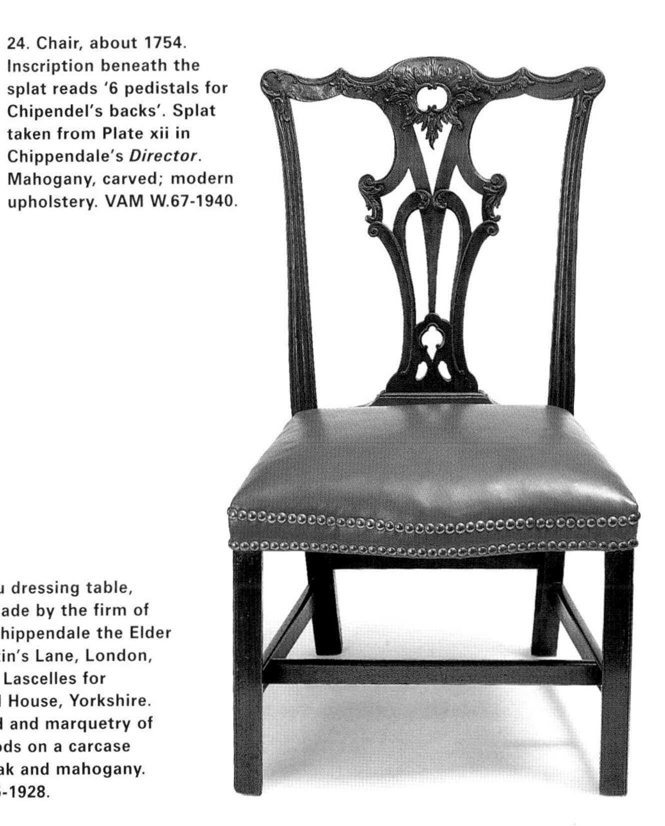

25. Bureau dressing table, 1771–5. Made by the firm of Thomas Chippendale the Elder in St Martin's Lane, London, for Edwin Lascelles for Harewood House, Yorkshire. Rosewood and marquetry of other woods on a carcase of pine, oak and mahogany. VAM W.55-1928.

5. Public art and design

The foundation of the Royal Academy was one move in a trend towards the general opening up of visual culture. In today's world, bombarded with visual stimuli of all types, it is difficult to imagine the situation before about 1730. With the notable exception of what could be seen in churches, paintings and sculpture were largely invisible, locked up in private houses, and high-design decorative schemes and objects were accessible only to the few. Paintings could also be seen in salerooms or at picture dealers, but works of art were most easily consumed second hand through prints. From about 1700 the world of the printed image, encompassing illustrated books and printed ephemera as well as loose prints, underwent a huge expansion. This exposed a wide public, including craftspeople and those learning the ways of politeness, to art and new ideas in design. The essentially commercial character of the print world was paralleled in other areas, most notably in the field of public entertainment.

One of the most significant developments in such visual culture was at the Vauxhall Pleasure Gardens in London. Opened by the 1660s, they had sunk into scandal as a venue for prostitution and debauchery by the 1720s. For the gardens' new proprietor, Jonathan Tyers, raising their tone was an astute commercial move answering the rising demand for polite entertainment. In addition to introducing new attractions and improving the buildings, including adding a new orchestra to provide the essential music, he set up what was in effect the first public art exhibition in England. The first move, in 1738, was the erection of a statue of the composer George Frederick Handel, by the sculptor Roubiliac. While public sculpture of living monarchs was not unknown, commoners were generally shown only on their tombs after death. But here was a living composer of the popular Italian opera, portrayed in relaxed dress as a modern Orpheus or Apollo. Tyers's intentions were made clear in a newspaper article published just before the statue's installation. The civilizing qualities of Handel's music would be enhanced by the effigy of the composer himself, set next to the orchestra 'where his harmony has so often charm'd even the greatest crouds into the profoundest calm and most decent behaviour'.

A month after it was unveiled, the statue was illustrated in a songsheet decorated by Gravelot. Some two years later more art appeared in the gardens, in the form of large paintings of moral and literary subjects by Hayman and after Hogarth. This move is usually attributed to the influence of Hogarth, and certainly involved the St Martin's Lane group, which also made itself felt in other ways: the metal tickets for the gardens were designed by Yeo, and the rococo relief wall ornament of the Music Room was designed by Moser. The 1740 art initiative at Vauxhall was probably a response to the recently opened Ranelagh Gardens, on the other bank of the Thames. Ranelagh, which became the most fashionable of the pleasure gardens, pioneered a new type of public spectacle. It contained no art, but its huge rotunda presented a remarkable architectural interior. It was unmatched in size and design among secular public buildings until the opening in 1772 of the Pantheon in Oxford Street, described by the musical historian Charles Burney as 'the most elegant structure in Europe, if not on the globe'. The effect on taste of such public spaces must have been considerable: the Pantheon, for instance, was probably the most easily accessible neo-classical structure in London at a time when the style was just taking hold among the general public.

26 *Jonathan Tyers*, about 1740.
By Louis François Roubiliac. Terracotta.
[h. 71.1cm]. VAM A.94-1927.

27

28

27 *Vauxhall Gardens showing the grand walk at the entrance of the garden and the orchestra with musick playing*, about 1751. By Johann Sebastian Muller after Samuel Wale. The statue of Handel is to the right of the orchestra; paintings are hung on the walls of the supper boxes to the left. The daylight in this scene is misleading – Vauxhall was an evening and night-time venue. Etching and engraving, coloured by hand. VAM W.27BB-1947.

28 *View of the Pantheon, London*, about 1772. Attributed to William Hodges and Johann Zoffany. The Pantheon, built 1769–72, was designed by James Wyatt. Oil on canvas. © Leeds Museums and Galleries.

29

In 1781 the Royal Academy moved into purpose-built premises in Somerset House on the Strand in London, designed by the academy's treasurer and co-founder, the architect Sir William Chambers. Although it served as a civil-service office block and a home for the learned societies, Somerset House's consciously neo-Palladian exteriors marked it out as a national monument. The premises of the Royal Academy at Somerset House were a place to see and be seen, like the pleasure gardens, theatres, assembly rooms, concert halls, exhibitions and other settings for the social round. All these were, to varying degrees, also taste-forming spaces, but the academy was significantly different, for by virtue of its location and ambitions it had a national status. In this context it was notable that it was controlled not by connoisseurs like the Society of Dilettanti (who had refused to support the fledgling academy of 1755) but by the member artists and architects, who designed and decorated the rooms, thus establishing themselves as arbiters of taste.

29 *Portraits of their Majesty's and the Royal Family viewing the exhibition of The Royal Academy 1788*. Etched and engraved by Pierre Antoine Martini. The portraits drawn by John Henry Ramberg. Etching, stipple etching and engraving. VAM E.3648-1923.

6. Neo-classical networks

The neo-classical stylistic revolution showed very clearly the forces of taste formation that were in place by the 1760s. It emerged and spread via the operation of a network of overlapping and mutually reinforcing interests, involving designers, enterprising manufacturers and men and women of taste. The activities of three key personalities make the process clear: the architect Robert Adam and the manufacturers Josiah Wedgwood and Matthew Boulton.

Adam stamped his version of neo-classicism upon the nation, but the story is a revealing one. His letters from Italy in 1757 show that he had decided to become the most prominent architect in Britain. This was a normal aspiration for a young British architect on the Grand Tour, but Adam was unusual in wanting to bring to Britain what he called the 'one true grand and simple style'. Unlike Burlington, Adam did not have a ready-made network of noble friends and relations and was too busy learning to draw to make the contacts that would provide clients for his future practice. This was in marked contrast to William Chambers, whose path he briefly crossed and whom Adam immediately recognized as a future rival. But what he lacked in contacts, Adam made up for in drive and determination, combined with a strong dash of good luck.

On his return to Britain in 1758 Adam took properly furnished rooms at a good address to display his Italian drawings. The fashionable world soon flocked to see them and they played a key part at a crucial meeting with Lord Scarsdale, at which Adam secured the management of Scarsdale's grounds at Kedleston Hall. Later, at dinner with Scarsdale, Adam showed him more drawings. Scarsdale was particularly excited by a grand Roman design, 'the Nabob's palace'. The following year Adam was invited to Kedleston, where a house by the neo-Palladian architects Mathew Brettingham and James Paine was already under construction. James Stuart, another pioneer of neo-classicism, was working on the interiors (*see 3:33*). Unlike Adam, he had actually been to Greece and published a book on the subject. Adam was nevertheless able to have him dismissed on the grounds of his designing ability, attacking Stuart's pioneering neo-classical designs as 'so excessively and ridiculously bad they beggared all description'. Adam's Scottish origins also played a crucial part, for it was his good fortune that several of the ministers of the future George III, who came to the throne in 1760, were his countrymen. A number became his clients, and one, Lord Bute, lay behind his appointment as royal architect, together with Chambers. But Adam's success with his noble clients does not fully explain the widespread adoption of his style. For that we must look at the nature of the style, at the Adam firm and his publications.

30

31

30 *Robert Adam*, about 1770–5. Attributed to George Willison. Oil on canvas. National Portrait Gallery, London.

31 *Sir William Chambers*, 1788. By Carl Fredrik von Breda. Oil on canvas. Royal Institute of British Architects.

Two aspects of his style were crucial. Notwithstanding Adam's concern with architectonic concepts of visual 'movement', the essence of the style lay in the use of ornament. This was acknowledged by Robert's brother and architectural partner James, who called ornament the 'great secret in architecture', and by Sir John Soane, who looked back in 1812 to when Adam had introduced ' . . . a light and fanciful style of decoration . . . This taste soon became general; everything was Adamitic . . . ' The second aspect was Adam's insistence on stylistic coherence across every element of his interiors. Total control of the client was achieved by the production of enticing drawings setting down every detail. As everything had to be in the new style, nothing could be 'off the peg'. Thus makers in many fields (like the cabinet makers Mayhew and Ince) experienced the new style directly from Adam's own designs or (like Thomas Chippendale) were obliged to produce their own versions for Adam interiors. Either way, it was only a matter of time before the style passed to customers who were not Adam's clients.

Interestingly, Robert Adam at first experienced difficulty in getting things done in the way he required – for instance, finding it impossible to get ceiling plasterers to work in the 'stiff angly manner' he had seen in Italy. The solution was to import Italian artists for decorative painting, and to train workers in other trades. As with the workmen who carried out the decoration of the churches designed by Sir Christopher Wren and his office, the small group of

33

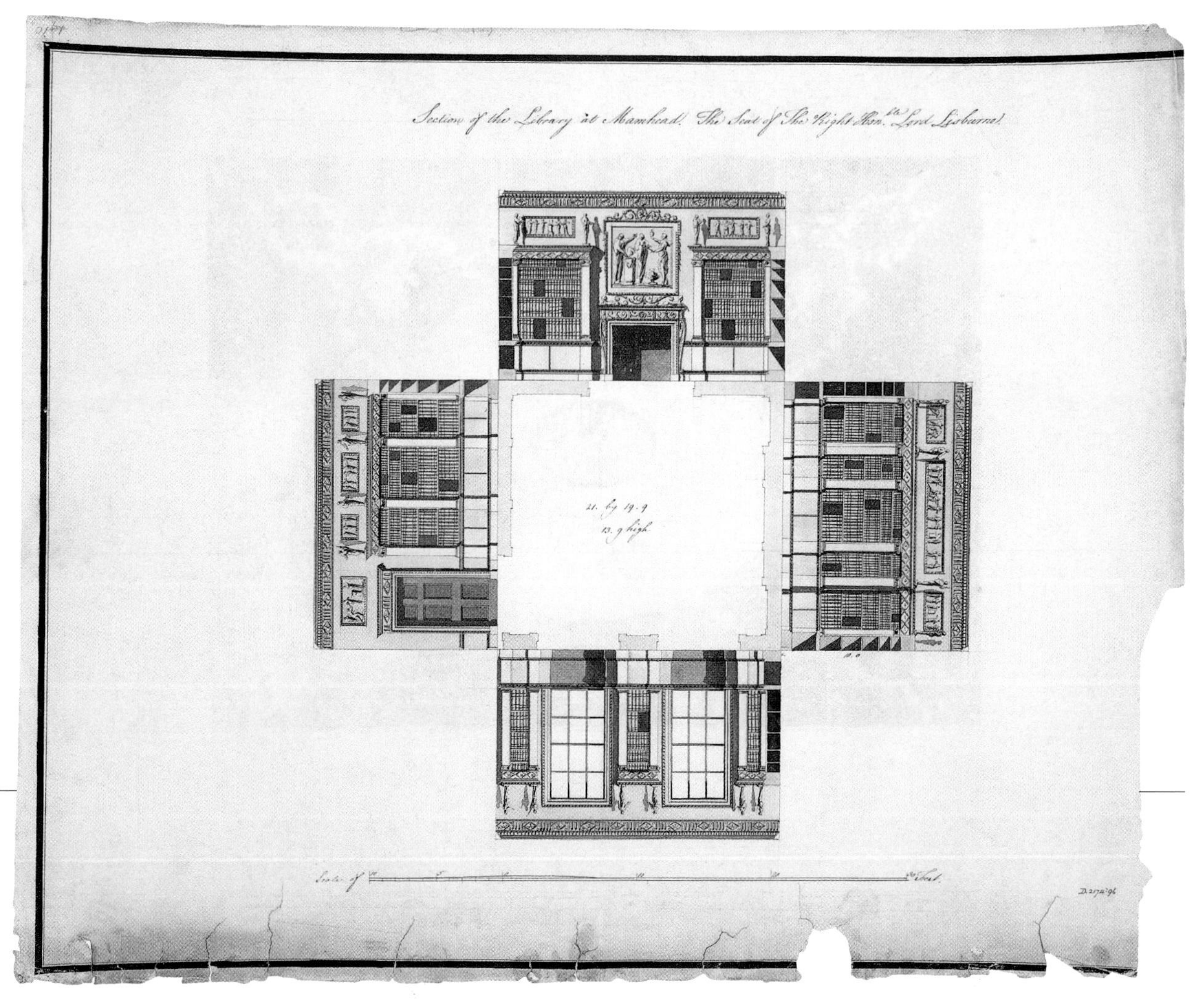

32

34

32 *Design for the walls of a library for Mamhead House, Devon*, 1766. Designed by Robert Adam, the drawing by an Adam office draughtsman. This and 3:34 were drawings made for the client, Lord Lisburn. Pen, ink and wash. VAM D. 2174-1896.

33 *Design for decorating a state room at Kedleston, Derbyshire*, about 1757–8. By James Stuart. Pen, ink and wash. The National Trust, Kedleston Hall.

34 *Design for the ceiling of a drawing room for Mamhead House, Devon*, 1766. Designed by Robert Adam, the drawing by an Adam office draughtsman. Pen, ink, water and body-colour. VAM D.2171-1896.

35

Adam building craftspeople, such as the plastering family of Rose, inevitably carried the style beyond their Adam commissions. The activities of the Adam firm had the same effect. Robert was not only the senior partner in a large architects' practice, but also the creative genius behind a huge family building firm busy with urban speculation. William Adam & Company, set up in 1764, owned brick works, patented a form of exterior cement and at one point employed some 3,000 workmen. Only a national bank crash prevented it from reaping success from the vast Thameside development at the Adelphi (named for the word 'brothers' in Greek).

The Adams' lavish publication, *The Works in Architecture*, published in parts from 1773, played a significant but less than obvious role in the dissemination of their style. Its characteristically boastful text, which credited the complete change in national taste to the brothers, certainly established their reputation for the future. The illustrations encouraged the idea of the total interior, for they were soon followed by print sets clearly reflecting the same idea.

On the other hand, isolated examples of Adam style and other neo-classical style decoration had begun to appear in ornament prints from the mid-1760s. These were mainly produced not by craftspeople but by a new breed of professional draughtsmen or designers, like Matthias Darly, or by self-professed architects, like John Crunden, whose publication of 1766, entitled the *Chimney-piece Maker's Daily Assistant*, contained perhaps the first example of the style in print.

35 *The London riverfront between Westminster and the Adelphi*, about 1771–2. By William Marlow. On the right is the Royal Terrace of the Adelphi development under construction. Oil on canvas. The Museum of London.

36 *View of the Third Drawing Room at Derby House*, 1777. Engraved by B. Pastorini after Robert Adam. Plate from *The Works in Architecture of Robert and James Adam*, volume II, 1779. Adam remodelled the interior of Derby House, Grosvenor Square, London, for Lord Stanley, 1773–4. Engraving. VAM 11.RC.GG.2.

37

38

36

7. Boulton and Wedgwood

Enterprising manufacturers played a key role in the spread of neo-classicism. Especially important were the Birmingham metalworker Matthew Boulton and the Staffordshire potter Josiah Wedgwood, who were friends as well as occasional commercial rivals. Operating far from the centre of fashion in London, their ingenious methods of obtaining new ideas and of selling clearly show how the market in fashionable goods worked. It was not a matter of originality in design, but of recognizing the key importance of the nobility as consumers, as Boulton wrote to the Earl of Findlater in 1776: 'I only wish to excell in the execution of that taste which my employers must approve'. But the real purpose of having such customers was to increase the consumption of high-design goods lower down the social scale. Wedgwood's 'Queen's Ware' was one example, while Boulton happily copied for sale a clock originally made for the King and designed by Chambers, the King's architect.

39

37 *Matthew Boulton*, 1814. By Peter Rouw the Younger. Wax. VAM 1858-1871.

38 *Section of a room with Greek Ornaments*, 1770. Plate by Matthias Darly. The garlanded medallions and rosettes strongly resemble the decoration of interiors by Sir William Chambers. Engraving. VAM E.2252-1908.

39 Table clock, 1772. Made by Matthew Boulton, after a design by Sir William Chambers, from the moulds prepared for a clock supplied to George III in 1771. It was bought for Sir George Cornewall of Moccas Court, Herefordshire. Ormolu, Derbyshire flourspar and glass. Courtauld Institute Gallery, London.

JOSIAH WEDGWOOD

Hilary Young

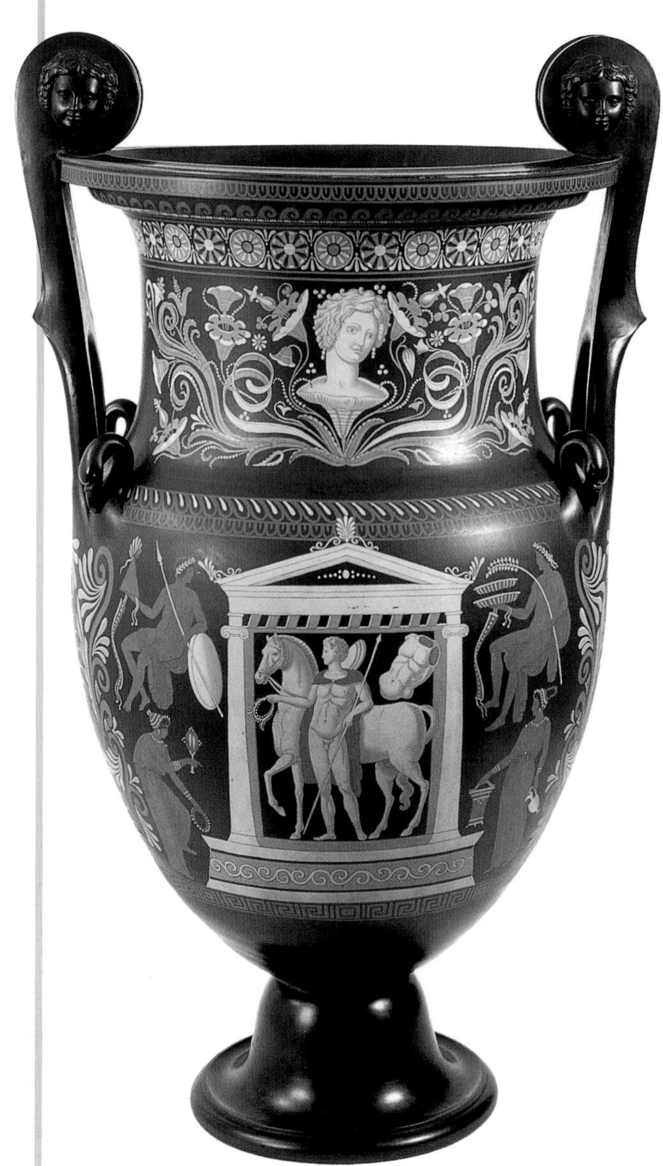

The remarkable success of the potter Josiah Wedgwood (1730–95) can be attributed to a unique combination of personal qualities. Firstly, he had a rare grasp of the chemistry and physics of the potter's craft: this, and his passion for experimentation, led him to invent or improve a number of ceramic materials and glazes. Secondly, he was sensitive to shifts in fashion and he responded by introducing new designs and product lines, the excellence of which won him a leading place in the market. Finally, he possessed exceptional entrepreneurial skills and had the vision and daring to promote his wares in a bold and often innovative manner.

The crucial years were 1768–80, when he was in partnership with the cultivated Liverpool merchant Thomas Bentley, who introduced Wedgwood to a circle of antiquarians, architects and collectors. Under their influence he adopted the classical styles then becoming fashionable in interior decoration. These men allowed Wedgwood to copy designs from their books and antiquities and did what they could to promote his wares. Striving to make modern pottery in the revived classical taste, Wedgwood introduced new materials, notably Jasper and Black Basalt, and such novel pottery goods as vases, chimney tablets and portrait medallions. These were almost the first items made in English pottery that were intended to be viewed and valued as works of art.

42. *Sir William Hamilton*, about 1772. Modelled by Joachim Smith and made at Josiah Wedgwood's factory, Etruria, Staffordshire. Unglazed white stoneware. [h. 16.51cm]. VAM 275-1966.

43. Teapot, 1785–90. The reliefs designed by Lady Templetown. Made at Josiah Wedgwood's factory, Etruria, Staffordshire. Jasper with green dip and applied reliefs. VAM 414:1152&A-1885.

40. Volute krater vase, about 1785. Made at Josiah Wedgwood's factory, Etruria, Staffordshire. Black Basalt with 'encaustic' enamel painting. [h. 87.31cm]. VAM 2419-1901.

41. Punch bowl, about 1795. Made at Josiah Wedgwood's factory, Etruria, Staffordshire. Creamware ('Queen's Ware') painted in enamels. VAM 3229-1853.

Much of Wedgwood's success stemmed from his flair for marketing and publicity. Early in his career he capitalized on a royal commission to market his improved creamware pottery as 'Queen's Ware', realizing the importance of the correct connotations for his wares. Wedgwood marked his pottery with his name: this became accepted as a guarantee of high quality, enabling him to charge higher prices than his

45. ***The Wedgwood Family in the grounds of Etruria Hall,*** **1780. By George Stubbs. Oil on canvas. The Wedgwood Museum, Barlaston.**

46. Dish painted with a view of the lake at West Wycombe Park, Buckinghamshire, 1773. Made at Josiah Wedgwood's factory, Etruria, Staffordshire, and painted at his decorating studio in Chelsea, London. From the 'Frog Service' made for Catherine the Great of Russia. Creamware ('Queen's Ware'), painted in enamels. VAM C.74-1931.

competitors. He opened exclusive London showrooms, where he entertained and cultivated the custom of 'shoals of ladies'. Here he held exhibitions of his finest work and most prestigious commissions, notably the 'Frog Service', made for Catherine the Great, and his copy of the Portland Vase. He consistently targeted above all the wealthy, believing that the 'middling sort' would follow the example of their 'betters'. Wedgwood was the first British potter to publish trade catalogues, which were issued in English and foreign-language editions. These helped him win huge export markets, which accounted for an astonishing 80 per cent of his business by the 1780s.

Admission
to see Mr. Wedgwood's Copy of
THE PORTLAND VASE
Greek Street, Soho,
between 12 o'Clock and 5.

44. Ticket to the exhibition of the copy of the Portland Vase at Wedgwood's showroom, 1790. Engraving and aquatint. VAM 96.M.23.

Wedgwood and Boulton moved towards the antique style in the late 1760s, seeking ideas for new designs everywhere. Taking them from rivals was an old trick. Boulton visited London 'toyshops' and silver retailers and bought or had drawn what he saw. But copying cut both ways, and Boulton suggested that his proposed private London showroom should have curtained showcases to guard against spies or 'pimps' from Sheffield, Birmingham and London. Objects and works of art were also to be seen in private collections. In 1770, for example, Boulton waited on the Duke and Duchess of Northumberland. After drinking chocolate together, the Duke showed Boulton 'his great picture gallery and many of his curiositys. He made me sit down with him till 3 o'clock and talked about various arts.'

Both Boulton and Wedgwood bought or borrowed the all-important illustrated source books on antiquity. Wedgwood was particularly careful to cultivate 'the legislators of taste'. These included Sir William Hamilton, whom he flattered with a cameo portrait. Hamilton in turn responded by attributing the diffusion of 'a purer taste of forms and ornaments' to the products of the Wedgwood factory, modestly downplaying the effect created by his own collection of antiquities and its publication in 1766–7 in a book written by Baron d'Hancarville.

Noble clients could give access to architects, and vice versa. Wedgwood saw the importance of having fashionable architects as 'proper sponcors', regretting in a letter to his partner Bentley that 'we were really unfortunate in the introduction of our jasper into public notice, that we could not prevail upon the architects to be godfathers to our child'. Ideally, architects would also be directly involved in the design of products. A scheme in which the Adam brothers were to design Boulton's goods (and set up a London showroom together) unfortunately came to nothing. Sir William Chambers, however, designed Boulton's ormolu and James Wyatt formed a distinctive neo-classical style for his silver. An essential part of Wedgwood's design policy was the employment of skilled modellers, who included the young John Flaxman, later to become the leading sculptor of his generation.

But the ultimate impact of both Wedgwood's products and those of Boulton was the result of brilliant marketing. Assiduous courting of the nobility and gentry through direct contact and the establishment of showrooms and auction sales in London were matched by the production of printed catalogues of the firms' more ordinary products. Wedgwood's Etruria factory in Staffordshire and Boulton's Soho works in Birmingham were also promoted as fashionable and instructive tourist sights in their own right, attracting huge numbers of British and foreign visitors, who could buy the goods as well as see them made, assisted by the wonderful technology of water and steam power.

47

8. Shops and shopping

Boulton's and Wedgwood's showrooms, exhibitions and auction sales joined a rapidly increasing number of similar events drawing the London crowds, including museums of curiosities and art exhibitions, both temporary and permanent. Part of the general movement towards a more sophisticated polite culture, they became leading areas of taste promotion. Shops were increasingly significant. Since the late seventeenth century they had been becoming more fashionably decorated inside. At the same time glazed shop-window displays turned London's chief shopping streets into a major tourist sight, as a German visitor, Johanna Schopenhauer, observed in 1803: 'The brilliant displays of silverware, the beautiful draperies of muslin . . . behind large plate glass windows, the fairy-tale glitter of the crystal shops, all this bewitches the visitor.' Fashions, new styles and the products of a new breed of 'artistic manufacturer' were also brought to the public through fashion magazines and the first British style magazines. Among the latter was Rudolph Ackermann's *The Repository of Arts*, begun in 1809. As with such magazines today, it was

47 Painting on an ancient Greek vase. Plate from *Catalogue of Etruscan, Greek and Roman Antiquities from the cabinet of the Hon. W. Hamilton*, vol. I, by Pierre Hugues d'Hancarville, 1766–7. Coloured etching. VAM 64.G.44.

48 *Interior of the Shakespeare Gallery, London*, 1790. By Francis Wheatley. The gallery was created in 1789 to promote history painting, by exhibiting Shakespearean subjects and having them engraved. The fashionable crowd shown here includes the Dukes of York and Clarence, the Duchess of Devonshire and Sir Joshua Reynolds. Watercolour. VAM 1719-187.

49 *The Strand from the corner of Villiers Street, London*, 1824. By George Scharf. Watercolour over pencil with black ink. The British Museum.

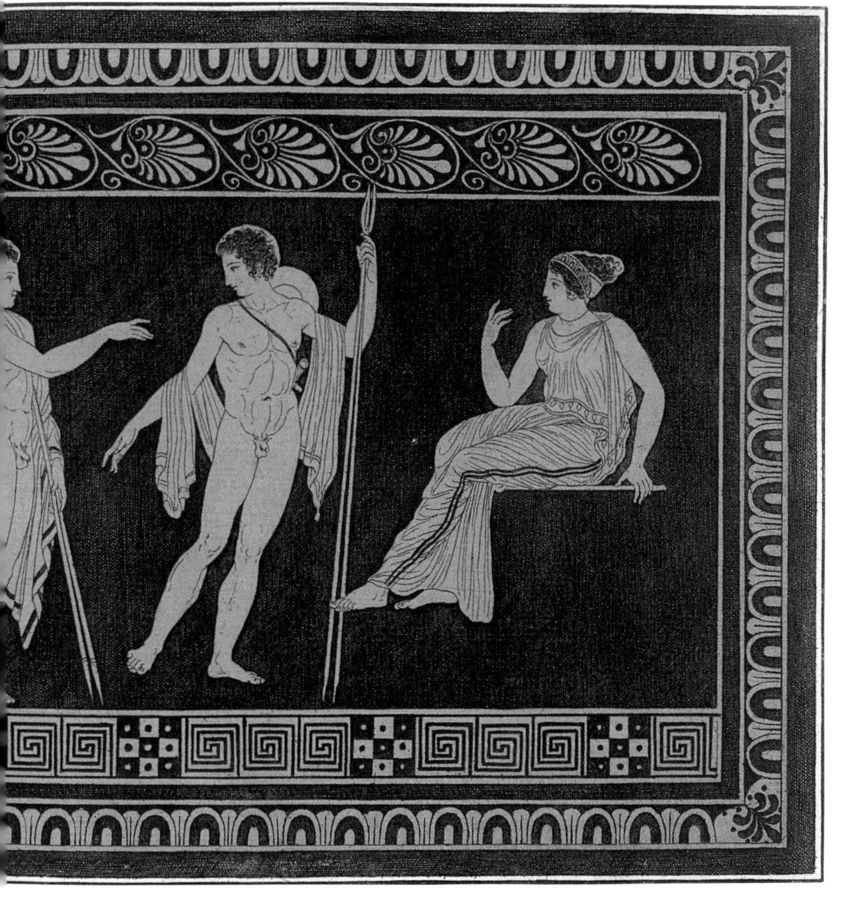

48

Stick no Bills
VILLIERS
Street near the Strand
DRURY, SILVERSMITH & JEW
MANCHESTER
HOUSE
CARLEY GROCER

49

FASHION MAGAZINES

Rachel Kennedy

The first publications to illustrate fashion were sixteenth-century German costume books or *Trachtenbücher*. They depicted the styles of dress that were characteristic of different countries. By the early eighteenth century the traditional costume book had been replaced by images of fashionable men and women in contemporary dress, sold as single fashion plates. In London a burgeoning print culture and rising levels of literacy, combined with improved access to these publications through circulating libraries and print shops, ensured that these images reached a wider audience than ever before.

By the mid-eighteenth century the increasing demand from well-to-do women of all ages and backgrounds for information on, and representations of, fashionable clothing and accessories was met by the ladies' pocket book. One of the earliest was *The Ladies Complete Pocket Book*, published for the year 1758–9 by John Newbery in London.

Derived from almanacs, these were small, portable and relatively inexpensive etiquette books dispensing 'useful' advice on fashion to elegant ladies, as well as providing entertainment in the shape of puzzles, songs and stories. The fashion content consisted of one or two simple engravings depicting a lady in court dress in the style of the previous year. Pocket books were also produced in provincial centres, such as Bury St Edmunds, Canterbury, Birmingham, Newcastle, Norwich and Exeter.

By the end of the eighteenth century pocket books had been supplemented by monthly magazines such as Nicolaus von Heideloff's *Gallery of Fashion*, begun in 1794. These

50. Plate from *Gallery of Fashion*, April 1796. Published by Nicolaus von Heideloff. Printed by W. Bulmer & Co., London. She walks in St James's Park, London, with the Queen's House (now Buckingham Palace) behind. Hand-coloured aquatint. VAM L.255-1943.

51. Page, dated 1792, from an album of textile cuttings and printed fashion sources put together by Barbara Johnson, 1746–1822. VAM T.219-1973.

52. *A Fashionable Full Dress*. Plate from *Le Beau Monde*, 1806. Hand-coloured etching. VAM E.3038-1888.

53. *Evening Dress*. Plate in Rudolph Ackermann's *Repository*, April 1819. Hand-coloured engraving. VAM RC.R.25.

54. *The Optic Curls or The Obligeing Head Dress*, 1777. By Matthias Darly. Engraving. VAM E.2292-1966.

publications were more visually appealing than pocket books, reflecting the increasing sophistication of their readers. The fashion plates were larger and hand-coloured, and the text accompanying them gave a detailed description of the materials used, as well as where and when the particular outfit should be worn. Unlike annual pocket books, monthly magazines were able to contain up-to-date information about the latest developments in fashion both in London and on the continent.

By the early nineteenth century magazines like Rudolph Ackermann's *The Repository of Arts, Literature, Commerce, Manufactures, Fashions and the Politics* (produced between 1809 and 1828) were providing both the male and female reader with information on contemporary fashions, as well as articles on politics, new developments in science, the latest furniture, exhibition reviews and even actual samples of furnishing fabrics.

56. *Seated man*, 1745. Engraved by Thomas Major after Hubert-François Bourguignon, called Gravelot. Engraving. VAM E.2440A-1886.

55. *A Lady in The Dress of the Year*, 1757. Plate from a pocket book. Engraving. VAM E.486-1902.

58

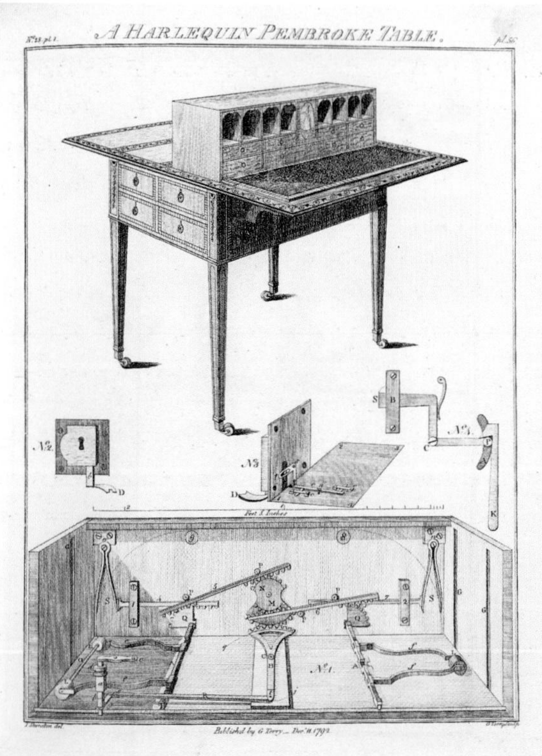

57

closely connected to shops and other suppliers, as well as being linked to his establishment of the same name (based on James Lackington's bookshop, the 'Temple of the Muses'), which sold and lent oil paintings and watercolours, published prints, sold artists' materials and fancy articles and included a drawing school. The tone and approach of *The Repository*, with its critical and illustrated advice on current style and where to obtain it, were matched by a new generation of illustrated technical manuals and pattern books. Bigger and more detailed than before, they included several publications by Thomas Sheraton, a drawing master and specialist furniture designer, whose first book, *The Cabinet-maker and Upholsterer's Drawing Book*, appeared from 1791, as well as works by the designer George Smith. A key figure for Smith (who claimed to be his upholsterer), for Sheraton (who illustrated his latest work) and for Ackermann (who dedicated his *Repository* to him) was George, Prince of Wales, Regent from 1811 and King from 1820.

57 *A Harlequin Pembroke Table*, 1793. Engraved by G. Terry after Thomas Sheraton. Plate from *The Cabinet-maker and Upholsterer's Drawing Book* by Thomas Sheraton. Sheraton illustrated the mechanical furniture that was then much in vogue, in this case a Pembroke table (for taking breakfast) that converted into a writing table for ladies. Engraving. VAM 11RC.J.23.

58 *Messrs Morgan and Sanders's Ware-Room, Catherine Street, London*. Plate from *The Repository of Arts* by Rudolph Ackermann, 1809. Engraving. The Museum of London.

60

9. Royal taste

George III had studied under Sir William Chambers and was a serious promoter of architecture and the visual arts, but his ultimate impact on national taste – if we except the Somerset House enterprise – was negligible. His eldest son was the precise opposite; the first taste-leading English monarch since William III and the most visually cultivated since Charles I. A prodigious builder, collector and patron, his reckless spending, restless pursuit of fashion and his connoisseurship set stylistic trends that exactly matched the mood of the time. On a more permanent level, his promotion of palace building and related town-planning schemes, chiefly executed by John Nash, turned London into a metropolis befitting its status as the most populous city in the world, and a major shopping and commercial centre.

When George came of age in 1783 he was given Carlton House, a run-down royal residence off Pall Mall in London. He immediately set about modernizing it, with the aid of the architect Henry Holland and decorators and furniture makers brought over from France. The first schemes introduced a French-influenced style, which replaced the Adam manner and prepared the ground for the group of styles often described as Regency. Holland's chaste interiors were repeatedly changed, attaining, under the decorator Walsh Porter in the 1810s, a rich luxuriance heavy with textiles. In all these changes the

59

59 *The County Fire Office and the Quadrant, Regent Street, London*, built 1819–20. Designed by John Nash. Engraved by Dale after Thomas Hosmer Shepherd. Plate from *Metropolitan Improvements* by James Elmes, 1827. Engraving. VAM 237.F.44.

60 *The Crimson Drawing Room, Carlton House, London*, 1816. By Charles Wild. Watercolour. © The Royal Collection.

Prince played a very active role: indeed, Porter said when taxed with overspending, 'I have not added or *branched* out into a single thing that was not plan'd by the Prince himself (not *me*).' Carlton House was demolished in 1827, but by then the chief royal residence had become Buckingham House, which was rebuilt as Buckingham Palace, with interiors richly decorated in a heavy Roman style. Every detail, said Nash, 'is the subject of a distinct drawing, submitted for previous approbation'. At Brighton, Holland built the Prince a classical 'marine pavilion'. The whole house was eventually converted into the Chinese style inside, with reconstructed exteriors in the Mogul manner. 'I do not believe that, since the days of Heliogabalus, there has been such magnificence and such luxury,' wrote the Princess Lieven. At Windsor, the Gothic style was adopted for furniture in the castle, which was comprehensively restored with new suites of state rooms and given the impressive silhouette that we see today. A simple lodge was also converted by Nash into a huge thatched *cottage orné*.

62

61

61 The Royal Lodge, Windsor, 1828. Designed by John Nash, built 1813–16. Hand-coloured aquatint. © The Royal Collection.

62 Model of the Marble Arch, London, about 1826. Perhaps after a wood and clay original model. Designed by John Nash and John Flaxman. The Marble Arch, now at the north end of Park Lane, was originally erected in front of Nash's Buckingham Palace. Plaster. VAM A.14-1939.

The Prince's collecting of paintings and *objets d'art* also had a profound influence on national taste. He led the trend away from the Italian Old Masters and Grand Tour objects of the past towards an interest in more modern French products, seventeenth-century Dutch painting and modern British art. His patronage also played a key role in encouraging the manufacture of British luxury goods. The most characteristic example was that of the royal goldsmiths, Rundell, Bridge and Rundell, who set about remaking and expanding the royal plate from 1806. Royal patronage had, of course, long been important to makers and retailers, but Rundells typified a new trend. They actively publicized their royal link, not only at their shop in Ludgate Hill, but also on every piece they made, which bore their title, in Latin, as goldsmiths to the Prince and King. They became the biggest, most influential manufacturing goldsmiths in the country.

This firm clearly demonstrates the changes in status and practice of craftspeople and retailers, and the rising position of the applied arts since the mid-eighteenth century. An earlier goldsmithing firm like that of Paul de Lamerie was certainly innovatory in pioneering the rococo style in silver, but it did not make artistic claims for its products. Rundells, on the other hand, saw advantages in being artistic. As well as useful plate, they made pure art works, like the Shield of Achilles, John Flaxman's reconstruction of a famous ancient work described by Homer. Although this was a risky speculation, it certainly enhanced the status of the firm, as the reaction of the *European Magazine* testified on a visit to Rundells: 'It appears that, highly to the credit of the taste, discernment, and liberality of Messrs Rundell and Bridge, this has been entirely a speculation of their own.' Even in their more useful silver (the *European Magazine*'s 'many gorgeous and valuable articles'), the trend towards more sculptural design based on ancient forms demanded unprecedented levels of artistic skill in design and execution. Rundells responded by setting up their own design studio, headed for many years by the sculptor John Theed. In addition to Flaxman (who had worked for Wedgwood), it employed the sculptors Edward Baily and Sir Francis Chantrey, and the painter and book illustrator Thomas Stothard.

63 *The premises of Rundell, Bridge and Rundell, Ludgate Hill, London*, 1826. By John Clement Mead. The shop, designed by Mead, was built in 1825. Watercolour. Corporation of London.

64 The Shield of Achilles, with London hallmarks for 1821–2. Mark of Phillip Rundell. Designed and modelled by John Flaxman, and made by Rundell, Bridge and Rundell. © The Royal Collection.

10. Taste reform

Extremes of taste and fashion in the years around 1800 were matched by an unprecedented amount of criticism. While Jane Austen satirized the horrors of the Gothic novel in *Northanger Abbey*, brilliant caricatures by James Gillray and others linked the Prince Regent's stylistic excesses to his financial extravagance, his unpopularity and his immorality. The extraordinary performance of George IV's coronation in 1821, with its side-show of the excluded but popular Queen Caroline, only confirmed these notions. With typical royal attention to detail, the entire cast was clothed in historicizing dress, while the accoutrements were designed to match. The coronation helped to establish a fatal link between bad taste and immorality, which lay at the root of the design debates of the Victorian era. It was the last coronation on such a scale until the needs of Empire created another in 1911.

But the move towards design reform had begun some 20 years earlier in the work of Thomas Hope (whose London house is discussed in Chapter 2). Hope was a new kind of patron. Like Lord Burlington, he aimed single-handedly to influence and reform fashionable artistic taste, but his banking background and his very public methods reflected the shifts in the consumption of visual culture towards the ever-growing urban, business élite. Hope's interests encompassed literature as well as visual culture, from furniture and paintings to gardens and architecture. His London house at Duchess Street was a demonstration (open to the public) of his ideas in art, taste and decoration. In 1807 he published *Household Furniture and Decoration Executed from Designs by Thomas Hope*, illustrating the interiors and contents of the house (*see 2:44*). The illustrations alone would have made it a new kind of design book, but it was also accompanied by a polemical text setting out Hope's reforming manifesto on design and craftsmanship.

Hope's London house, the illustrations in his *Household Furniture* and *Designs of Modern Costume* (1812), which he inspired (*see 2:63*), were the main agents for the general adoption of the pure classical style during the Regency period. In the long term, however, it was Hope's text that was most significant, setting out, as his son Alexander wrote in 1862, ' . . . the idea of art-manufacture, of allying beauty of form to the wants and productions of common life'. By promoting craftsmanship, avoiding the excesses of the division of labour and by employing (according to Thomas Hope) 'the talent of the professor of the more liberal arts; the draughtsman, the modeller, the painter, and the sculptor', it would be possible to give not only 'new food to the industry of the poor, but new decorum to the expenditure of the rich'. The resulting rise in design standards would lead 'not only towards ultimately increasing the welfare and the commerce of the nation, but refining the intellectual and sensible enjoyments of the individual'. The continuing story of these ideas belongs in the Victorian era.

65

65 *The Unexpected Visit, or more free than Welcome*, 1820. By William Heath. The rejected Queen Caroline arrives in Brighton, surprising the Prince Regent and his mistress Lady Conyingham. Hand-coloured etching. Corporation of London.

66 *The Coronation Banquet of George IV*, 1821–2. By George Jones. Oil on canvas. © The Royal Collection.

CHAPTER 4

Fashionable living

MICHAEL SNODIN

1. The spread of luxury

In 1771 Tobias Smollett, in his novel *Humphry Clinker*, looked back on a changed London. He did not like what he saw. 'In the space of seven years I am credibly informed that eleven thousand houses have been built in one quarter of Westminster . . . Pimlico and Knightsbridge are now almost joined to Chelsea and Kensington; and if this infatuation continues for half a century, I suppose the whole county of Middlesex will be covered with brick.' According to Smollett, 'the daily increase in this enormous mass' had been created by a single 'grand source of luxury and corruption' – the spread of the trappings and habits of elegant living from the nobility to the merchants and professionals of London, and thence to social ranks lower down:

> About five and twenty years ago, very few, even of the most opulent citizens of London, kept any equipage, or even any servants in livery. Their tables produced nothing but plain boiled and roasted, with a bottle of port and a tankard of beer. At present, every trader in any degree of credit, every broker and attorney, maintains a couple of footmen, a coach-man, and postilion. He has his own town-house, and his country house, his coach, and his post-chaise. His wife and daughters appear in the richest stuffs, bespangled with diamonds. They frequent the court, the opera, the theatre, and the masquerade. They hold assemblies at their own houses; they make sumptuous entertainments, and treat with the richest wines . . . The substantial tradesman, who was wont to pass his evening at the ale house for fourpence half-penny, now spends three shillings at the tavern, while his wife keeps card-tables at home; she must likewise have fine clothes, her chaise, or pad, with country lodgings, and go three times a week to public diversions . . . The gayest places of public entertainment are filled with fashionable figures; which, upon inquiry, will be found to be journeymen tailors, serving men, and abigails [ladies' maids], disguised like their betters.

Smollett's attack on luxuries as both morally dangerous and socially destabilizing was an old refrain. In 1755, the time to which he was looking back, the newspaper *The World* had followed a similar line: 'Thanks to the foolish vanity which prompts us to imitate our superiors . . . every tradesman is a merchant, every merchant is a gentleman, and every gentle-man one of the nobles. We are a nation of gentry.' These shifts in consumption were among the most characteristic features of the Georgian period, in which the civilizing codes of gentility and polite living spread from the upper to the middling classes, and sometimes beyond. As Smollett suggests, the effects were to be seen in every aspect of life, from building to eating and drinking, from clothes to modes of travel, the last a significant cost item: maintaining an equipage of coach and horses could cost as much as running a helicopter today. It was not simply a matter of consumption, but of the closest attention to manners and deportment, as Lord Chesterfield made clear when writing to his son in 1751: 'take particular care that the motions of your hands and arms be easy and graceful, for the genteelness of a man consists more in them than in anything else . . . '

1 Detail of *A Millener's Shop. Mrs Monopolize, the Butcher's wife, purchasing a modern Head Dress*, 1772. Coloured mezzotint on glass. VAM E.620-1997.

2 *To Offer or Receive*. Plate from *The Rudiments of Genteel Behaviour: An introduction to the Method of attaining a graceful Attitude, an agreeable Motion, an easy Air and a Genteel behaviour* by François Nivelon, 1737. Engraved by Louis-Philippe Boitard after Bartholomew Dandridge. Engraving. VAM L.766-1876.

The chief arena for such manners, and of the increased sociability that they promoted, was the rapidly expanding and changing area of entertainment, both public and private. Greater sociability was especially linked to a progressive decrease in heavy formality. This applied to public areas such as Vauxhall Gardens, but also to the more private sphere, in which genteel activities like tea drinking (and the accompanying conversation) grew into an important social ceremony, while the noble ceremonials of formal dining tended to decline.

2. Changing spaces

In the private sphere, the demands of genteel sociability were closely reflected in house planning and furnishing. One of the key factors was the development of new forms of social gathering, in particular the 'assembly', which had both private and public forms. The early private assemblies were small and decorous affairs; in 1751 they were defined as a 'stated and general meeting of polite persons of both sexes, for the sake of conversation, gallantry, news and play'. By then, however, assemblies were sometimes being called 'routs' – 'a colossal

3 The music room from Norfolk House, London, 1748–56. Designed by the architect, Matthew Brettingham, Thomas Clark and Giovanni Battista Borra. VAM W.70-1938.

3

caricature of an assembly', involving dancing, conversation and cards. The lack of large enough rooms soon began to make itself felt, although in older country houses an existing room could sometimes be adapted as the desired 'Great Room'. At Temple Newsam House, Yorkshire, between 1738 and 1745, the seventh Viscount Irwin and his wife Anne altered, refurnished and redecorated the virtually derelict Jacobean Long Gallery in the latest neo-Palladian and rococo styles as a great room for company. The movable furniture consisted of 20 chairs, two settees, a daybed, two pier tables and eight candlestands. The fixed decorations were two pairs of pier tables, two wall sconces and 83 pictures.

In new country houses more radical solutions were possible: a case in point was the Palladian-style Houghton Hall, Norfolk, begun in 1722. Instead of adopting the linear baroque enfilade of multi-room apartments extending from one or two great state rooms, the plan of the first floor wrapped four 'apartments' around the great hall and saloon. Two of the apartments could be joined to the hall and saloon as public spaces. By 1731 one apartment included one of the earliest state dining rooms, not only ousting the hall or saloon as the setting for great dinners, but also starting a process of equalization in the status of rooms. In London, as the architect Isaac Ware noted disapprovingly in *A Complete Body of Architecture* in 1755, the solution was more difficult: 'In houses which have been some time built, and have not an out of proportion room, the common practice is to build one on to them: this always hangs from one end or sticks to one side, of the house . . . The custom of routs has introduced this absurd practice.'

A better answer came with Norfolk House in London's St James's Square. On the first floor the Duchess of Norfolk's state bedchamber and a dressing room, together with an ante-room, a music room, two reception rooms and a great room formed a circuit around the main staircase. The whole run was in use at the opening assembly in 1756. 'All the earth was there,' wrote Horace Walpole, 'you would have thought there had been a comet, everybody was gazing in the air and treading on each other's toes. You never saw such a scene of magnificence and taste. The tapestry, the embroidered bed, the illumination, the glasses, the lightness and the novelty of the ornaments and ceilings are delightful.' As the army captain William Farrington noted, 'Every room was furnished with a different colour, which used to be reckoned absurd, but this I suppose to be the standard.' The decorations were equally varied, with different ceilings and wall treatments and an 'entirely Chinese' dressing room, but apart from a general increase in magnificence in the great room, marked by its decoration with tapestries, the general aim was equality of use. Cards could be played in any room, and the dining tables and seating were equally movable.

4

4 The Picture Gallery, Temple Newsam House, Leeds, created 1738–45.

TAKING TEA

Rachel Kennedy

Tea was introduced to Britain in the mid-seventeenth century. Samuel Pepys noted the first time he encountered tea in his diary in 1660, describing it as 'a China drink of which I never had drank before'. Within a century the practice of 'taking tea' had become a widespread national custom.

It was not until the early eighteenth century that tea overtook coffee and chocolate as the nation's favourite hot drink. It became enormously popular for several reasons: it was easier to prepare than either coffee or chocolate; it could thus be served anywhere, from large social events such as public balls and concerts to more intimate gatherings among family and friends; above all, by the early eighteenth century it was cheaper than the alternatives.

At first, though, tea had been prohibitively expensive and only the very wealthy could afford to buy it. The tea paraphernalia or 'equipage' required to indulge in this pastime reflected the drink's early social exclusivity. Tea caddies, tea services, kettles and stands were made from expensive materials, such as silver, and were considered luxury items. Equipages were commissioned from leading craftspeople of the day and might be embellished with the owner's family crest or

5. *A Family of Three at Tea*, about 1727. By Richard Collins, possibly painted in Leicestershire or Lincolnshire. Oil on canvas. VAM P.9-1934.

6. Tea tray, 1743. Probably made in London. Tin-glazed earthenware. [diam. 35.5cm]. VAM 3864-1901.

7. Teawares, 1683–1731. From left to right: sugar bowl, with London hallmark for 1730–1. Mark of Edward Cornock. [h. 8cm]. Tea caddy, with London hallmarks for 1722–3. Mark of Bowles Nash. Tea bowls and saucers, about 1683–1722. Made in the Jingdezhen kilns in Jiangxi Province, China. Spoon tray, with London hallmarks for 1722–3. Teapot, with London hallmark for 1705–6. Mark of Simon Pantin (about 1680). Silver, and porcelain decorated in underglaze cobalt blue. VAM M.164-1939, M.180-1919, C.777-1910, C.778-1910, M.318-1962, M.172-C-1919.

8. Tea equipage, with London hallmarks for 1735–6. Marks of Paul de Lamerie. Engraved with the arms of Jean Daniel Boissier and Suzanne Judith Berchere. Silver. © Leeds City Museums and Galleries.

9. Kettle, probably 1730–2. Made in London in the workshop of Charles Kandler for the banker Littleton Pointz Meynell. Cast, chased and engraved silver with basketwork handle. VAM M.49-1939.

coat of arms. Specialist tea wares were also imported from China and Japan. As tea became cheaper, British potters began to make tea wares in cheaper materials. In the second half of the eighteenth century tea drinking became universal.

By the start of the Georgian period the habit of taking tea had become particularly associated with women. Men tended to drink coffee in coffee houses. Collecting Chinese porcelain, of the kind imported into Britain for drinking tea, was already regarded as an especially female activity. But the association between women and tea may also have arisen because taking tea fitted so well with the new custom of visiting, which developed in the late seventeenth century, especially in London. Tea could easily be served by the mistress of the house herself to a group of female friends around a small, intimate tea table. So close was the link between women and tea during the Georgian period that the tea table itself came to be regarded by some writers as a symbol of unwelcome female power and influence. Several artists played with this idea, such as the caricaturist George Cruikshank, who portrayed tea-drinking women as dangerous gossips or 'slandering elves'.

10. Chelsea tea service, about 1759–69. Made at the Chelsea porcelain factory, London. Soft-paste porcelain and painted in enamel colours and gilt. Marrow scoop, 1748–9. Teaspoons, about 1730–80. Sugar nips, about 1750. Silver. VAM 517-522-1902, 144-1903, M.65-1910, M.39&41-1928, M.11-1976, 1118-1902, Circ.8386-1956.

11. *A Curious Junto of Slandering Elves*, early 19th century. Copy by an unknown artist after a caricature by George Cruikshank, from a drawing by E.H.L. Hand-coloured engraving. VAM E.501-1955.

3. Neo-Palladian planning

The Palladian notion of the *piano nobile* meant that the most important rooms at Norfolk House were on the first floor. The more everyday rooms on the ground floor included the Duke's bedroom and dressing room and the everyday dining and drawing rooms. The example of Norfolk House helped to free the log-jam of formal planning for both town and country houses. On constricted town-house sites, neo-classical architects like Robert Adam and Sir William Chambers devised ingenious sequences of grand public rooms, varied both in shape and decoration and precisely adapted to their role as a glittering setting for a nocturnal assembly or morning levee. Adam took particular credit for this development, noting that 'the parade, convenience, and social pleasures of life, being better understood, are more strictly attended to in the arrangement and disposition of apartments'. A key element was the staircase. Usually top-lit, it became a processional way to the great rooms above. In smaller urban houses the same precepts held, for they increasingly had to accommodate large social gatherings. The standard internal arrangement for terraced houses – two rooms and a closet on each floor – was adapted to fit the concept of the *piano nobile*. On the first floor lay the drawing room and sometimes the dining room, but the latter was more often on the ground floor. The hall and staircase that linked them often impressed foreign visitors by their neatness, relatively large size and carpeted stairs. Bedrooms, too, could be on the first floor and were often provided with closets or dressing rooms that functioned as more intimate social spaces.

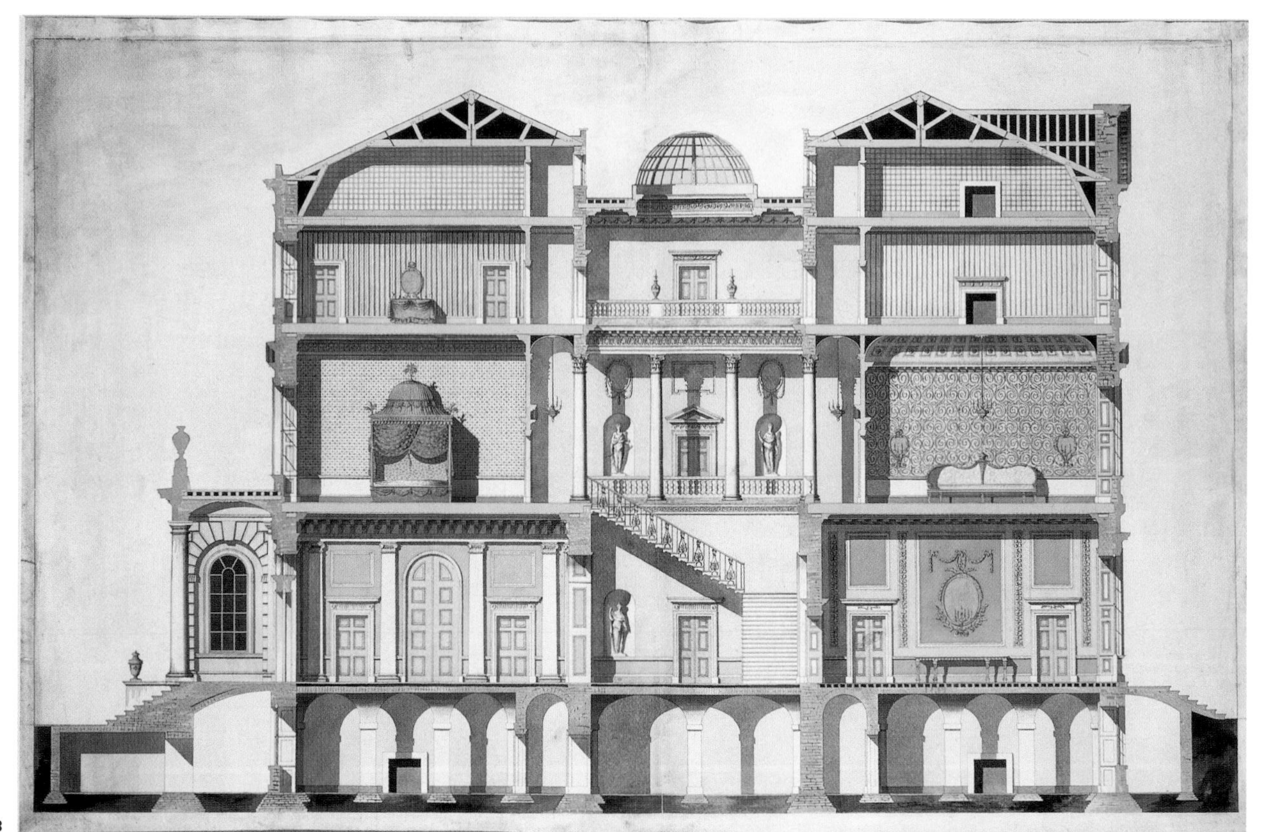

12 The staircase hall, Fairfax House, York, about 1755–62. Designed by John Carr of York for the ninth Viscount Fairfax.

13 *Design for a town mansion*, 1774. By John Yenn. Pen, ink and watercolour. © Royal Academy of Arts.

Central to the Palladian style was a hierarchy of decorative treatment. This stemmed from the notion of the classical orders, ranked in status, as described by Vitruvius and elaborated by Palladio and other Renaissance theorists. In a design for a town mansion by Chambers's pupil, John Yenn, the basement is Doric, the most primitive of all the orders. The entrance porch is Tuscan and leads into an Ionic hall. This connects with a top-lit staircase, in which a ring of Corinthian columns announces the *piano nobile* and the state bedroom and drawing room, or saloon, with its coved ceiling. A smaller house, lacking columns or pilasters, would express the same hierarchy in mouldings and ceiling heights.

Yenn's general decorative finishes reflect contemporary ideas on the appropriate treatments for certain types of room. The entrance hall is a grand introduction for the even nobler staircase. But as both places are not for lingering in, except by servants, their walls comprise plain plaster with minimal ornament. The great dining or eating room off the stairs is plastered in panels. The room's relatively austere stateliness reflects not only the concern that soft wall coverings absorbed food smells but also the idea that this was a male sphere. This was linked to the custom of drinking in the dining room at the end of dinner after the women retired to the drawing room. The dining room tended to become, by extension, the locus of family history, where silver and older portraits were displayed, and somewhere that changed less quickly with shifts in taste. The drawing room or great room, by contrast, came to be regarded as part of the feminine sphere. It was the seat of taste and fashion and the chief setting for large social gatherings. Yenn's drawing room announces its superior status with walls hung in patterned textiles and its feminine function with an elegant sofa.

Yenn's state bedchamber is less profusely decorated, but in reality such grand bedchambers were often elaborately furnished with textiles, with the curtains matching the bed hangings and the walls hung with tapestries or Chinese wallpaper. The attached dressing rooms, not shown by Yenn, were often just as richly and curiously decorated. They were the site of business or social meetings, which took place while the occupant dressed. Yenn's upper bedrooms, though better furnished than the servant's bedrooms in the attic, show that even in grand houses ordinary family bedrooms could be relatively modest in design.

4. Floors, walls and furniture

In 1749 the architect John Wood, who began Bath's transformation into the elegant city we see today, described the advances in furniture and furnishing that he had observed since the 1720s. His list of signs of modernity in a provincial context emphasized solidity, quality and expense: floors, made of the 'finest clean Deals or Dutch Oak Boards', were for the first time carpeted, while 'the Rooms were all Wainscoted and Painted in a costly and handsome Manner; Marble slabbs and even Chimney Pieces, became common; the Doors in general were not only made thick and substantial, but they had the best sort of Brass Locks put on them'. The furniture told the same story: 'Walnut Tree Chairs, some with Leather, and some with Damask or Worked Bottoms supplied the place of such as were Seated with Cane or Rushes.' Oak tables and chests of drawers were exchanged for mahogany or walnut ones, while 'handsome Glasses were added to the Dressing Tables, nor did proper Chimneys or peers [spaces between the windows] of any of the rooms long remain without Well Framed Mirrours of no inconsiderable Size; and the Furniture for every Chief Chimney was composed of a Brass Fender, with Tongs, Poker, and shovel agreeable to it'.

14

14 *Mr B. Finds Pamela Writing*, 1743–4. By Joseph Highmore, from a set of four scenes from *Pamela, or Virtue Rewarded* by Samuel Richardson, published in 1740–1. The room shown, though probably imaginary, has many of the features listed by John Wood in 1749. Oil on canvas. © Tate, London, 2003.

15

15 *The Lady's Last Stake*, 1759. By William Hogarth. The walls are hung with woven silk damask. Oil on canvas. [Overall size: 91.6 x 105.6cm]. Albright-Knox Art Gallery, Buffalo, New York. Gift of Seymour H. Knox, Jr, 1945.

Wood's insistence on the modernity of wainscot in 1749 would have surprised fashionable Londoners. Wainscot had been introduced to replace textile hangings; by 1750 it was itself being ousted in grander rooms by woven textiles, especially damasks, or their imitations in wallpaper. Wallpaper was becoming increasingly important. For two centuries it had imitated more expensive forms of wall covering, especially textiles. By the 1740s it was intensely fashionable, eventually displacing not only wainscoting but also moulded and modelled plasterwork. Much of its appeal lay in its high-quality colour printing, enabling it to match closely the surrounding curtains and upholstery.

As Wood's remarks show, a decoratively treated fireplace was relatively uncommon in ordinary homes until neo-Palladianism introduced standard types of chimneypiece. These not only provided an area for the display of ornaments, but also formed the decorative focus in standard room compositions. Elegant as neo-Palladian fire surrounds were, the grates remained very inefficient, although coal burning allowed for more attractive designs. Although cast-iron stoves were introduced to heat larger areas, it was not until the early 1800s that the Rumford grate, or 'stove', increased the efficiency of the ordinary fireplace.

5. From formal to informal

Wood's comments also indicate the arrival into more ordinary contexts of two features that had been developing in great houses for some 40 years: an increased use of soft seating and the introduction of sets of furniture of matched design, formally arranged. This not only emphasized the architectural character of room design, but also reflected changing room functions and social customs. Thus by the 1740s the spaces, or 'piers', between windows were often filled with mirrors and matching fixed pier tables. Seating, including chairs and sofas (the latter now more numerous than before), was arranged around the walls when not in use, set against the protective chair-rail. Tables were stored out of sight or against the wall when not needed.

Towards the end of the eighteenth century a new informality became evident in house planning and furnishing. This was partly the product of ideas of the Picturesque, which encouraged asymmetry and an easy connection between the interior of the house and the 'natural' park or garden outside. Humphry Repton, in his *Fragments on the Theory and Practice of Landscape Gardening* of 1816, used his famous before-and-after technique, and a verse, to illustrate the effects of the new informality. The 'cedar parlour's formal gloom' had become the new 'living room', 'where guests to whim, to task or fancy true/Scatter'd in groups their different plans pursue'. The ideal place for the principal rooms became the ground floor, 'so that you may instantly be outdoors', as Mrs Powys noted approvingly at Longford Castle in 1776.

16 Wallpaper from Doddington Hall, Lincolnshire, about 1760. Colour print from woodblocks. VAM E.474-1914.

17 *Mrs Congreve and her children*, 1782. By Philip Reinagle. The seating is arranged around the walls, except for the armchair, which is temporarily pulled up in front of the fire. Oil on canvas. National Gallery of Ireland.

18

In Jane Austen's *Persuasion*, the daughters of the house informalize the wainscotted 'old fashioned square parlour, with small carpet and shiny floor' through sheer activity, 'gradually giving the proper air of confusion by the grand piano forte and harp, flower-stands and little tables placed in every direction'. Such activities demanded light furniture of new types, like 'the nest of tables for ladies' described by Robert Southey in 1807: '... you would take them for play things, from their slenderness and size, if you did not see how useful they find them for their work'. 'Quartetto' tables were part of a new range of multi-functional furniture, which had of course existed for a long time; the bureau-bookcase, a compact combination of bookcase, desk and chest of drawers, was an innovation of the first half of the eighteenth century. But the general increase in such furniture matched a heightened demand for elegant high-design goods intended for use in confined spaces.

At Petworth House, Sussex, built in the 1690s, the state apartments were already on the ground floor. In the late 1770s the windows were lengthened, allowing direct access to a new terrace. With no *piano nobile*, all the bedrooms could be placed upstairs. In the extra space, the ground floor developed as a set of principal rooms with distinct functions. Many of the room-types were new, including breakfast rooms, billiard rooms and conservatories. Designs for their permanent furnishing show drawing rooms filled with comfortable, heavy sofas and tables and chairs, arranged in informal conversational groups, while dining rooms introduced massive permanent tables and monumental sideboards.

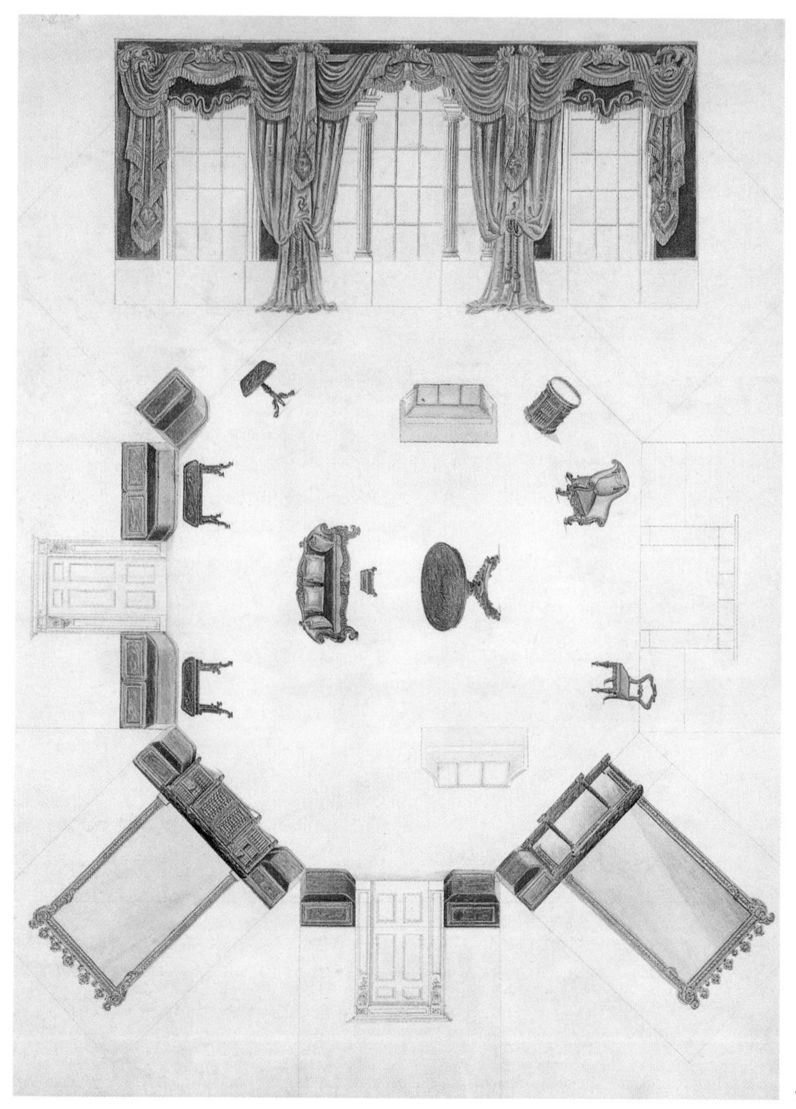

19

18 *The cedar parlour and the modern living room*. By Humphry Repton. Plate from *Illustrations from Fragments on the Theory and Practice of Landscape Gardening*, 1816. The transition from living room to exterior was eased by an attached conservatory. Aquatint. The British Library.

19 *Design for furnishing an octagonal drawing room*, about 1825. Made for Gillow & Co. Pen, ink and watercolour. VAM E.42-1952.

Dec. 20, 1873.] THE BUILDER. 1007

NORTHUMBERLAND HOUSE, STRAND: THE STAIRCASE. [See p. 998, *ante*.

21

20

Meanwhile, in London's West End, a handful of great houses were being brought to a state of hitherto unparalleled opulence. At Northumberland House, in the early 1820s, especially large sums were spent on lighting, by then a key consideration, as dinners, routs and balls were all held after dark. At a more modest level, the shift from afternoon to evening dining was reflected in the widespread adoption of the previously unusual branched candlestick for the table. The need to increase the number of reflective surfaces also led to the insertion of mirrors and refractive glass wherever possible. At Northumberland House, £720 – about the annual income of a lesser-ranking landed gentleman – was spent on enriching the four gallery chandeliers with 64,000 'spangles etc'. While these were lit by candles, and other lights by oil, the two three-metre candelabra on the stairs (£2,000) were lit by gas, which had been introduced as street lighting in 1809. Especially valued for lighting factories and shops, gas was rare in domestic contexts until the 1840s.

20 A set of quartetto tables, about 1800. Rosewood, with green-stained legs. By courtesy of H. Blairman & Sons, Ltd.

21 *The staircase at Northumberland House, London*, fitted out in 1823. Illustration from *The Builder*, December 1873, engraved by F. George Williams after J. R. Brown. Wood engraving. VAM PP.19.G.

22

23

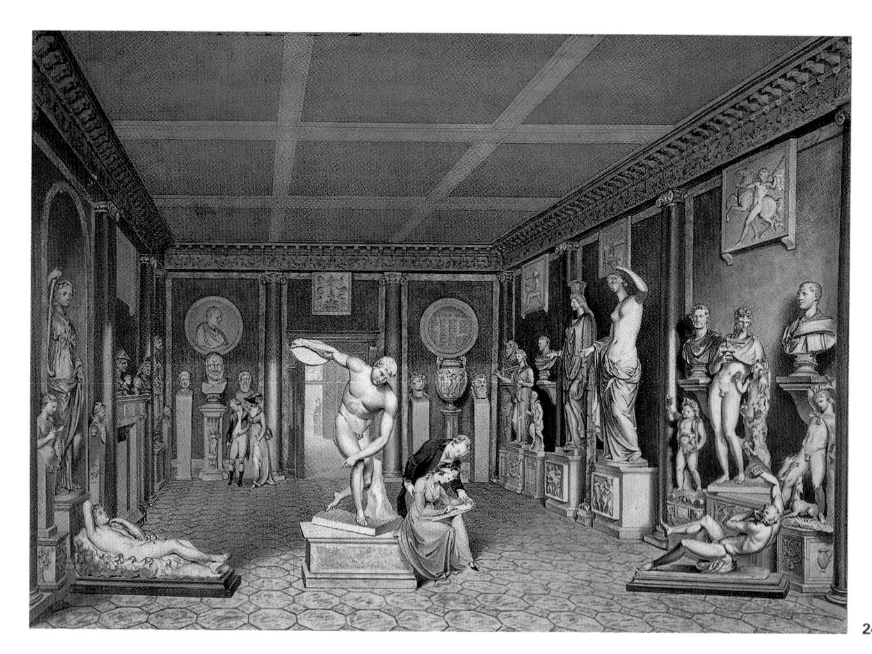

24

6. Special rooms for special needs: collecting art

Among the pictures in Lord Irwin's saloon at Temple Newsam in 1750 were the best of the 40 paintings bought in Venice in 1705 by his grandfather, 'to furnish my great rambling house'. Pictures had long adorned the walls of great houses, but they had been mainly portraits and their display was usually more dynastic and political than artistic in intention. Before 1700 collecting art for its own sake was a connoisseurial activity limited largely to the few who had been abroad, and especially on the Grand Tour. But with increasing numbers of people going on the Grand Tour, the collecting of Italian painting and ancient sculpture became an essential demonstration of taste, and their display a significant form of decoration in the grandest spaces of the neo-Palladian house. Those who had not travelled bought works through dealers or salerooms in London, which were singled out by William Hogarth and others as feeding an obsession with badly painted (and probably fake) Old Masters at the expense of modern British art.

The rising prestige of British painting and sculpture in the second half of the eighteenth century, and the study of the aesthetics of ancient art associated with neo-classicism, had an impact in both public and private spaces. Private sculpture galleries, largely inspired by Roman examples, were a case in point. One of the pioneering ventures, the Duke of Richmond's gallery of plaster casts at Richmond House, London, set up in 1758, was for the use of students. From 1774 the collector Charles Townley filled his London house with a great collection of antique art. The dining room was specially adapted for its display, the walls being set out with columns imitating porphyry. Galleries built specifically to take the spoils of the Grand Tour became a feature of country houses, like that at Newby Hall, Yorkshire, designed by Robert Adam, and the gallery at Woburn Abbey, Buckinghamshire, which culminated in a temple for Canova's *Three Graces*.

22 *Project for the decoration of the saloon at Houghton Hall, Norfolk*, 1725. By William Kent. Sir Robert Walpole's great picture collection was sold to Catherine the Great of Russia in 1779. Pen, ink and wash. Private collection.

23 *The Great Library, Cassiobury Park, Hertfordshire*, about 1815. By Augustus Charles Pugin. Figures engraved by Meyer, aquatint by F. Lewis. From *The History and description of Cassiobury Park* by John Britton, 1837. Etching and aquatint. Stapleton Collection.

24 *The Dining Room at Charles Townley's house at 7, Park Street, Westminster*, 1794. By William Chambers. Watercolour. The British Museum.

But owners could be fickle in their tastes. In 1771 the Earl of Shelburne, on a visit to Rome, decided to turn his projected music room at Shelburne House, in London's Berkeley Square, into a sculpture gallery. A design was commissioned, and the painter and antiquary Gavin Hamilton was contracted to dig up statues for the next four years. A year later the Earl changed his mind; the space was to become a library for his remarkable collection of books, manuscripts and other material. The shift is not as surprising as it may at first seem, for libraries, suitably decorated with busts of writers and other significant figures, had become an important demonstration of taste, growing from a private scholarly sanctum into a large and useful social space.

Sculpture galleries, too, served a social function: the gallery at Petworth House, formed in 1754–63, was frequently used for large dinners for the tenantry and local yeomanry. In 1824 a large top-lit picture gallery was added. Significantly only 24 of the pictures were Old Masters, the remaining 67 being modern British and American works, which were displayed alongside modern sculpture. The gallery's purpose was the serious display of art, and it borrowed many features from the Dulwich Picture Gallery, opened in 1811 as Britain's first public art gallery. In other contexts, notably the great London houses from about 1820, richly decorated picture galleries became the principal social room.

25

25 *The North Gallery, Petworth House, Sussex*, about 1827. By J. M. W. Turner. Watercolour and gouache. © Tate, London, 2003.

Collecting and the Grand Tour

Malcolm Baker

By 1730 a tour through France to Rome was already well established as part of a British nobleman's education. As well as allowing young men to complement their knowledge of Greek and Latin texts with first-hand experience of the monuments and antiquities of ancient Rome, a 'voyage to Italy' was seen as a progress through 'the common stages of the journey of life'. As the classical scholar Conyers Middleton put it in 1729, 'At our setting out through France, the pleasures that we find, like those of our youth, are of the gay fluttering kind, which grow by degrees, as we advance towards Italy, more solid, manly, and rational, but attain not their full perfection until we reach Rome.' Later in the century the tour extended as far south as Naples and the newly excavated sites of Pompeii and Herculaneum and attracted increasing numbers of men (and women) of more modest means.

Tutors as well as guide books were available to indicate what antiquities and works of art were to be particularly admired – whether antique sculpture, the paintings of Raphael or the marbles being carved in the studios of contemporary sculptors. The Grand Tour served to consolidate and expand the canon of antique sculpture that was regarded as the height of aesthetic achievement for both connoisseurs and those many artists who flocked to Rome and Florence. Some major works were bought by the wealthy British, but as it became steadily more difficult to export such pieces, collectors made do with marble copies, plaster casts and even smaller-scale reproductions in ivory, which could be mounted in furniture made at home.

26. Cabinet, about 1743. Designed by Horace Walpole, perhaps in collaboration with William Kent, for his collection of miniatures. The figures on the top by James Francis Verskovis show the sculptor François Duquesnoy and the architects Andrea Palladio and Inigo Jones. The reliefs on the front, made in Rome by Andrea Pozzo, show classical subjects. The cabinet attributed to William Hallett. Veneered with padouk on a pine carcase with oak drawer linings, carved ivory plaques and figures. [h. 156cm]. VAM W.52-1925.

27. *Antonio Canova in his Studio with Henry Tresham and a Plaster Model for his sculpture of 'Cupid Awakening Psyche'*, about 1788–9. By Hugh Douglas Hamilton. Tresham, a painter and dealer, was in Rome accompanying Colonel John Campbell, who had commissioned *Cupid Awakening Psyche*. Pastel on paper. VAM E.406-1998.

28. ***The Three Graces*****, 1814–17. By Antonio Canova. Carved in Rome for John, sixth Duke of Bedford. In 1819 it was installed in a specially built Temple of the Graces at Woburn Abbey, Bedfordshire. Marble. [h. 173cm]. VAM A.4-1994.**

29. ***Edward Howard with his dog, leaning against a parapet overlooking the Roman campagna*****, 1764–6. By Pompeo Batoni. Edward Howard was the son of Lord Philip Howard. Oil on canvas. VAM W.36:1-1949.**

Another way of importing antiquities was to have them included in a portrait of oneself by a fashionable Roman painter, such as Pompeo Batoni; set in a neo-classical British interior, this would serve as a record of a visit usually made only once in a lifetime, and as a demonstration of the owner's taste and cultivation. British visitors took advantage of the wealth of art in Italy – foreign as well as Italian – to purchase and commission many modern neo-classical works of sculpture and painting, the most distinguished being sculptures such as Canova's *Three Graces*.

30

7. Collecting and the antiquarian interior

Collecting was also taking place across a broader field. A key event was the publication in 1784 of *The Description of Strawberry Hill*, an illustrated account of Horace Walpole's villa in Twickenham. Walpole was the younger son of Sir Robert Walpole of Houghton. He had catalogued his father's great collection of Old Masters, but his own collecting interests went beyond art and classical antiquities, to ceramics, metalwork, arms and armour, enamels, *objets de vertu* and engraved portraits, often collected more for their associational or historical value than for their beauty. Except that it excluded natural history specimens, Walpole's collection was in a direct line of descent from the cabinets of curiosities and prototype museums of the previous two centuries – places that were, as he wrote, 'an Hospital for everything that is *singular*'.

31

Walpole's innovation was to combine his collection with his domestic environment. While some rooms were consistently thematic, most contained a mix of objects of widely differing origin, quality and date. In the Refectory or Great Parlour, the furniture included a remarkably forward-looking set in the Gothic style to match the fixed decoration of the room. Like other eating rooms, this contained family portraits, but the chimney carried an ancient Greek vase flanked by two East Asian pots. More Asian pots stood on the floor under the lacquered desk, which carried a modern French clock. The Gallery, the main formal space of the house, combined Gothic decoration with modern furniture in the rococo, classical and Gothic styles, bronzes, classical sculpture and sixteenth-century and modern ceramics. The walls were hung with portraits in the manner of a Jacobean long gallery. Walpole's carefully contrived interiors, with their historical atmosphere (he also wrote the first Gothic novel, *The Castle of Otranto*, in 1764), pioneered a style of informal mixed furnishing and helped to establish a certain range of obsolete old things as 'antiques'.

32

30 *The Refectory or Great Parlour, Strawberry Hill*, 1788. By John Carter. Watercolour. Courtesy of the Lewis Walpole Library, Yale University.

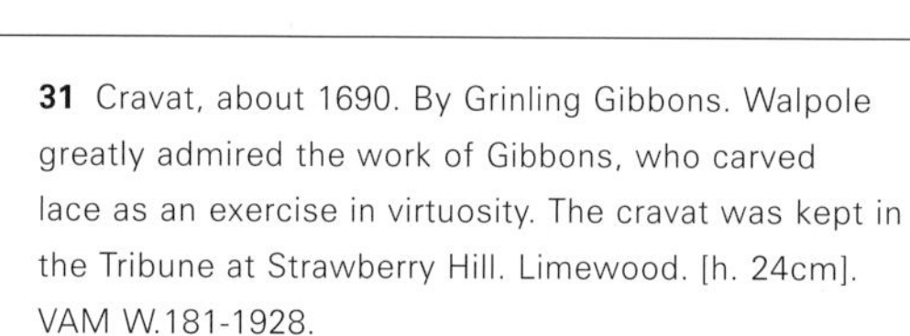

31 Cravat, about 1690. By Grinling Gibbons. Walpole greatly admired the work of Gibbons, who carved lace as an exercise in virtuosity. The cravat was kept in the Tribune at Strawberry Hill. Limewood. [h. 24cm]. VAM W.181-1928.

32 Chair, 1755. Designed by Horace Walpole and Richard Bentley. Probably made by the firm of William Hallett, Senior, for the Great Parlour at Strawberry Hill. Beechwood, painted black to imitate ebony; modern replacement rush seat. The back formerly carried a finial. [h. 125cm]. VAM W.29-1979.

33

34

33 *The Antiquary's Cell*, 1835. By Edward William Cooke. To make the painting, Cooke collected material from antique dealers in London's Wardour Street and elsewhere. Oil on panel. VAM FA.42.

34 *The Gallery at Strawberry Hill*, 1781. By Thomas Sandby and Edward Edwards. Watercolour. VAM D.1837-1904.

35 *A dinner party of fourteen: The first course.* Diagram from *The Footman's Guide* by James Williams, 1840. VAM 215.D.65.

8. Special rooms for special needs: eating and drinking

For a member of the fashionable élite like Walpole, the term Great Parlour was probably used self-consciously to convey the idea of an old-fashioned great house. However, in the houses of the merely genteel, in both town and country, parlours performed the same function as the drawing rooms of the fashionable, although they had far less money spent on their furnishing and equipment than dining rooms did. In addition to a sideboard, a table and a set of chairs meant to last a lifetime, at least two sets of eating wares and utensils had to be provided. Elizabeth Shackleton of Colne in Lancashire, the widow of a landowner and now the wife of a merchant, divided her ware and equipment for eating and drinking clearly into 'common' and 'best', used in different combinations of utensils and spaces according to the occasion. Servants and tenants would eat in the kitchen on common ware, while superior tradesmen and -women, such as milliners and mantua makers, would be given tea in the parlour or dining room, but on the same common ware. Only guests of Mrs Shackleton's status, or above, used the dining room adorned with silver and laid with the best blue-and-white Chinese export dinner service on a damask tablecloth.

Increasingly genteel modes of eating and drinking were marked by a huge rise in the number of specialized vessels and utensils, as well as in the range of materials employed in their manufacture. Many of these new types were French in inspiration, following the fashion for service *à la française*, which required diners to help themselves or their companions to food already set out on the table. Of the new types of vessel, those introduced by 1730 included bottle coolers, tureens for soup and boats for sauce. By the end of the century a wide range of specialized smaller items had appeared, including dishes for pickle and asparagus, cruets for a new range of sauces and novel implements, from soup ladles to fish servers. New breakfast equipment included toast racks

36 Wine cooler, with London hallmarks for 1727–8. Marks of Paul de Lamerie and Paul Crespin. Britannia Standard Silver. [h. 26.5cm]. VAM M.1-1990.

and egg stands. The custom of drinking after dinner, with the tablecloth removed, created the bottle holder or coaster, an item unknown on the continent. The most impressive object was the centrepiece, a complex structure that could be adapted to the main and dessert courses. Its decorative function was enhanced by the addition of either sugar or porcelain figures to the table, especially during the dessert course. By 1800 a mirrored stage-like plateau had been added.

The spread of genteel dining was greatly aided by the arrival of new materials. From the 1760s fused 'Sheffield' plate brought the look of silver to many tables, while the range of materials that was available for plates and other vessels was increased to include porcelain (either British-made or imported from China or the continent) and cream-coloured earthenware. This last material had the most profound effect on dining. Since the 1760s it had replaced, according to George Robertson in 1829, 'the old, clumsy Dutch delft-ware, and the more ancient pewter plates' at Scottish farmers' tables: 'being fully as cheap as any of those kinds of table service mentioned, . . . [it] was highly agreeable to the females of the house'.

37 Centrepiece, with London hallmarks for 1743–4. Mark of Paul de Lamerie. Given as a wedding present to Sir Roger and Lady Newdigate in 1743. It is here set up with dishes for the presentation of dessert. For the main course the central bowl served as a tureen and the branches supported candles. [h. 25.3cm]. Silver. VAM M.149-1919.

38 Top, from left to right: pewter plate, about 1760–1800. Possibly made in London by John Townsend and Thomas Giffen. Creamware ('Queen's Ware') plate, transfer-printed in black enamel, about 1780–90. Made at Josiah Wedgwood's factory, Etruria, Staffordshire. Bottom, from left to right: soft-paste porcelain plate, painted in underglaze blue, about 1780–90. Made at the Caughley porcelain factory, Shropshire. Soft-paste porcelain plate, painted in enamels and gilt, about 1773. Made at the Derby porcelain factory, part of a service sold to Philip Egerton of Oulton, Cheshire. Porcelain plate, decorated in overglaze enamels and gilt. Qing dynasty, about 1772. Made in China, the porcelain made at the Jingdezhen kilns and the decoration either added there or in Canton. VAM M.41-1945, 2302-1901, C.151-1921, C.23-1978, C.71-1932.

SPITALFIELDS SILKS AND THE SPREAD OF FASHION

Clare Browne

39. *Design for a woven silk*, 1708. By James Leman for his father, the master weaver, Peter Leman. Commissioned by the mercer Isaac Wittington. Watercolour. VAM E.1861.52-1991.

During the later seventeenth century the European market for fashionable dress silks had been dominated by material from France. The developing English industry expanded to meet this competition. It was significantly helped by refugee Huguenot families, who contributed both textile skills and business acumen. Huguenots were among large numbers, both from within England and from abroad, attracted to the capital, and by 1700 the London silk industry had spread east from the City to Spitalfields. Until the 1770s there was almost continuous progress in its production, stimulated by a considerable export market and constant innovation in fashionable design.

The Spitalfields designers and weavers had to keep up with changes in fashion and technical advances in France in order to earn a share of the market, but English silks came to develop their own individual style. One of the leading designers in the early eighteenth century was also a manufacturer, James Leman. Born into a weaving family of Huguenot descent, he produced his own accomplished designs from his early years of apprenticeship to his father, and as a master weaver later commissioned them from other leading pattern drawers.

The silks designed and woven in Spitalfields in the middle years of the eighteenth century displayed a particularly English interpretation of the rococo style, with a realistic depiction of botanical details in flowers scattered across an open or subtly patterned ground, usually in an asymmetrical arrangement, and with clear, true colours. Anna Maria Garthwaite's designs from the 1740s epitomize this style. She worked freelance, selling her work to a number of the leading London mercers and master weavers for a period of 30 years. More than 800 of her dated silk designs survive, vividly illustrating the progression of fashionable taste in dress silks during those years.

40. *Lady Walpole Wemyss*, 1754. By Allan Ramsay. Oil on canvas. In the collection of the Earl of Wemyss.

41. Silk dress fabric, 1749. Designed by Anna Maria Garthwaite for the master weaver Daniel Vautier. Brocaded silk. VAM T.192-1996.

42. Detail of a waistcoat, about 1734. Made from silk woven in Spitalfields, London. Silk brocaded with coloured silks and silver thread. VAM T.72-1951.

43. *Sir Thomas Kennedy of Culzean, 9th Earl of Cassilis*, 1746. By William Mosman. Oil on canvas. National Trust for Scotland, Culzean Castle.

The complex patterns and variety of surface effects achieved in the silks were fully exploited in fashions for both men and women. Satins, damasks, lightweight taffetas treated to achieve a high lustre (known as lustrings or lutestrings), heavier paduasoys and gros de Tours, cut and uncut velvets, tissues with different textures of gold and silver thread – all of these could be brocaded, or 'flowered', in brightly coloured silks or with more gold and silver for extra visual impact. Women's sack-back dresses with their pleated lengths of silk falling from the shoulders and men's long waistcoats, often the focal points of their outfits, allowed the intricate, balanced designs to be seen to full effect.

44. Detail of a sack-back gown, about 1755–60. Made from silk woven in Spitalfields, London. VAM T.426-1990.

9. Consuming taste

'Not Rachel, weeping for her children, could show more sorrow than Mrs Garrick,' wrote the actor David Garrick in 1775 to his influential friend Guy Cooper. 'Not weeping for her children for children she has none . . . What does she weep for then? It is for the loss of a chintz bed and curtains . . . she had prepared paper, chairs, etc. for this favourite token of Indian Gratitude.' A gift from 'the Gentlemen at Calcutta', the chintz was impounded by Customs under an Act of 1721 forbidding the import of Indian cottons. Eva Maria Garrick was unlucky, but such experiences were not unusual among people of fashion trying to import foreign luxuries, for fines or high duties controlled other luxuries, including French porcelain and furniture.

The Garricks were a fashionable couple, whose social and cultural circles ranged from the Duke of Devonshire to William Hogarth. Of relatively humble background and unencumbered by inherited goods, they were keen consumers of the latest fashions, from clothes to architecture, and avid collectors of books and modern paintings. In 1772 they took a London house in the best part of the new Adelphi development, beside that of its designer, Robert Adam, before the rest of scheme was completely built (*see 3:35*). The Adam interiors were matched by Chippendale furniture, while the movable goods included a remarkably large best tea and coffee set in the same fashionable style. Three years later Adam modernized the Garricks' villa at Hampton, further up the River Thames. Chippendale was probably again responsible for the suite for the chinoiserie best bedroom (which eventually received the troublesome chintz), combining imitation lacquer with the latest neo-classical styling.

46

45

47

45 Bed hanging, about 1775. The cotton made in a factory of the English East India Company at Masulipatam in Madras, India. Used by David Garrick and his wife for the principal bedroom of their villa at Hampton, Middlesex. Painted cotton. VAM W.70i-1916.

46 Tea and coffee service, with London hallmarks for 1774–5. Marks of James Young and Orlando Jackson. Commissioned by David Garrick and engraved with the arms of Garrick and his wife. Silver. VAM M.24-1973.

47 Robe and petticoat, 1760–5. Robe made in England of silk woven and painted in China. Owned and worn by Mrs David Garrick, née Eva Maria Veigel. Chinese painted silk. VAM T.593-1999.

48

50

49

48 Bergère chair, about 1772. One of a pair, supplied by Thomas Chippendale to Mr and Mrs David Garrick for their drawing room at No. 6 Royal Terrace, Adelphi, London. Painted beech; modern upholstery. [h. 96.5cm]. VAM W.41-1977.

49 Ceiling about 1772. Designed by Robert Adam, painted by Antonio Zucchi and possibly David Adamson. Removed from the drawing room of No. 6 Royal Terrace, Adelphi. Plaster and painted paper; the decorative parts partially restored after being painted over. VAM W.43-1936.

50 *David Garrick and his Wife by the Temple to Shakespeare at Hampton*, 1762. By Johann Zoffany. Oil on canvas. Yale Center for British Art, Paul Mellon Collection.

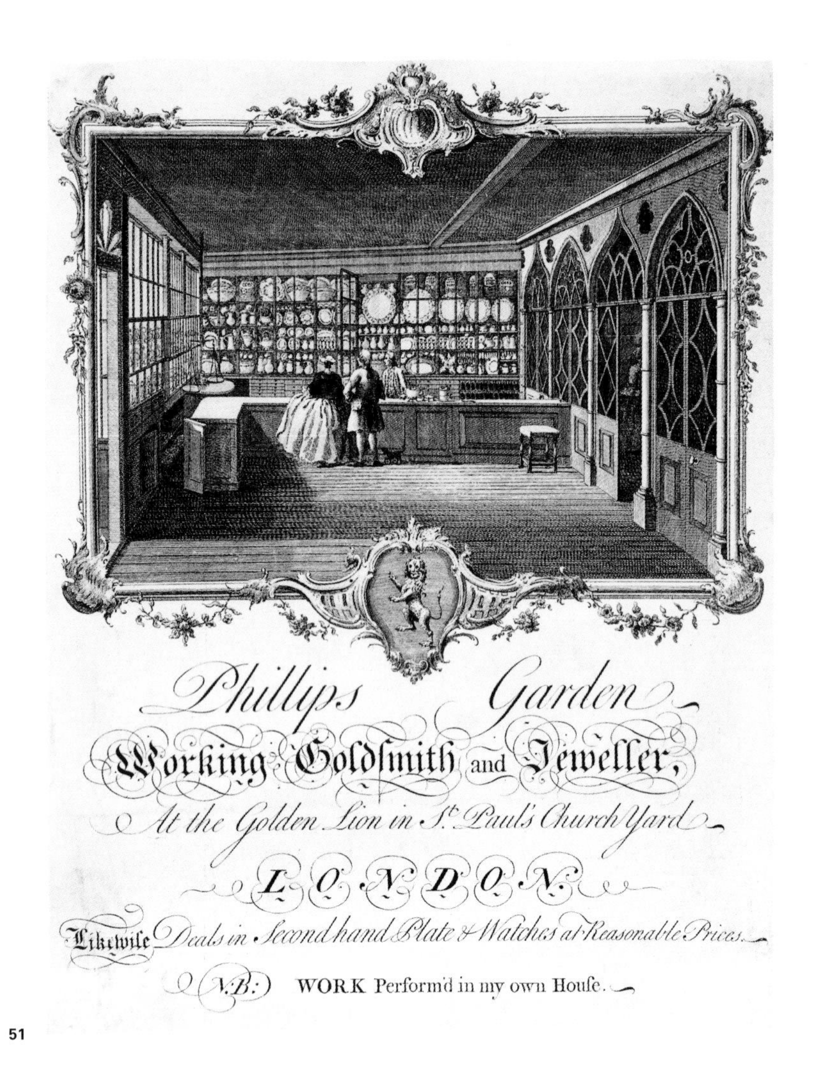

51

52

Mrs Garrick was not exceptional in taking charge of the furnishings at Hampton. Just as households at all social levels (except the very highest) were managed chiefly by women, so genteel women often took the leading role in choosing household furniture and furnishings, as they did other household goods. For Mrs Shackleton of Colne – self-consciously genteel, but lower down the social and fashion scale than Mrs Garrick – such choices may have stopped at the expensive suite of dining furniture that was ordered by her husband from the successful cabinet makers Gillows of Lancaster, but did include smaller, locally made pieces of furniture. At the top end of society the active role of women could include dealing directly with architects, as Lady Shelburne did with the normally dominating Robert Adam over Shelburne House: ' . . . with [Mr Adam] I consulted on the furniture for our painted antichamber, and determined that it should be pea green and satin spotted with white and trimmed with a pink and white fringe, it was entirely my own thought and met with his entire approbation'. On the other hand, it was with her husband that Lady Shelburne visited suppliers:

> . . . we went first to Zucchi's, where we saw some ornaments for our ceilings, and a large architecture painting for our antichamber, with which, however, my Lord is not particularly pleased. From there to Mayhew and Inch [Ince] where is some beautiful cabinet work and two pretty glass cases . . . From thence to Cipriani's where we saw some beautiful drawings and crayon pictures and where Lord Shelburne bespoke some to be copied for me, to complete my dressing room . . . From thence to Zuccarelli's where we also saw some large pictures doing for us and from thence home it being half past four.

Outside the metropolis, learning about fashion and acquiring fashionable goods was a more complex business. Elizabeth Shackleton, like many genteel provincial consumers, used friends and relatives living in London to advise and act for her in the purchase of such items as tableware. London contacts, newspapers and a network of observant informants in the bigger northern towns, like York and Pontefract, kept her well apprised of the latest in fashionable dress. Such local centres had their own social calendars, some being

51 Trade card of Phillips Garden, working goldsmith and jeweller, about 1750. A man and a woman are shown shopping together at a fashionable London goldsmith's. Engraving. The British Museum.

52 Page from an album of textile cuttings and printed fashion sources put together by Barbara Johnson. At the top left is a cutting from a sack (a loose, tube-shaped dress) made for attending the races at Stamford, Lincolnshire, in June 1767. VAM T.219-1973.

linked, like London, to a 'season' (that at the spa of Tunbridge Wells occurred in the summer) or to regular events, like the races or the assizes, which naturally brought people together.

The London season, which ran from November to May, was set by the timing of the court and Parliament. Although by the end of the eighteenth century an actress like Mrs Abington could set tastes in fashionable dress, the key events in the London fashion calendar continued to be those associated with the court. Especially important were the balls and 'drawing rooms' marking the King's and Queen's birthdays, at which the dazzling clothes worn were described in great detail in the newspapers. The textiles used were just as closely observed as the changing cut and other details. In the case of silks, their patterns changed at least twice a year. Clothes worn at court were at the top of a carefully graduated scale of fashionable clothing divided into two main areas: the formal 'dress' and more everyday, although often no less elaborate, 'undress'. In addition there were special clothes for riding and various types of gowns and hats for relaxation. The cut and cloth of clothes, as well as hats, hair, wigs and accessories, announced the social position of the wearer, as Lord Chesterfield acidly observed: 'A gentleman is every man who, with a tolerable suit of clothes, a sword by his side, and a watch and snuff box in his pockets, asserts himself to be gentleman . . . '

While court dress became to some extent fossilized, retaining into the 1820s the very wide hoops of the 1750s, it shared a general tendency towards the informal. In the 1780s the relaxed lines of informal 'chemise gowns' found their way into women's 'undress'. At the same time, men's 'undress' was gradually taking on a new simplicity under the influence of everyday country riding and sporting wear. This culminated in the restrained elegance codified by George 'Beau' Brummell. His chief aim, according to his biographer, ' . . . was to avoid anything marked; one of his aphorisms being that the severest mortification that [a] gentleman could incur was to attract attention in the street by his outward appearance'. The result was a simplified form of men's dress with close-fitting coats and pantaloons, the immediate ancestor of the modern suit. While a small élite followed every seasonal shift in taste, the reaction of Mrs Shackleton and many like her was to resist the dictates of fashion by maintaining a middle course. But even for her, clothing was the element most subservient to changes in taste, with tableware coming next and furniture, which was expected to go on for a lifetime, last. The kind of sudden shift to genteel manners and consumption that became the common butt of metropolitan satire must have been extremely rare.

53

54

53 Mantua and petticoat, about 1740–5. English. This mantua was made to be worn over the very wide hoops characteristic of the mid-18th century. Silk embroidered with coloured silk and silver thread. [h. 170cm]. VAM T.260-1969.

54 *Farmer Giles and his Wife shewing off the daughter Betty to their Neighbours on her return from School*, 1809. By James Gillray, after an amateur. The drawing room of 'Cheese Hall' is fashionably decorated, while 16-year-old Betty's genteel accomplishments are much in evidence. Hand-coloured etching. VAM 1232(73)-1882.

PUBLIC ENTERTAINMENTS

Kate Newnham

The Georgian period saw the emergence in Britain of a new kind of public entertainment, the commercial pleasure ground. There, for a modest admission charge, visitors could promenade, listen to music and take refreshments. This new form of leisure brought people together in an environment expressly designed to promote gentility and politeness. There were 64 pleasure grounds recorded in London alone, the most successful of which – Vauxhall, Marylebone and Ranelagh Gardens – were imitated in towns across Britain and Europe.

Horace Walpole described Ranelagh when it opened in 1742. 'There is a vast amphitheatre, finely gilt, painted and illuminated, into which everybody that loves eating, drinking, staring, or crowding is admitted for twelvepence.' He remarked, too, on the unprecedented social mingling that took place, embracing the nobility and gentry as well as the various ranks of London's middle classes.

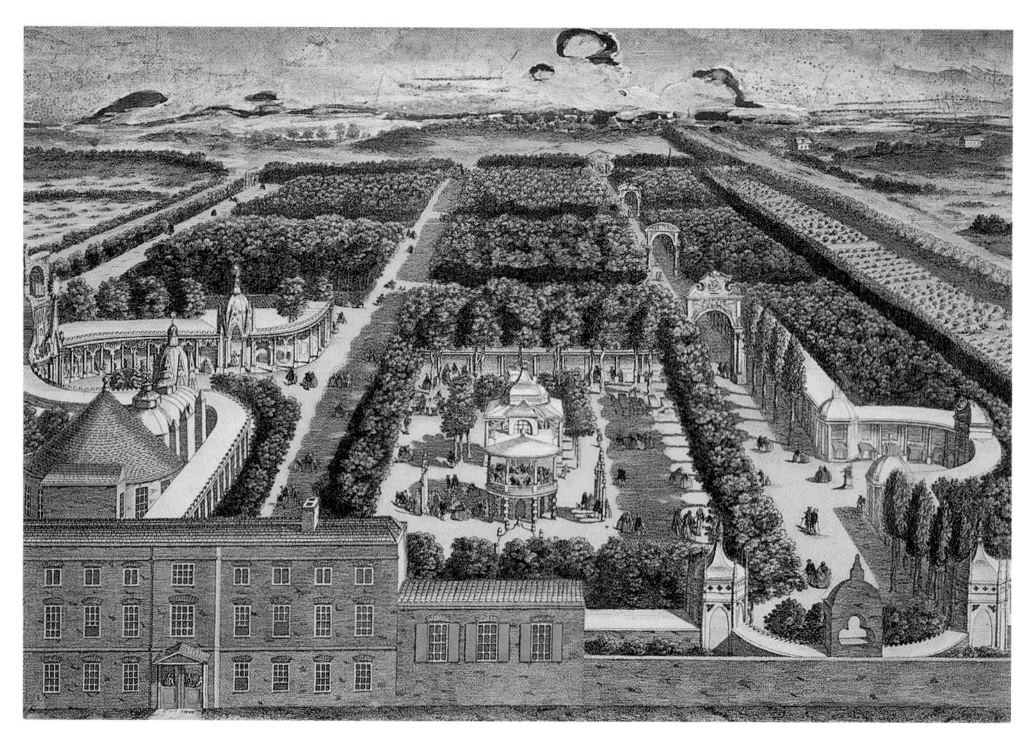

55. *A General Prospect of Vauxhall Gardens, shewing at one View the disposition of the whole Gardens*, 1751. By Johan Sebastian Muller after Samuel Wale. Hand-coloured engraving. VAM E.809-1903.

Of all the pleasure grounds, Vauxhall Gardens was the longest-lasting and the most famous. It was built on the site of the old 'Spring Gardens' on the south bank of the River Thames near Lambeth. The area of park and woodland had been open to the public since the 1660s, but had gained a dubious reputation. In 1728 the young entrepreneur Jonathan Tyers bought the lease to the land, made improvements and reopened the pleasure grounds in 1732 as a more refined attraction. The high wall round the gardens and entrance gate enabled him to control the number of visitors and extract admission charges from them.

Each evening, from late spring to early autumn, two programmes of orchestral and vocal music were performed, with works by leading composers of the day, such as George Frederick Handel, William Boyce and Thomas Arne. On 21 April 1749 a crowd of 12,000 attended a rehearsal of Handel's *Music for the Royal Fireworks*, stopping the traffic for three hours. Between the programmes, visitors could explore the five hectares of gravel walks, pavilions and triumphal arches or take a meal in one of about 50 'supper-boxes'. The Irish writer Oliver Goldsmith wrote in 1760, 'I found every sense overpaid with more than expected pleasure; the lights every where glimmering through the scarcely-moving trees; the full-bodied concert bursting on the stillness of the night.'

56. *Vauxhall Gardens*, 1784. Madame Weischel singing to a crowd including Dr Johnson and the Prince of Wales. By Thomas Rowlandson. Watercolour. VAM P.13-1967.

59. *Interior of the Rotunda at Ranelagh*, 1754. By Antonio Canaletto. Oil on canvas. © The National Gallery, London.

58. *George Frederick Handel*, 1738. By Louis François Roubiliac. Made for Vauxhall Gardens. Marble. [h. 153.5cm]. VAM A.3-1965.

57. *The Milkmaid's Garland, or Humours of Mayday*. Painting for a supper box at Vauxhall Gardens, 1741–2. By Francis Hayman. Oil on canvas. VAM P.12-1947.

60

61

10. Public arenas

Christian Goede, a German visitor to London between 1802 and 1804, noted that in Bond Street, London's chief area for luxury goods, the foot pavement was 'so perfectly covered with elegantly dressed people as to make it difficult to move', while 'the gentlemen pass up and down the street on horseback so as to see and be seen'. Shopping was but one of a growing number of public cultural activities in which fashionable town dwellers could indulge, as Tobias Smollett made clear in his attack on the citizens of London. To his 'Court, the opera, the theatre, and the masquerade' should be added public assemblies, clubs, circulating libraries, exhibitions and pleasure gardens. As Goede's comments about the fashionable West End of London suggest, the regular planning of Georgian towns tended to encourage genteel sociability. In cities like London, Bath and Edinburgh, as well as smaller towns, the refined and unified appearance of the classical street façades was matched by the airy squares and crescents in which they were laid out. Such outdoor spaces had a definite social purpose. In London, according to Goede, the squares 'fill with ladies in morning dress, presenting lovely groups to the observation of the passengers'. After shopping, 'all the world hurries to Hyde Park' to promenade until about four or five in the afternoon, the end of the fashionable 'morning'. In smaller cities a 'town walk' sometimes served the same function. The chief purpose of these activities – both outdoor and indoor – was to observe, and be observed by, the fashionable. At indoor entertainments like the theatre this was made possible by lighting the auditorium as much as the stage.

As the eighteenth century advanced, the social rituals of the London season, with their emphasis on polite visual culture, were increasingly matched by similar

60 *Stand coachman, or the Haughty Lady well fitted*, 1750. By an unknown artist. The print depicts a traffic incident outside the toy shop of Mrs Chenevix at Charing Cross, London. Items of stock are shown carefully displayed in the shop's windows to catch the attention of the throng of passers-by, many of them well dressed. Engraving. The British Museum.

61 *A London Street Scene*, 1835. By John O. Parry. The array of posters exemplifies the huge range of sensational entertainment available at the end of the Georgian period. Oil on canvas. The Alfred Dunhill Museum and Archive.

experiences on country estates, with their neo-Palladian houses and their landscape gardens. Such gardens of the mid-century provided more fully developed versions of the mix of buildings and walks to be found in London pleasure gardens. Their circuitous paths, dotted with buildings and other convenient resting places, were intended to promote philosophical contemplation, as well as providing an opportunity for exercise and sociability. Later landscape parks, with their invisible sunk fences and artfully remodelled topography, drew the whole visible countryside into fashionable culture. Getting into the real countryside for reasons other than sport became for the first time a widespread genteel activity. But such cultural tourism was not restricted to the well-trodden round of picturesque sights. Between 1765 and 1775 Elizabeth Shackleton was far from unusual in setting out to see such modern wonders as the Leeds cloth hall, the new turnpike road and the locks on the Leeds to Liverpool canal.

62 *The Prospect Before Us*, 1791. By Thomas Rowlandson. A performance of the ballet *Amphion et Thalie* at the King's Theatre at the Pantheon, London. Hand-coloured etching. VAM Beard collection.

63 Detail of *Buckingham House, St James's Park*, 1790. By Edward Dayes. Hyde Park took over from St James's Park (and the Mall) as the principal place of fashionable parade in London. Buckingham House was acquired in 1762 as the royal family home. Watercolour. VAM 1756-1871.

CULTURAL TOURISM AND THE APPRECIATION OF THE NATIVE LANDSCAPE

Malcolm Baker

64. *A scene on the River Wye*, 1770. Plate from *Observations on the River Wye* by William Gilpin, 1789. By Francis Jukes. Hand-coloured aquatint. VAM L.1860-1914.

65. *The Ruins of Rievaulx Abbey, Yorkshire*, 1803. By John Sell Cotman. Watercolour. VAM FA.496.

66. A Claude glass in its case, 1775–1800. Blackened mirror glass. [h. 21cm]. VAM P.18-1972.

The idea of Britishness entered public thinking during the eighteenth century and became defined in large part through contrast with the French. One expression of it was the cult of national heroes, such as Nelson and Wellington; another was a growing appreciation of Britain's native landscape. With the French Revolution of 1789 and subsequent wars with France, continental travel became more difficult and tourists began to enthuse about the scenery of Wales and the Lake District.

The tourist parodied by Thomas Rowlandson in his illustrations to William Combe's three volumes of tours by 'Dr Syntax', *Dr Syntax in search of the Picturesque*, *Dr Syntax in search of Consolation* and *Dr Syntax in search of a Wife*, stood for those many visitors who set out for these regions, keen to see antiquities and the remains of a national past and to record Britain's native scenery in their own drawings. A model was provided by William Gilpin's *Observations...Relative Chiefly to Picturesque Beauty*, which played a crucial role in forming a taste for the 'picturesque' landscape, with its qualities of roughness, irregularity and variety. One effect was to replace the idea of landscape as property with the notion of scenery as native land.

Amateur artists such as Lady Farnborough executed 'sketchbooks' with finished views of sites celebrated for their antiquarian or natural interest, often drawing with the help of a Claude glass (a tinted, curved mirror named after the painter Claude Lorraine), which concentrated the composition. Such images represent the British countryside seen through the eyes of an increasingly urban population at a time when the rural economy was in a state

67. *Dr Syntax drawing a waterfall at Ambleside*. By Thomas Rowlandson. Watercolour. VAM Dyce 813.

of flux. These same subjects also attracted the attention of professional artists, especially those like Thomas Girtin and John Sell Cotman, who developed the watercolour into a major and distinctively British genre suitable for ambitious compositions that were prominently exhibited at the Royal Academy. This tradition of British landscape painting reached its apogee in works such as John Constable's *Salisbury Cathedral*, which continues to epitomize a certain notion of Britishness. However, these were images of nature intended for exhibition to urban viewers – landscape as elevated public art.

68. *View of Arundel Church*, from a sketchbook with finished views of Sussex towns and villages, 1800–25. By Amelia Long, Lady Farnborough. Pencil and ink wash. VAM E.21080-1957.

69. *Salisbury Cathedral from the Bishop's Grounds*, 1823. By John Constable. Commissioned by John Fisher, Bishop of Salisbury. Oil on canvas. VAM FA.33.

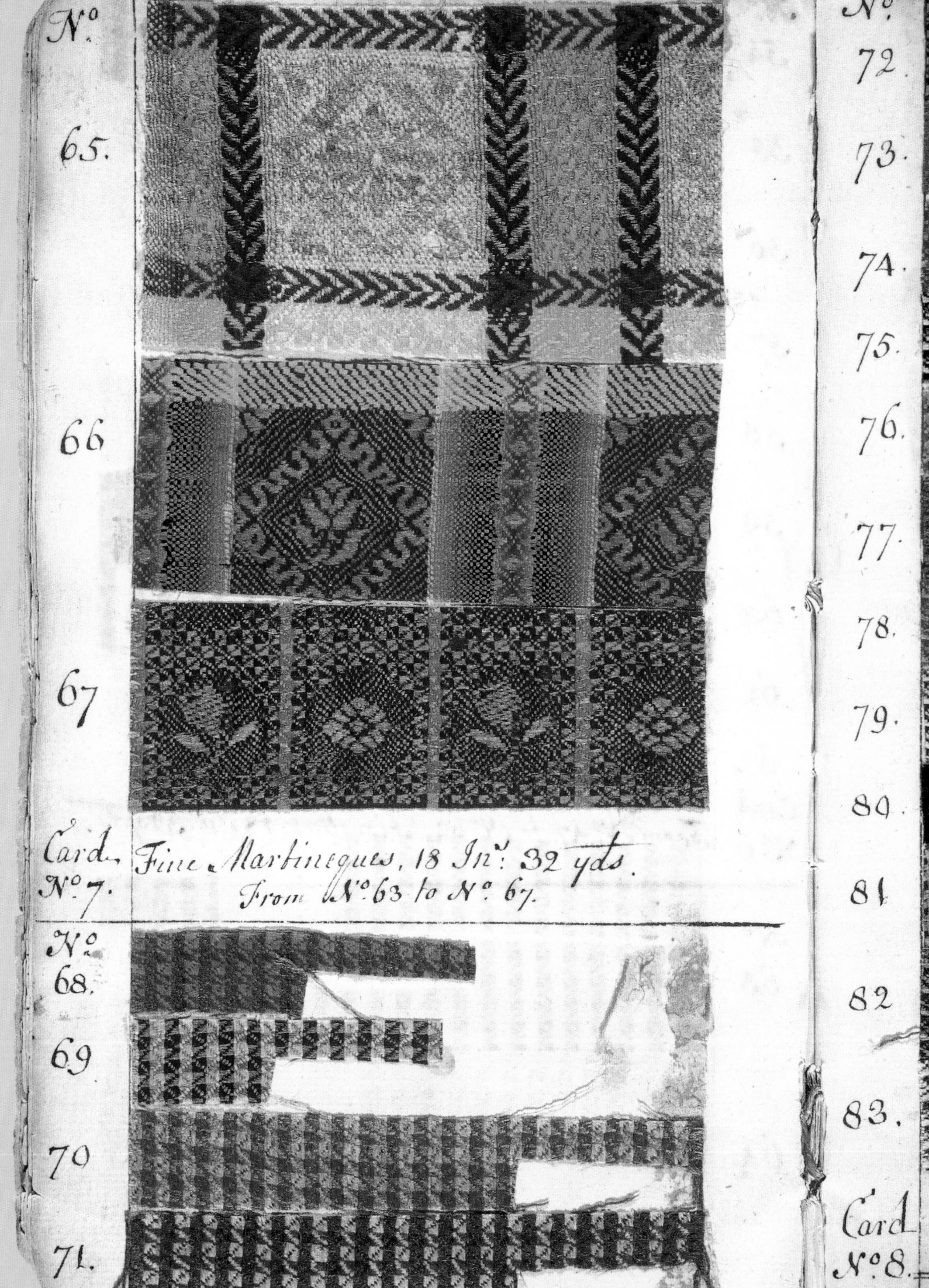

No.
65.
66
67
Card No. 7.
Fine Martineques, 18 Inᵗ 32 yds.
From No. 63 to No. 67.
No.
68.
69
70
71.
No.
72
73.
74.
75.
76.
77.
78.
79.
80.
81
82
83.
Card
No. 8.

CHAPTER 5

What was new?

JOHN STYLES

1. The view from abroad

In 1784 François Lacombe, the author of a guide book for French visitors to London, listed 'the objects that no people can furnish in such a range and quality as the English', along with the goods that the English exported 'in profusion' to France, much 'to the shame of the ministry at Versailles'. The list was a long one, testimony to Britain's growing industrial might, especially as most of the goods could reach their customers in France only by being smuggled through French customs. It included a host of high-design products – cotton, woollen and silk textiles, decorative metal buttons and boxes produced in Birmingham, iron railings and grates, scientific instruments, clocks, furniture such as tea stands and mahogany tables, tin-glazed pottery and the new white earthenware, and even coaches.

1 Page of a textile sample book for the Spanish and Portuguese markets, 1763. Produced for John Kelly, a Norwich worsted manufacturer. The export of worsted dress and furnishing fabrics was very important to the textile industry in Norwich. This book is the 'counter-part', or matching copy, of one sent to Seville and Lisbon, where customers would order from the numbered samples. Worsted (wool) samples mounted on paper. VAM 67-1885.

2 An unknown man, 1780s. By John Russell. The man in this portrait wears a full complement of the steel buttons fashionable in the 1780s. Pastel on paper. VAM P.33-1952.

3 Snuff box, about 1765–75. Made in the West Midlands, probably Birmingham. Enamelled copper painted in colours on a green ground with raised dots and cartouches, in a chased gilt-metal mount. [h. 3.5cm]. VAM C.470-1914.

4

5

5 *Voiture Inversable*, 1782. Drawn by G. Robertson. Engraved by Peter Benazech. An advertisement in French for the non-overturning carriage invented by the British coach maker John March of Grosvenor Place, London. Engraving. VAM 19402.

6

The list demonstrates the vast improvement in Britain's reputation as a producer and exporter of quality manufactures that had taken place since the seventeenth century. At the same time it registers the wealth of innovation – in products, materials, manufacturing techniques and design – that transformed British manufactures during the Georgian era. Lacombe's list embraces many novel kinds of artefact, from cut glass to creamware dinner services. It also includes products – both old and new – that employed new materials, like mahogany or Turkey red dye; new techniques, like transfer printing or power spinning of yarn; and new design ideas, like those developed in the Staffordshire potteries or the coach-building workshops of London. Above all, the list reveals Georgian Britain's capacity for invention and improvement, a phenomenon that astonished, delighted and sometimes, as in Lacombe's case, disturbed foreigners.

This tide of innovation bears witness to profound changes in the ways things were made in Britain. In retrospect, our view of these changes has been dominated by the new steam engines and textile machines that, brought together within the forbidding walls of the factory, have come to define the Industrial Revolution for subsequent generations. Yet it was only in the 1830s and 1840s that the notion of an Industrial Revolution, defined in this way, was developed. Even then, its currency was largely confined to continental European observers, concerned to analyse Britain's extraordinary economic success so that they could learn from it. It was they who coined the term 'Industrial Revolution', making an analogy between the social transformation wrought by the French Revolution on the continent at the end of the eighteenth century and what they regarded as an equivalent transformation wrought by the new manufacturing technologies invented in Britain at

4 Automaton clock made for the China trade, about 1780. By William Carpenter. Clocks like this one were mostly produced for the Chinese market. Clock case, mechanized figures and bells, made from gilt-brass with enamelled and glass paste decoration. [h. 88.9cm]. VAM M.1108-1926.

6 Cut-glass cruets in a cruet frame, with London hallmarks for 1789–90. Frame with mark of John Scofield. Silver-gilt frame with cast and engraved decoration; cut lead-glass cruets. VAM M.46-1960.

7 *Arkwright's Cotton Mills by Night*, about 1782–3. Painted by Joseph Wright. An atmospheric night-time depiction of the two water-powered mills erected by Richard Arkwright in 1771 and 1776 on the banks of the River Derwent at Cromford in Derbyshire to house his cotton spinning machines. Oil on canvas. Private collection.

the same period. The French economist Adolphe Blanqui wrote in an appropriately apocalyptic vein in 1837:

> Just as the French Revolution witnessed great social experiences of earth-shaking proportions, England began to undergo the same process on the terrain of industry. The end of the eighteenth century was signalled by admirable discoveries which were destined to change the face of the world and increase in an unforeseen manner the power of their inventors. The conditions of labour underwent the most profound alteration since the origin of societies. Two machines, henceforth immortal, the steam-engine and the spinning machine, overthrew the old commercial system and gave birth, almost at the same moment, to material goods and social questions unknown to our fathers.

Those Britons who lived through the period did not perceive these developments as an Industrial Revolution in the quite the way Blanqui did. This is not to suggest that they were blind to the manufacturing changes that were taking place all around them. On the contrary, they were obsessed with these changes. Indeed many, like the Luddite machine breakers, were violently hostile to them. For much of the Georgian period, however, those who wrote about innovation tended to treat it as something affecting a wide range of industries and processes, rather than focusing on the all-transforming effects of just two innovations, the steam engine and the spinning machine. The characteristic view was captured by the potter Josiah Wedgwood in 1766 when he wrote to a friend about 'the extensive capability of our manufacture for further improvement'.

7

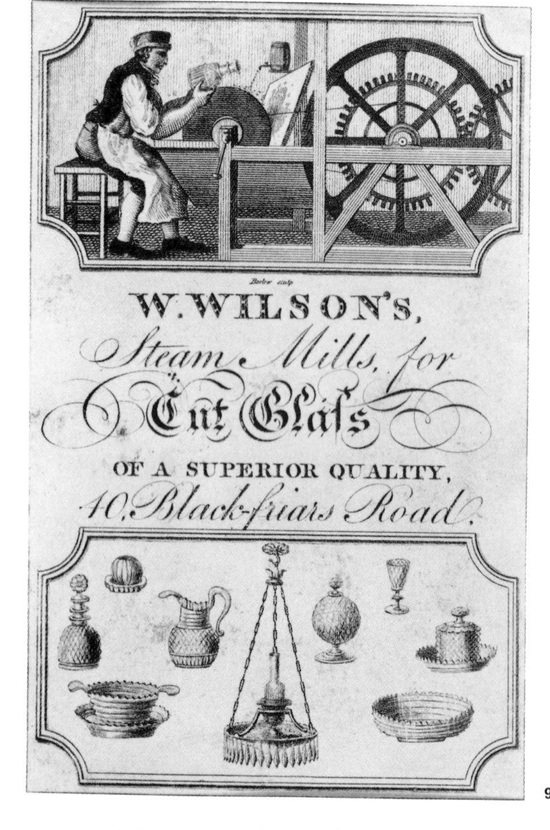

A glance at Lacombe's list of the most competitive British products indicates why the British tended to take a broad and inclusive view of the country's burgeoning industrial innovations. Published in a decade when the new textile machines were beginning to be introduced in some numbers and the first rotary steam engines were being installed, the list contains only three types of goods whose manufacture was to be fundamentally changed over subsequent decades by these particular technologies – cotton textiles, some types of woollen textiles and cast-iron railings and grates. This was because the range of industries transformed by the application of steam and powered machinery was narrow, confined principally to textiles and the production of raw iron. The other manufactured goods in Lacombe's list continued to be made by hand tools or hand-driven machines for the rest of the Georgian era and, in many cases, on into Victoria's reign. This was especially true of the more intricate, fashionable high-design goods. Their manufacture demanded a combination of great manual dexterity and frequent changes in specification, which often proved impossible to mechanize. The persistence of hand techniques does not, however, indicate a lack of innovation. In the case of almost all the hand-made products mentioned by Lacombe (as well as many other artefacts that he did not mention, including entirely new kinds of goods), hand making was itself profoundly changed by innovations in technique, materials and design.

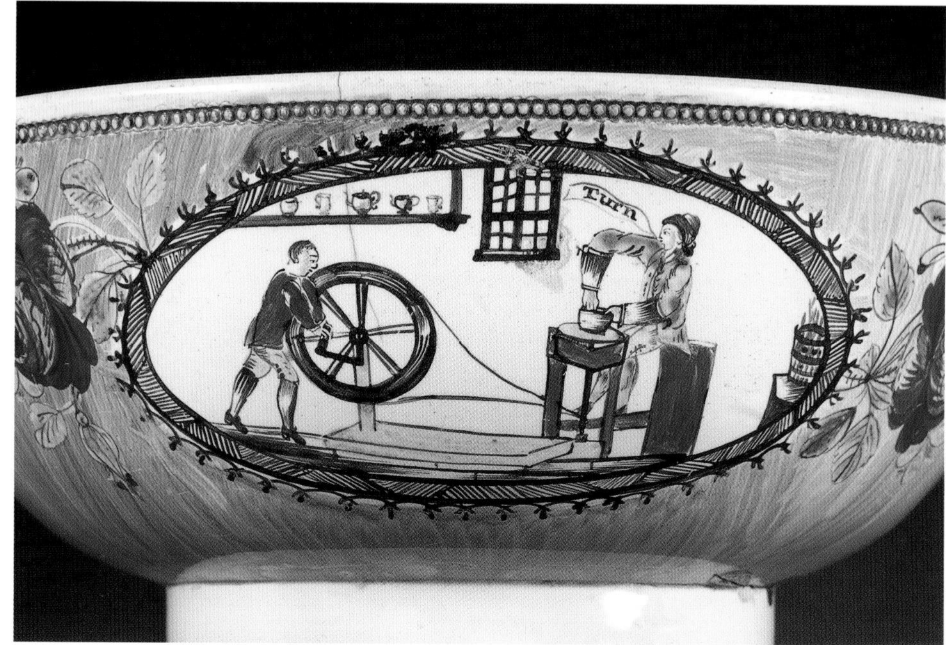

8 Balcony from 12 John Adam Street, Adelphi, London, 1775. Designed by the Adam brothers and probably made by Carron Iron Co., near Falkirk, Scotland. Cast iron. VAM M.429-1936.

9 Trade card for the steam-powered glass-cutting mills of W. Wilson, Blackfriars Road, London, about 1807. Glass cutting was one of the few high-design manufactures to which steam power was applied, although much of the skill remained with the operator. Steam power facilitated deep cutting, but tended to limit the range of cutting styles. Engraving. Corning Museum of Glass.

10 Detail of a bowl, about 1770. Made at the Leeds pottery. The bowl depicts the process of hand throwing in a pottery factory. Turning the potter's 'great' wheel was traditionally a job for boys. Creamware with red enamel decoration. VAM C.22-1978.

2. The size and organization of manufacturing enterprises

Innovation in design and the decorative arts in Georgian Britain was predominantly market-driven. All the manufactured goods on Lacombe's list were produced by commercial firms. The pattern of innovation reflected the commercial opportunities identified by entrepreneurs and inventors and their capacity to use the ideas, skills and resources available in Britain to exploit those opportunities. Britain did not have the state-sponsored manufactories producing prestigious high-design goods that existed in a number of continental European countries, like the Gobelin tapestry works in Paris or the Meissen factory near Dresden in Saxony, where the European discovery of the secret of porcelain was applied for the first time.

This is not to suggest that other influences were unimportant. Innovation benefited in a variety of ways from the protection and encouragement of the British state. The state provided tariff barriers that protected British industries from foreign competition; ferocious laws against the export of machinery and the emigration of skilled workers; a patent system designed to ensure that inventors reaped their due rewards from their new ideas; and, in 1787, the first copyright legislation for design, which gave three months' protection to patterns for printed textiles. Innovation also benefited from a cultural milieu that encouraged the country's élite to take an active interest in scientific, technical and artistic improvement. It became fashionable to visit industrial sites, attend scientific lectures and art exhibitions, join philosophical societies and sponsor design competitions. Nevertheless, the main driving force propelling innovation in materials, techniques, products and design remained commercial profit.

Yet commerce had many faces. Understandably, our received image of commercial manufacturing during the Industrial Revolution tends to be dominated by the big cotton factory, with its hundreds of workers toiling to the rhythm of powered machines. But commercial manufacturing in Britain during the Georgian era was extremely diverse, both in its scale and in the ways that businesses were organized. There is little doubt that the largest industrial firms and their plant grew bigger. The application of the new powered technologies in iron works and textile mills accounts for a good deal of this increase in scale. The 85 largest Lancashire cotton mills in 1841 each employed 500 or more workers. Nevertheless, in most sectors of manufacturing the majority of enterprises continued to remain small. Even in 1841 nearly half of Lancashire's 975 cotton mills employed fewer than 100 workers. Elsewhere textile factories tended to be smaller still.

The small size of most businesses should not blind us to the growing scale of the web of commercial relationships that entwined them. Men like the independent village linen weaver, working up locally grown materials on an artisanal, jobbing basis for his neighbours, became fewer. Even the smallest manufacturing firms were enmeshed in chains of supply and demand that became ever more extensive. To secure both raw materials and customers they came to rely increasingly on the packhorse tracks, turnpike roads and canals that carried goods to every corner of Britain, and on the fleets of British

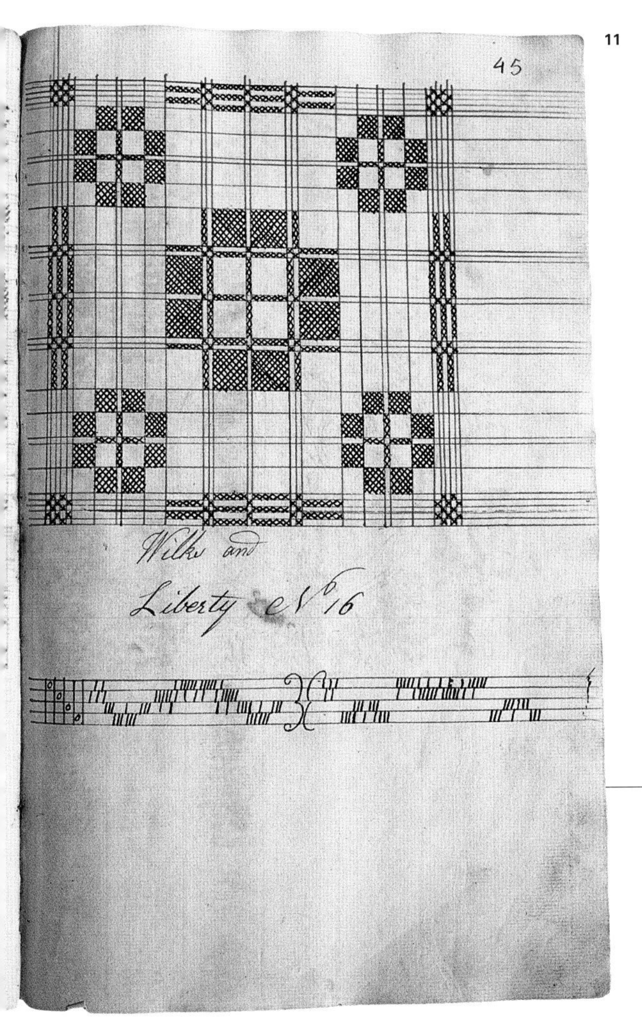

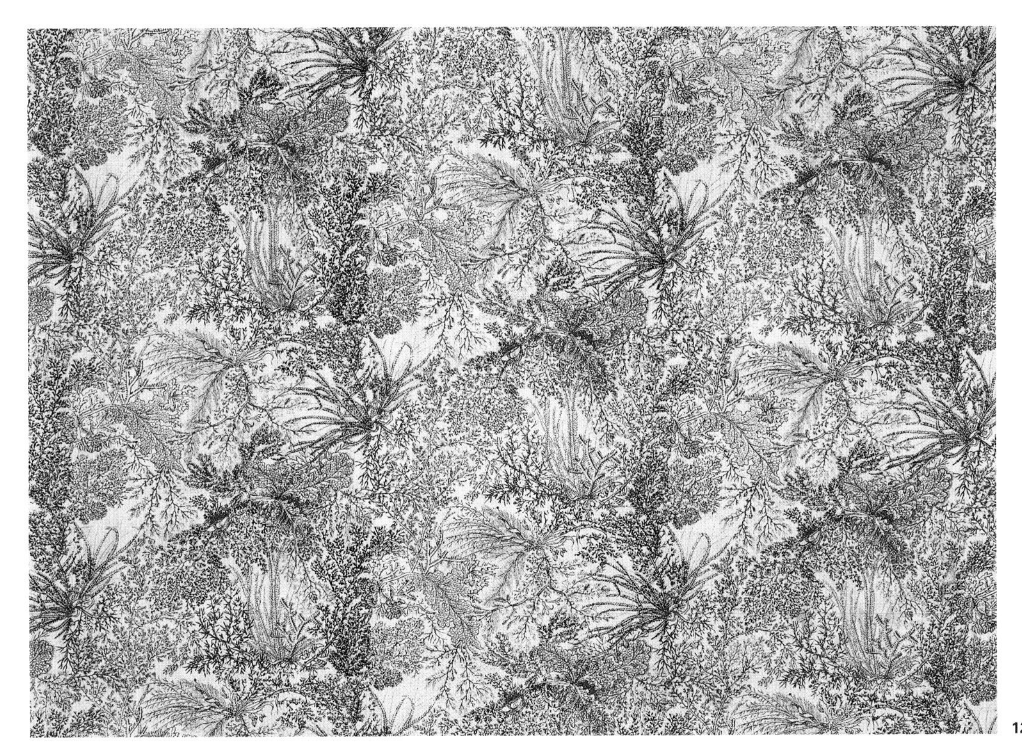

11 *Wilks and Liberty No. 16*, late 18th century. A design for a woven linen cloth drawn by the jobbing linen weaver Ralph Watson of Aiskew, near Bedale, North Yorkshire. From the book of designs compiled by Watson, which he circulated among his local customers to secure orders. Ink on paper. North Yorkshire County Record Office.

12 Printed cotton dress fabric, about 1790. Possibly designed by William Kilburn, one of the London-based designers of printed textiles who lobbied Parliament for copyright legislation in 1787. VAM T.84-1991.

merchant vessels that plied the sea routes to continental Europe and beyond. Increasingly, therefore, purchasers of manufactured goods were reliant on distant, anonymous suppliers. This trend was already well established at the start of the Georgian period and was noted by the author Daniel Defoe in 1726: 'Suppose the poorest countryman wants to be clothed, or suppose it be a gentleman wants to clothe one of his servants, whether a footman in a livery or suppose it be any servant in ordinary apparel, yet he shall, in some part, employ almost every one of the manufacturing counties of England, for making up one ordinary suit of clothes.' The same was true of the household furnishings of a country grocer's family: 'It is scarce credible to how many counties of England, and how remote, the furniture of but a mean house must send them; and how many people are everywhere employed about it.'

Large manufacturing enterprises had, of course, existed long before the emergence of the first water-powered cotton-spinning factories in the 1770s and after that date they were not confined to industries that employed the new powered technologies. There were many large firms that made goods with a high visual design content exclusively by means of hand techniques. In the silk industry of Spitalfields in London, for instance, where the finest patterned fabrics for men's and women's clothes were woven, some master manufacturers in the first half of the eighteenth century employed hundreds of hand-loom weavers. John Sabatier, one of the leading masters, recalled that he began 'to trade for himself in the year 1750, and then employed about fifty looms; that afterwards took a partner, and increased his looms to one hundred'.

14

Each loom required the labour of three or four workers. Many of these weavers were employed on piece rates in their own homes under the putting-out system, under which the master manufacturer retained ownership of the raw materials, but put them out to the employee to work up into a finished product. This form of organization was widespread and embraced more women workers than men. It was characteristic of the production of most textiles, including woollens, worsteds, linens and lace, and of the manufacture of ready-made clothes like stockings, shoes, hats and gloves. It was also widespread in many branches of metalworking, including watches, buttons, buckles and domestic utensils.

13

13 *Matthew Boulton's Soho Works*, about 1781. Aquatint. Birmingham City Archives.

14 *Woman spinning*, 1814. By George Walker. Etched by R. and D. Havell. Plate from *The Costume of Yorkshire* by George Walker, 1814. A woman spins by hand at the fireside in her home. Etching and aquatint. VAM 11.RC.F.19.

Equally large enterprises in the high-design sector were organized as single-site manufactories employing skilled hand labour. The new porcelain factories built in the 1740s and 1750s used little or no powered machinery, but employed hundreds of workers. Earlier, the tin-glaze potteries of Lambeth in London and of Bristol had employed similarly large numbers. In 1786 the London furniture maker George Seddon employed 400 workers in a building with six wings. Around Birmingham the larger workshops making japanned goods, buttons and other decorative metalwares employed 200 or 300 workmen in the 1760s. The largest of all, Matthew Boulton's Soho works, employed more than 600 people soon after it opened in 1766.

Large single-site manufactories like this aroused huge public interest in the eighteenth century, appealing to the taste among the educated for scientific knowledge and national advancement. High-design products were, however, most commonly made by producers working on a smaller scale. In some cases, like the Sheffield cutlery trade, goods of this kind were manufactured by individuals who ran independent businesses virtually alone – buying their raw materials, working them up in a workroom in their own houses, with the assistance perhaps of a single apprentice, and then selling the finished product to dealers who coordinated sales throughout Britain and beyond. But the scale of enterprise associated with high-design trades was typically somewhat larger than this, characteristically taking the form of a free-standing workshop, run by a master manufacturer employing waged workers and apprentices, who were usually numbered in single figures or tens, not hundreds. This sort of business was found in an enormous range of industries, from goldsmithing to coach building, from type founding to cabinet making. Workshops of this kind could be found in most major towns in Britain, but it was London that had the greatest concentration, despite a tendency for some high-design trades, such as cotton printing, to move away from the capital to the provinces.

16

15 *China Painters: The Painting Room of Mr Baxter, no. 1 Goldsmith Street, Gough Square*, 1810. By Thomas Baxter junior. Baxter senior was a painter and gilder who in 1797 set up a porcelain-decorating workshop in London, buying porcelain blanks directly from the manufacturers. The standing figure is Thomas Baxter junior; his father is the seated figure decorating a saucer. For the plate depicted in the foreground, *see 1:24*. Watercolour over pencil. VAM 782-1894.

16 *View of Mr Hatchett's Capital House in Long Acre*, 1783. By John Miller. This engraving depicts the workshop of John Hatchett, the coach maker, in Long Acre, London, the centre of the coach-building trade. Coaches can be seen on display inside the open street front of the workshop. Engraving. Corporation of London.

The Printed Illustrated Catalogue

Helen Clifford

The origin of the printed trade catalogue lies in the engraved books of patterns produced in continental Europe in the sixteenth and seventeenth centuries. These were sources of ornament for use by makers of all kinds of high-design goods. Out of them developed publications like Thomas Chippendale's path-breaking *The Gentleman and Cabinet Maker's Director* of 1754, which served not just as a source of designs for other cabinet makers, but as an advertisement to wealthy customers of his cabinet-making business. Trade catalogues, by contrast, were intended for use by travelling salesmen and wholesale merchants, who acted as intermediaries between manufacturer and retailer. Their role became indispensable as high-design goods came increasingly to be made in long runs, according to a fixed range of pre-determined designs. In this respect, illustrated catalogues resembled the sample cards and swatches that textile manufacturers circulated in exactly the same manner. As with illustrated catalogues, textile samples showing the range of designs that a firm could produce were sent out to distant wholesale customers, both in Britain and overseas. The firm's production schedule was then set up according to the orders received.

19. Page from a catalogue of 'Queen's Ware' made by Josiah Wedgwood, Etruria, Staffordshire, 1774. Engraved by John Pye. Engraving. The Wedgwood Museum, Barlaston.

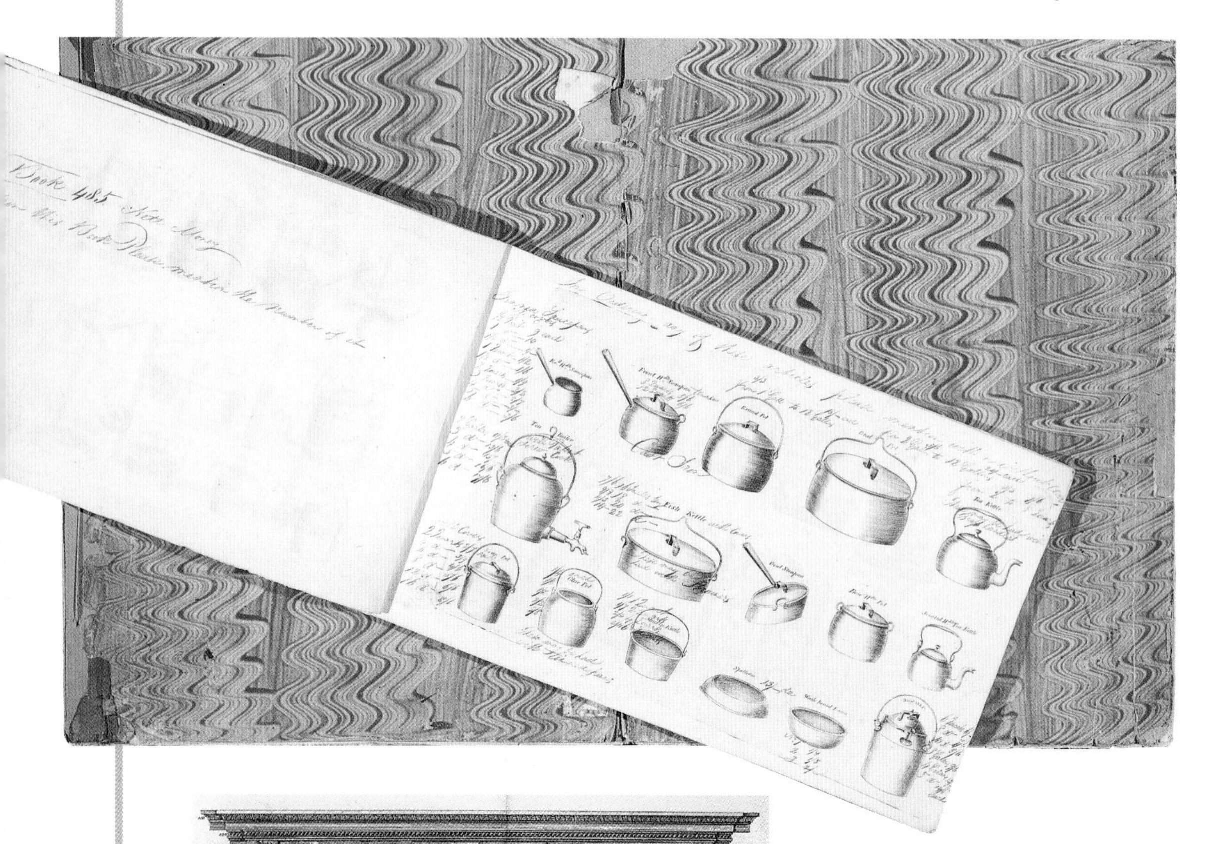

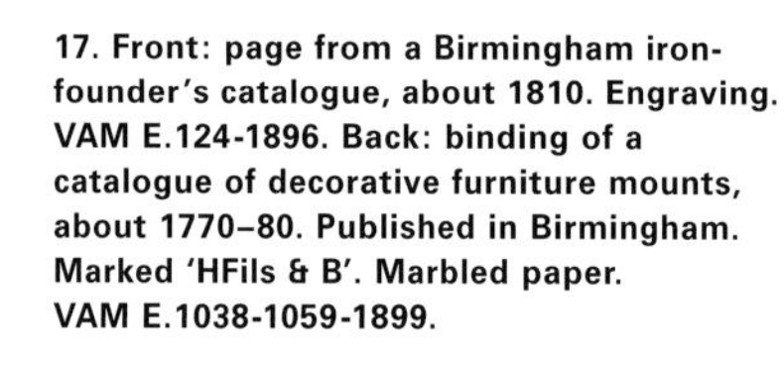

17. Front: page from a Birmingham iron-founder's catalogue, about 1810. Engraving. VAM E.124-1896. Back: binding of a catalogue of decorative furniture mounts, about 1770–80. Published in Birmingham. Marked 'HFils & B'. Marbled paper. VAM E.1038-1059-1899.

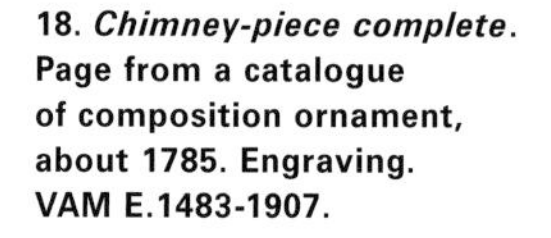

18. *Chimney-piece complete*. Page from a catalogue of composition ornament, about 1785. Engraving. VAM E.1483-1907.

The first British printed trade catalogues were for metalwares, particularly brass, and seem to have emerged in the mid-1760s. Birmingham was the leader in brass production and it can be assumed that many of these early catalogues were connected with Midlands firms. But the range of products marketed by means of catalogues quickly expanded. Josiah Wedgwood produced his first 'Queen's Ware' catalogue in 1774. Catalogues were usually anonymous, because it was often in the interest of wholesale merchants to keep their sources secret; they were marketing tools in frequent, hard use, and it is rare for the original binding, like the one illustrated above left, to survive. The catalogue whose binding appears in this illustration reveals enough about its user – 'HFils & B' – to show that it was intended for a foreign market.

20. Commode with English brass mounts, about 1766. Made in Amsterdam by Andries Bongen. Oak veneered with rosewood and other woods. Courtesy of the Amsterdam Historical Museum.

21. *To Make a compleat Commode sett*, 1780–5. Page from a brass-founder's trade catalogue. Probably made in Birmingham. Engraving. VAM E.2324-1910.

Such catalogues reveal a great deal about the market for high-design goods and the ways in which visual information was transmitted. English catalogues were rarely coloured, unlike later French examples; and some were crude. Early printed Sheffield-plate catalogues were simply engraved versions of earlier hand-drawn designs. Some provided a full-sized image of the objects for sale, and occasionally these can be matched with surviving objects, like the brass corner mounts and escutcheons on a Dutch commode of about 1766. Many catalogues simultaneously illustrated objects in a variety of styles, from the rococo to neo-classical, to suit the widest possible range of consumer preferences.

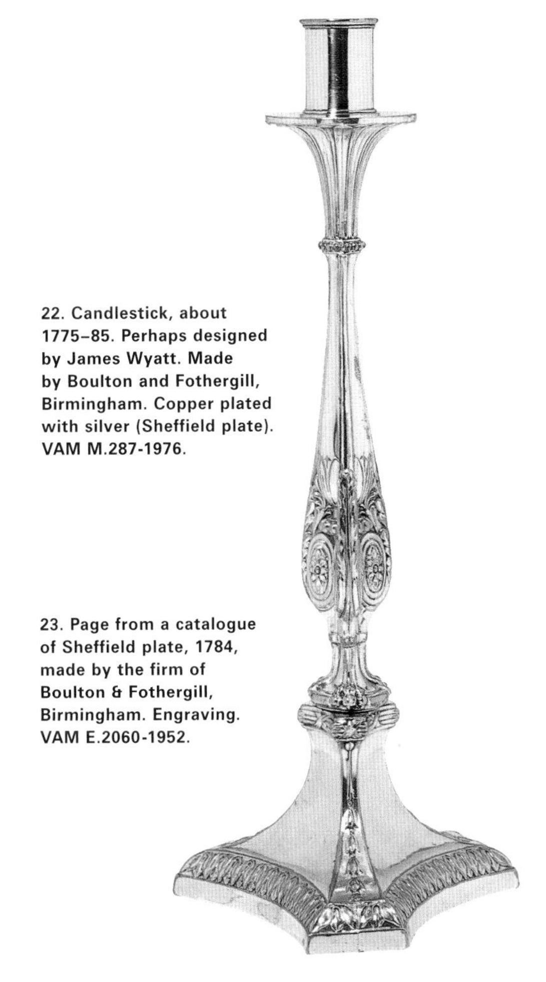

22. Candlestick, about 1775–85. Perhaps designed by James Wyatt. Made by Boulton and Fothergill, Birmingham. Copper plated with silver (Sheffield plate). VAM M.287-1976.

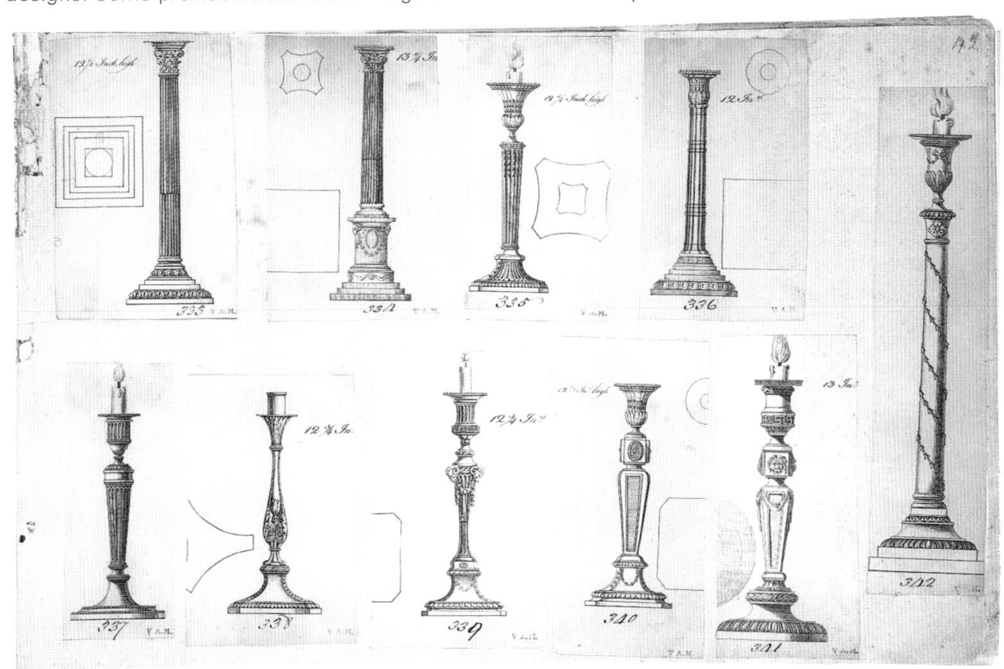

23. Page from a catalogue of Sheffield plate, 1784, made by the firm of Boulton & Fothergill, Birmingham. Engraving. VAM E.2060-1952.

3. Craft skill and the division of labour

Diverse though British manufacturing may have been in terms of the size of firms and the way they were organized, it did have a number of common features. Foreigners were especially alert to these. As Britain in the early Georgian years became an initiator of industrial innovation, rather than an importer of innovations from overseas, foreigners were attracted to discover the secrets of British industrial success. They identified a number of distinctive features of British manufacturing that seemed to make it so competitive. Among the characteristics most often mentioned were British inventiveness, British manufacturers' dedication to producing goods to high specifications for the middle and lower levels of the market, the use of coal as the prime source of heat for a host of manufacturing processes, the widespread application of labour-saving machinery (both hand- and power-driven) and the intensity of the division of labour between workers.

This last characteristic made a particular impact. Le Turc, a French industrial spy, reported in 1786 that 'there is no country where labour is so divided as here. No worker can explain to you the chain of operations, being perpetually occupied with one small part: listen to him on anything outside that and you will be burdened with error. This division is well-intentioned, thus resulting in inexpensive handwork [and] the perfection of the work.' Intense specialization of skills and work tasks was found throughout British manufacturing, but it was in the high-design industries in particular that the division of labour marked Britain out from her European neighbours. On the continent, guild regulations often insisted on a comprehensive training for skilled workers and imposed restrictions on the master manufacturers' ability to subcontract work to specialists. In London and other leading centres of high-design manufacture, guild regulation of the organization of production and the content of training was ineffectual by the Georgian period. The author of a review of the London trades recognized this in 1747 when he pointed out that:

> the goldsmith employs several distinct workmen, almost as many as there are different articles in his shop; for in this great city there are hands that excel in every branch, and are constantly employed but in that one of which they are masters. This gives us an advantage over many foreign nations in this article, as they are obliged to employ the same hand in every branch of the trade, and it is impossible to expect that a man employed in such an infinite variety can finish his work to any perfection, at least, not so much as he who is constantly employed in one thing.

As this description makes clear, there was a division of labour not simply within a single workshop, but between different workshops. Typical of the larger London goldsmiths was the firm of Parker and Wakelin, whose retail shop was in Panton Street, off the Haymarket in the West End. The firm operated a network of 75 subcontractors in the 1760s, most of them specialists in particular processes or in the making of specific types of object. What was true of goldsmithing was equally true of a host of other high-design trades, including those that made goods on a bespoke basis to individual customers' requirements, like the coach makers, and those that produced a limited range of products in batches to pre-set specifications, like the hatters. Subcontracting work outside the main workshop was the norm throughout the high-design sector, especially in London. It provided access to skills that were not required frequently enough to justify employment of a full-time specialist worker in the master's workshop. It also enabled masters to limit their own manufacturing activities or even to become pure retailers, while still handling a wide range of product types.

24

24 Tea canister, about 1765. Mark of John Parker and Edward Wakelin. This canister was sold through Parker and Wakelin's shop, but making it was the work of their subcontractors. James Ansill and Stephen Gilbert supplied the silver cubes for the tea tubs, as well as the cast finials; William Lestourgeon provided locks and lead linings; Robert Clee engraved them; Edward Smith made mahogany cases, when required. Silver, engraved, with applied castings. VAM Lonsdale: Loan:84.

25 Set of 12 plates depicting the division of labour in the manufacture of porcelain, 1813. From *The process of making China. Illustrated with twelve engravings, descriptive of the works of the Royal China Manufactory, Worcester*, 1813. The booklet was published by permission of the owners of the Royal Worcester Manufactory 'for the information of youth'. Engravings. VAM 60.S.145.

THE GRINDING MILL.
1
London Pub. Oct. 1.1810 by J. Wallis 13 Warwick Square

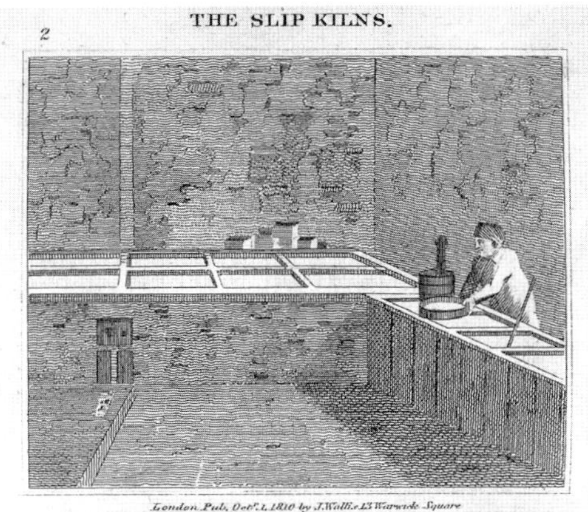
THE SLIP KILNS.
2
London Pub. Oct. 1.1810 by J. Wallis 13 Warwick Square

TEMPERING THE CLAY.
3
London Pub. Oct. 1.1810 by J. Wallis 13 Warwick Square

FORMING ON THE WHEEL.
4
London Pub. Oct. 1.1810 by J. Wallis 13 Warwick Square

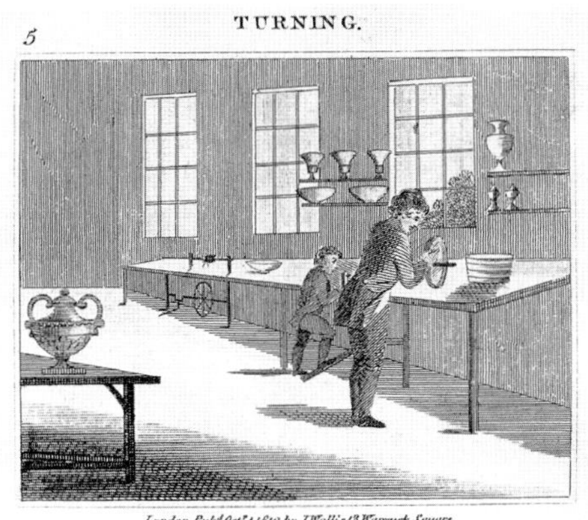
TURNING.
5
London Pub. Oct. 1.1810 by J. Wallis 13 Warwick Square

MODELLING.
6
London Pub. Oct. 1.1810 by J. Wallis 13 Warwick Square

THE BISCUIT KILN.
7
London Pub. Oct. 1.1810 by J. Wallis 13 Warwick Square

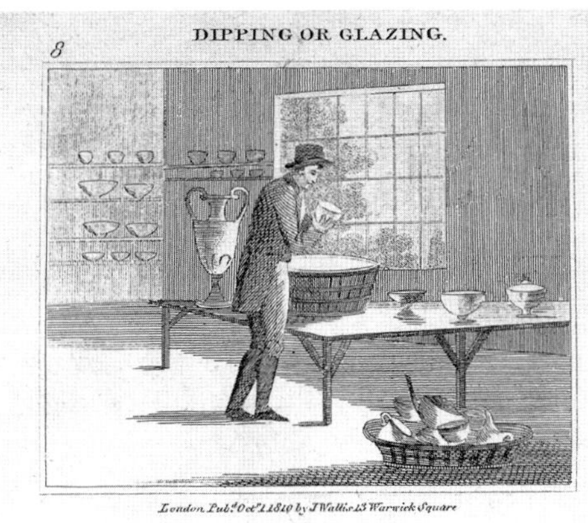
DIPPING OR GLAZING.
8
London Pub. Oct. 1.1810 by J. Wallis 13 Warwick Square

THE GLAZE KILN.
9
London Pub. Oct. 1.1810 by J. Wallis 13 Warwick Square

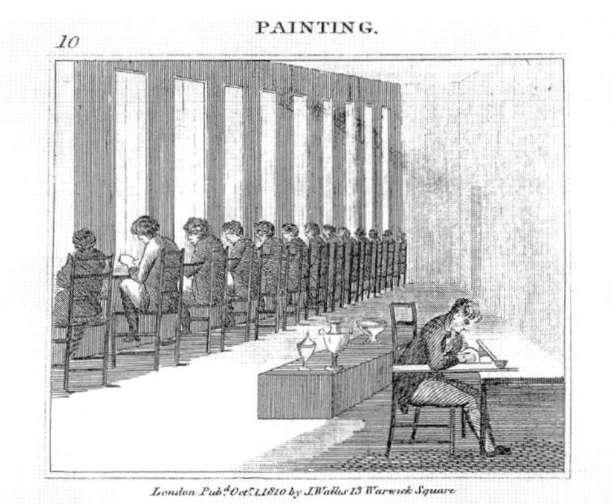
PAINTING.
10
London Pub. Oct. 1.1810 by J. Wallis 13 Warwick Square

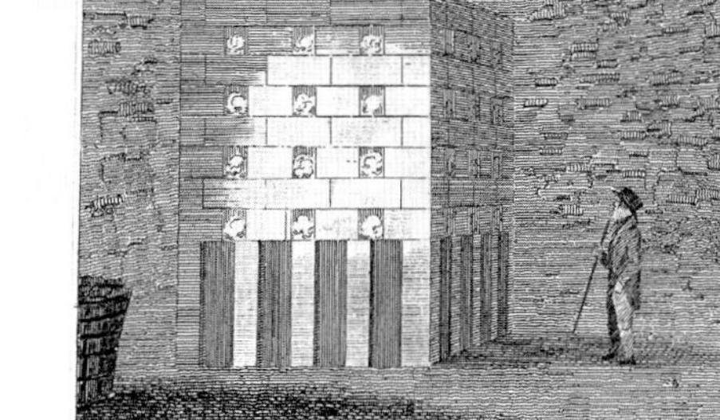
ENAMELLING KILN.
11
London Pub. Oct. 1.1810 by J. Wallis 13 Warwick Square

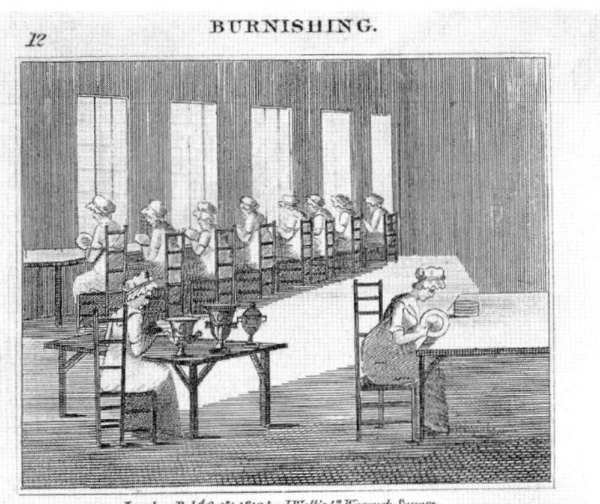
BURNISHING.
12
London Pub. Oct. 1.1810 by J. Wallis 13 Warwick Square

25

26

We often assume that the masters of Georgian workshops personally made the fine objects we now associate with their names. But famous individuals like Paul de Lamerie in goldsmithing or Thomas Chippendale in furniture making should be regarded first and foremost not as master craftsmen but as master manufacturers – entrepreneurs who organized production. When their businesses were at their height they can have handled – let alone crafted – very few of the large numbers of objects they sold that we now associate with their names.

Individuals like these may have played a part, often a key part, in designing the goods they sold, or at least in selecting and authorizing their design. Nonetheless, the work of hand crafting each object fell to a chain of specialist workers, each of whom was dedicated to the efficient execution of a limited task and was not necessarily under the master's direct supervision. Under these circumstances, determining the look of the object – its design – became one more specialist process. In most of the high-design trades it was not the creative work of an individual multi-skilled artisan who designed and made an object from start to finish.

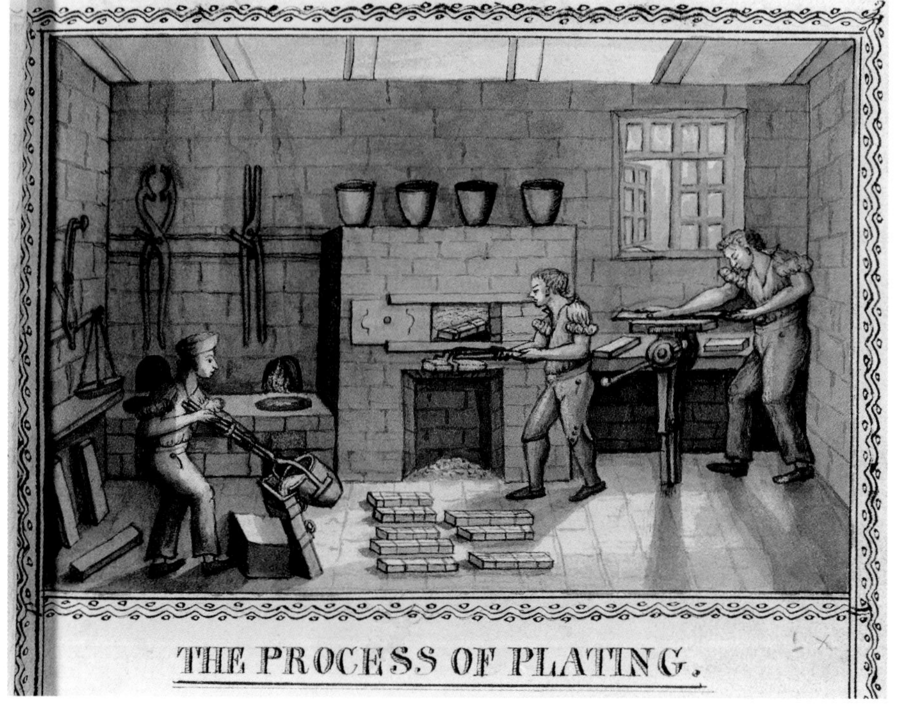

27

26 *Benjamin Vulliamy*, about 1790. By an unknown artist. Vulliamy is pictured in his shop in Pall Mall, next to one of the sculptural clocks he sold from the 1780s. He was best known as one of London's leading clock and watch makers at the end of the 18th century, but his firm also supplied ornamental plate, silver goods, other ornamental metalwares, diamonds and pearls. The firm's records show that most of the manufactured goods he sold were produced by subcontractors. Oil on canvas. Worshipful Company of Clockmakers.

27 *The Process of Plating*, 1830–2. Drawing in a manuscript by R. M. Hirst, 'A short account of the founders of the silver and plated establishments in Sheffield', 1830–2. The drawing depicts the making of Sheffield plate. Left: copper ingots being cast. Centre: silver sheets being fused to copper ingots in an oven. Right: ingots being filed. Ink on paper. Sheffield City Libraries.

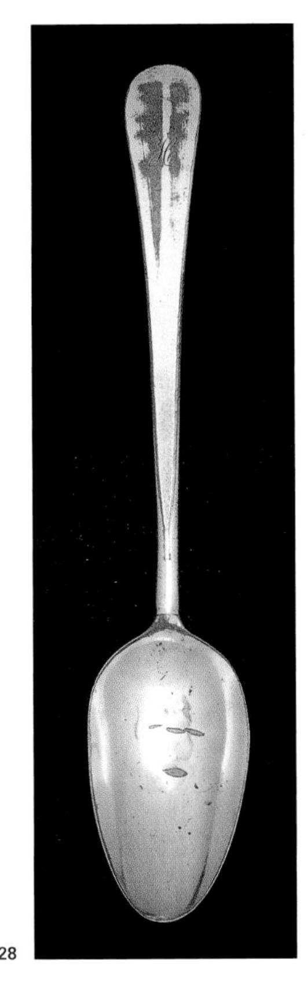

4. New materials

New materials were crucial to the burgeoning success of the high-design manufactures in Georgian Britain. They enabled manufacturers to make an ever-widening range of products, especially those produced to high specifications for the middle and lower levels of the market, a phenomenon that struck foreigners as being distinctively British. One such material was pinchbeck, an alloy of copper and zinc invented early in the eighteenth century that looked like gold, but at a fraction of its price. It was named after its inventor, Christopher Pinchbeck, a London watch and toy maker, and was much used for watch cases and jewellery. Sheffield plate, a fusion of silver and copper discovered in 1742, was another. It is a particularly impressive example, because objects made from Sheffield plate were visually indistinguishable from a huge range of pure-silver objects three or four times their price.

In the seventeenth century innovation in materials had often been a matter of import substitution – discovering how to make things that had previously been made abroad and imported into Britain. This process continued during the Georgian period, most prominently in the case of porcelain, where a whole new British industry was developed from the 1740s and seized much of the domestic market for this most prestigious of high-design products, from east Asian and European imports. But new materials continued to flow from overseas, particularly from the world beyond Europe as British trade and imperial conquest flourished. Mahogany – by the later eighteenth century the quintessential British furniture timber – is a prime example.

At the start of the eighteenth century British furniture makers were already very dependent on imported raw materials, especially walnut, then the most highly prized decorative timber. Mahogany grew extensively in the West Indies, including Jamaica, which became a British colony in 1655. Before the 1720s, however, hardly any mahogany was imported. Yet by 1792 mahogany worth nearly £80,000 and weighing about 7,000 tonnes was being imported into England annually and it had become the dominant timber used to make fine furniture. Imports of walnut had virtually ceased. Mahogany had a number of practical and stylistic characteristics that made it attractive. It was available in sizes large enough to make the dining tables that became an increasingly prominent feature of British high-style interiors. It could take the high polish required to show off table silver. It carved well, developed a deep, dignified colour and had the allure of the exotic.

However, mahogany's phenomenal success was not simply a matter of the wood's intrinsic qualities or the result of a change in public taste. It owed as much, if not more, to the economics of transatlantic shipping and the imperatives of government colonial policy. Crucial was the passing of the Naval Stores Act of 1721, which allowed West Indian timber to be imported free of duty, in order to improve the profitability of transatlantic shipping. This Act made it worthwhile for mahogany to be carried on ships returning from the West Indies to Britain when alternative, more lucrative cargoes were unavailable. The concerns of furniture and furniture makers played no actual part in this decision. It was simply a case of imperial economics shaping innovation in taste.

28 Sheffield plate dessert spoon, about 1800. The silver on this spoon has worn to reveal the copper underneath. Copper plated with silver. [l. 22 cm]. VAM M.47-1992.

29 Mahogany tripod tea table, 1737–8. Probably made in London by Frederick Hintz. The scalloped edges were designed to protect the tea wares, and the hinged top meant that the table could be placed flat against the wall when not in use. Mahogany with inlaid brass and mother of pearl. VAM W.3-1965.

PORCELAIN

Hilary Young

30. Vase, about 1760–5. Made at the Chelsea porcelain factory, London. Soft-paste porcelain, painted in enamels and with tooled and burnished gilding. VAM C.8-1996.

Although porcelain had been made on the continent for almost half a century, Britain did not succeed in making it until about 1745. The first factories were established at Chelsea, Limehouse and Bow in London, but many others followed soon after 1750. It is clear from the sudden birth and expansion of the industry that the possibility of making this white-bodied translucent ceramic material aroused an enormous amount of interest in mid-eighteenth-century Britain.

The earliest English wares were not true (or 'hard-paste') porcelains, but were imitations ('soft-pastes') made with a variety of ingredients in place of china clay and china stone. Bow's recipe included bone ash, which resulted in a tough, utilitarian material; Worcester used soaprock, which enabled exceptionally fine potting; other factories, such as Chelsea, made glassy-bodied wares suitable for light or ornamental use. It was not until 1767–8, at Plymouth, that an English factory succeeded in making hard-paste. Movement of workers and industrial espionage soon ensured that potting technologies spread from one factory to another.

33. Scent flask, about 1749–59. Made at the factory of Charles Gouyn, London. Soft-paste porcelain, painted in enamels, with gem-set gilt-metal mounts. VAM 2000-1855.

31. Salt cellar in the form of a crayfish and shell, about 1752–6 (Chelsea factory mark between about 1752 and 1758). Possibly modelled by Nicholas Sprimont, the design first made in silver by Sprimont in 1742–3 and repeated at his Chelsea porcelain factory, London, after 1745. Soft-paste porcelain, painted in enamels. [h. 5cm]. VAM C.73-1938.

32. Dish, about 1765. Made at the Bow porcelain factory, London. Soft-paste porcelain, transfer-printed in brown and painted in enamels. VAM 414:59/A-1885.

34. Trade card of Duesbury & Co., manufacturers of Derby and Chelsea porcelain, London, about 1775. Hand-coloured engraving. VAM E.1638-1907.

Much English porcelain was painted in cobalt blue before glazing, in the manner of imported Chinese wares; this was a relatively cheap method of decoration. Porcelain was also decorated by painting over the glaze in enamels (metallic oxides in a glassy medium) and by transfer printing. Both techniques were new to the English ceramic industry. Transfer printing was invented in Birmingham around 1750; at its best it allowed high-quality decoration at a low cost per unit. It involved printing an image on to a sheet of paper or gelatin, which was then used to transfer the design to the ware. Gilding was painted and fired-on, and at Chelsea it was often elaborately tooled in the manner of the French royal factory at Sèvres.

36. Plate, about 1755. Made at the Bow porcelain factory, London. Soft-paste porcelain, painted in underglaze blue. VAM C.595-1924.

Pottery figures had long been made in England, but the porcelain figure of the second half of the eighteenth century was a new and distinct ceramic genre. The conventions adopted for English porcelain figures were taken largely from Meissen figures, and many early English figures and wares were in fact directly copied from Meissen examples. After about 1760 Sèvres set the fashions for English porcelain luxury wares. Chinese blue-and-white wares were also copied throughout the second half of the eighteenth century, particularly for cheaper lines. There was no copyright protecting ceramic designs during this period and English factories did not hesitate to plagiarize the patterns of their rivals.

35. Figures of shepherds. Left: about 1750, modelled by Johann Joachim Kaendler and made at the Meissen porcelain factory, Germany. Hard-paste porcelain, painted in enamels and gilt. VAM C.147-1931. Right: about 1754, made at the Bow porcelain factory, London, imitating Meissen. Soft-paste porcelain, painted in enamels and gilt. VAM C.144-1931.

But in the Georgian period more and more new materials came to be invented in Britain. Often invention was a matter of chance. It was while repairing a knife handle that Thomas Boulsover, a Sheffield cutler, found that copper and silver fused under pressure, the key discovery that led to the creation of Sheffield plate. Much invention proceeded by a process of trial and error, developing recipes for dyestuffs or metal alloys in a manner more akin to cookery than modern laboratory science. Nevertheless, the rage for scientific enquiry among a broad, educated public did encourage the application of systematic techniques to the process of innovation. One of the most prominent exponents of such techniques was the Staffordshire potter Josiah Wedgwood, who believed that 'everything gives way to experiment'. During the 1750s, while still in his twenties, he embarked on a series of experiments to 'try for some more solid improvement, as well in the *Body*, as the *Glazes*, the *Colours*, and the *Form* of the articles of our manufacture'. These experiments resulted first in the development of a fine, transparent green glaze and in improvements in the variegated wares that imitated natural stones.

Next, in the late 1750s, Wedgwood turned his attention to improving the lead-glazed creamwares that had been invented in Staffordshire in the 1730s, combining a white English stoneware body and a lead glaze. His improved creamware was to be immensely influential, not least because of his own inspired marketing and the patronage of Queen Charlotte. By the early nineteenth century creamware and its successor pearlware, made by numerous potteries had become the standard ceramic materials for tableware among the middle and upper ranks of British society. Wedgwood went on, in the 1760s and 1770s, to develop more new or improved stoneware bodies. These

38

39

37

37 Tureen, cover and stand, about 1790–5. Made at Josiah Wedgwood's factory, Etruria, Staffordshire. Creamware ('Queen's Ware'), painted in enamels. VAM 344-1854.

38 Tea canister, cover and bowl, probably early 1760s. Probably made in Staffordshire by Josiah Wedgwood or Thomas Whieldon. Cream-coloured earthenware, with a green and orange-yellow lead glaze. VAM Schr.II.295.

39 Plate from *Designs for Sundry Articles of Queen's or Cream-Colour'd Earthen-Ware, Manufactured by Hartley, Greens and Co. at Leeds Pottery,* published in Leeds, 1794. The pattern book of the creamware products of the Leeds Pottery, one of the leading firms producing creamware for British and overseas customers in the 1790s, with title-pages and descriptive lists of the contents in English, French and Dutch. Engraving. VAM 96.A.41.

included black basalt and jasper, intended for use in ornamental pieces in the new neo-classical style, such as vases, plaques and portrait medallions. Perfecting jasper required thousands of meticulously recorded experiments, as well as the development of a specialized kiln and a thermometer to measure kiln temperatures. Wedgwood's life-long commitment to a systematic, experimental approach towards innovation was recognized in 1783 when he was elected a Fellow of the Royal Society.

41

5. New techniques

It was innovation in the way things were made that had the greatest impact on foreign visitors to Britain during the Georgian era. They identified two features of Georgian manufacturing as especially distinctive. The first was the use of coal, and its derivative coke, in virtually the whole range of industrial processes where heat was required, from the refining of metals to the firing of pottery kilns. For continental Europeans, familiar with the use of wood or charcoal for such purposes, this seemed odd, especially as coal was notorious for containing noxious impurities that could easily damage delicate, expensive materials. Readily accessible coal deposits were relatively rare on the continent, but coal was abundant in Britain. Its use freed British manufacturers from reliance on limited and increasingly expensive supplies of timber fuel.

In the course of the Georgian period it also became clear that coke allowed the processing of basic materials on a much larger scale, and therefore more cheaply, than was possible with charcoal. The development of huge blast furnaces for converting iron ore into pig iron, like those built at the Cyfarthfa works in Merthyr Tydfil in the 1790s, would have been impossible without the use of coke. Smelting iron ore with coke only became widespread after 1750, allowing a huge increase in the production of cast-iron grates and other decorative ironwares. But the initial breakthrough in iron smelting with coke had been made by Abraham Darby at Coalbrookdale in Shropshire in 1709 and it is important to remember that iron was almost the last of the major metals to be converted to smelting with a coal-based fuel. The application of coal and coke firing to the smelting and refining of copper, lead, brass and a host of other materials used in high-design manufactures had already been completed during the century before the accession of George I in 1714, principally by means of the reverberatory furnace, which separated the fuel

40

42

40 Tray of Josiah Wedgwood's jasper trials, about 1773–6. Each trial piece is marked with a number that corresponds to an entry in Wedgwood's 'Experiment Book'. Jasper trial pieces, mounted in a wooden tray. Wedgwood Museum, Barlaston.

41 Buckle with a jasper plaque, about 1780–90. Cut steel and jasper. VAM M.3-1969.

42 *Cyfarthfa Ironworks*, about 1795. By Julius Caesar Ibbetson the Elder. Men working hot iron at the Cyfarthfa ironworks, Merthyr Tydfil, south Wales, one of the largest ironworks of the period. Watercolour. Cyfarthfa Castle Museum and Art Gallery.

and its impurities from the material. The fact that this innovation began to excite the general attention of overseas commentators only in the Georgian period is testimony to the novelty of foreign interest in British manufacturing.

The second characteristic of Georgian manufacturing that foreigners picked out was the widespread use of labour-saving machinery. Specialist machinery combined with an intense division of labour could cut costs, not just by increasing output per worker, but also by simplifying tasks so that at least some processes could be taken over by lowly paid child or female workers. At the same time, the use of machinery ensured much greater consistency in the quality of the finished product. These features of British manufacturing were already stimulating foreign admiration well before the invention of the powered textile machines of the second half of the eighteenth century. The French priest Jean-Bernard le Blanc pointed out in 1747 that:

> England has more than any other country of those machines so useful to the state, which really multiply men by lessening their work; and by means of which one man can execute that which would take up thirty without such assistance. Thus by turning a wheel, a boy of ten years old gives a hundred things of steel, all at the same time, that beautiful polish, which few of our French workmen can imitate.

Labour-saving machinery was not confined to the metal trades. New hand-powered mechanical devices proliferated in textiles, too, from the flying shuttle invented by the Lancashire reedmaker John Kay in 1733, to speed up weaving, to the improvement to the stocking frame enabling it to knit ribbed stockings, patented in 1758 by the Derbyshire farmer Jedediah Strutt. Ironically, some of the much-admired hand machines and devices used in the Birmingham light-metal trades for making buttons, buckles, small boxes and other decorative items were already in use throughout Europe in mints, particularly mills for rolling metal into sheets, and fly presses and dies for stamping ornament on to soft metals. In a number of continental countries, including France, their use outside the mint for commercial purposes was restricted to safeguard the integrity of the coinage. Britain imposed no such restrictions, despite the circulation of distressingly large quantities of counterfeit coin, and such machinery was progressively improved and elaborated. Of course, not all labour-saving innovations involved machines, whether hand- or power-driven. Transfer printing, a hand technique invented in the early 1750s, did not require elaborate machinery. Nevertheless, it enabled highly sophisticated engraved decoration to be reproduced at a very low cost per unit, providing an alternative to the labour-intensive process of individually painting each object.

43 Hob grate, about 1790. Cast iron with steel fire grate. VAM M.424-1936.

44 Transfer-printed enamel plaques of the Gunning sisters: Elizabeth, Duchess of Hamilton and later Argyll, and Maria, Countess of Coventry, probably 1752. Transfer-printed decoration probably engraved by John Brooks after 1751 pastel portraits by Francis Cotes. Transfer printing was probably first developed in Birmingham around 1751. It was initially used to decorate enamelled plaques like these. The technique rapidly spread to other centres for the decoration of ceramics and enamels. White enamel on copper, transfer-printed in black with some overpainting also in black; gilt-metal frames. [h. 14cm]. VAM 414:1410-1885, 414:1411-1885.

If the extensive employment of labour-saving machines excited foreigners' attention throughout the Georgian period, it was powered machinery that came to dominate foreign perceptions of British manufacturing by the later Georgian years. The focus of attention was the power-driven machinery developed to spin cotton. This is not surprising. Although this chapter has emphasized that steam power and powered machinery had only a limited direct impact on the making of most Georgian high-design goods, their effect on the manufacture of British cotton textiles was immense. The two initial inventions in spinning, based on different principles, were made in the 1760s – the spinning jenny, invented by James Hargreaves, a hand loom weaver from Oswaldtwistle in Lancashire, and the water frame, invented by Richard Arkwright, a barber and wig-maker from nearby Preston.

The first cotton spinning factories relied on water, horse or, in the case of the spinning jenny, human muscle power, but from the 1790s the largest urban cotton mills began to install the new rotary steam engines invented by the Scot, James Watt. Power spinning brought about a massive reduction in the price of cotton cloth, which underpinned the astonishingly rapid growth experienced by the cotton industry in the late eighteenth century. By the early nineteenth century cotton textiles had overtaken woollen textiles – the traditional British staple – as the largest single manufacturing industry. Moreover, despite the fact that the weaving and finishing branches of cotton manufacture were still not completely mechanized at the end of the Georgian period, the earlier innovations in spinning had already transformed their production and reduced the cost of almost every type of cotton fabric, from plain coarse sheeting to the finest patterned cloths. As a result, during the late eighteenth and early nineteenth centuries cotton garments tended to replace many items of clothing made from linen, silk and wool in the wardrobes of rich and poor alike.

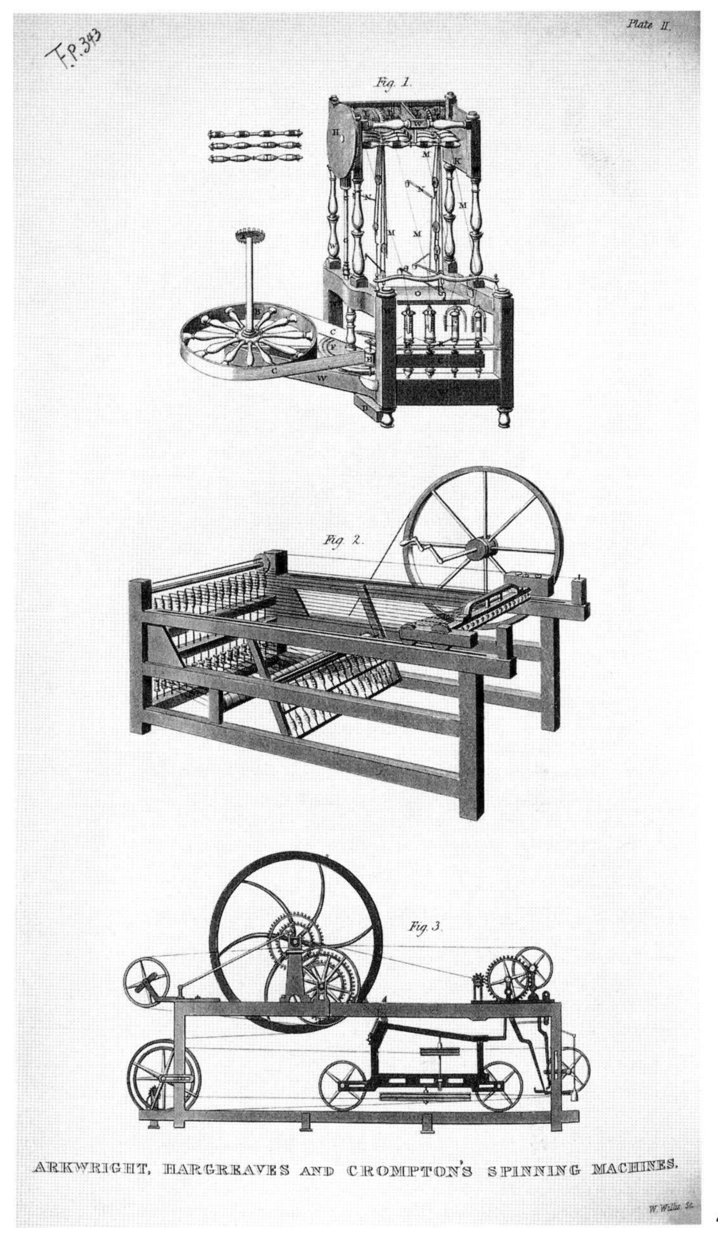

46

45

45 Model of a beam engine, 1821. Made by Peel and Williams of Manchester for the coronation of George IV. This model of a stationary steam engine incorporates the separate condenser and governor invented by James Watt. The linear motion of the piston is translated into a rotary motion, enabling engines of this kind to power factories. Iron and steel. [h. 41cm]. Science Museum, London.

46 *Arkwright, Hargreaves and Crompton's Spinning Machines*, 1857. Engraved by W. Willis. Plate from *History of the Worsted Manufacture in England* by John James, 1857. From top to bottom: Richard Arkwright's water frame of 1769; James Hargreaves's spinning jenny of 1764; Samuel Crompton's spinning mule of 1779. Engraving. VAM 43.E.8.

PRINTED TEXTILES

Clare Browne

By the mid-eighteenth century woodblock printing on cotton and linen textiles had developed to a high standard, even though the home market was affected by legislation protecting the silk and wool industries. The dyeing techniques used to produce the strong, fast colours on imported Indian chintzes, which had dazzled European customers in the seventeenth century, had been mastered and colour ranges were further developed with the introduction of 'pencilling' of indigo in the 1730s and 'china blue' by the early 1740s. A commentator on the state of British textile arts in 1756 wrote, 'chintz...can imitate the richest silk brocades, with a great variety of beautiful colours'.

Until this time, textile printing from engraved metal plates was restricted to the use of non-washable printers' ink. Francis Nixon from Drumcondra in Ireland was the first manufacturer to adapt the technique so that a mordant or dye could be printed from copper plates. He was advertising 'printed Linens, done from Metal Plates (a method never before practised)' in Dublin in 1752, and by 1757 he had brought the technique to England, joining in partnership with George Amyand at Phippsbridge in Surrey. Fine engraved designs on a large scale were now possible, and with the outstanding results that the technique achieved it was quickly adopted by textile printers around London. For the next 30 years plate-printed furnishings of high quality in terms of both design and production were manufactured at printworks like Bromley Hall. The standard of woodblock cutting also continued to be refined, achieving a crispness of detail that could realize the fine drawing of designers such as William Kilburn.

47. Page from a pattern book of printed textile designs, 1760–1800. From the factory run by members of the Ollive, Talwin and Foster families at Bromley Hall, London. The design taken from illustrations by William Kilburn in *Flora Londiniesis*, by William Curtis, 1777. Impression on paper from a copper plate. VAM E.458-1955.

48. Cuttings of dress fabrics, including printed cottons, 1780–1. From an album of textile cuttings and printed fashion sources put together by Barbara Johnson, 1746–1822. VAM T. 219-1973.

49. Furnishing fabric, 1803. Designed by I. Pincott. Printed at Bannister Hall, Lancashire. Block-printed cotton. VAM T.556-1997.

51. Furnishing fabric, 1770s. Printed by Nixon & Company, Phippsbridge, Surrey, using a copper plate engraved by Henry Roberts, originally for John Collins at Woolmers, Hertfordshire, 1765. Cotton, plate-printed in china blue. VAM T.612-1996.

52. Furnishing fabric, 1769. Made by Robert Jones & Co., Old Ford, London. Linen and cotton, plate-printed with additional colours added by block-printing and pencilling. VAM T.140-1934.

In 1783 a patent for printing from engraved metal rollers was taken out by Thomas Bell. The technique was initially confined to small patterned dress prints, but its potential for reducing labour costs and speeding up production was developed in the early nineteenth century, particularly in Lancashire. By 1815 roller printing was being used for larger-scale patterns, both furnishings and dress, alongside woodblock-printed chintzes, which had continued in popularity.

Chemical discoveries were also contributing to the change in appearance of printed textiles, whose colours had previously been achieved with vegetable dyes. Resist and discharge printing were developed and mineral colours were introduced, such as Ilett's single green – the first solid green available to British printers – and chrome yellow. In different combinations the new dyes and processes were fully exploited and incorporated into the increasing mechanization of the industry.

50. Furnishing fabric, 1818. Printed by Samuel Matley and Son, Hodge, Cheshire. Roller-printed cotton using Ilett's single green. VAM Circ.248-1956.

53. Detail from a design for printed cotton, about 1790. By William Kilburn. Body colour. VAM E.894-1978.

Power spinning triumphed even in the manufacture of fine muslins. At the start of the 1780s, as part of a general shift towards simpler styles in dress, muslin became fashionable for women's gowns and accessories. It was the most prized and expensive cotton fabric of the period, capable of the soft, light, flowing drape required for the styles of women's gown that predominated from 1780 to 1820. In the early 1780s almost all the muslin used in Britain was supplied from India by the East India Company. Muslin was woven from exceptionally fine yarn, but neither British hand spinners nor the new spinning machines could produce the degree of fineness regularly achieved by Indian hand spinners.

The invention of the spinning mule changed all this. The mule, invented in 1779 by Samuel Crompton, a jenny-spinner from Bolton in Lancashire, and so-called because it combined elements from the spinning jenny and the water frame, could spin exceptionally fine yarn. Initially hand machines (like the

54

55

54 *Lady Elizabeth Foster*, 1784. By Angelica Kauffmann. The sitter wears a muslin chemise dress. Oil on canvas. The National Trust, Ickworth House.

55 Muslin dress, about 1800. Fabric woven in India, dress made up in England. Through their cut, drape and colour these dresses made deliberate reference to the costume of classical Greece and Rome. Muslin embroidered in cotton thread. VAM T.785-1913.

spinning jenny), mules were being driven by water and steam power by the 1790s to produce ever-finer yarns. British-made muslins woven from mule-spun yarn began to drive out lower-quality Indian imports in the 1780s. In 1788 the East India Company reported, 'we are convinced however successfully the [British] manufacturers may have imitated the goods of the lower descriptions, that they will still find it very difficult to combat the high estimation in which our fine goods are held'. The Company was wrong. By the early nineteenth century the British could compete with the highest-quality Indian cloth. Rudolf Ackermann's *Repository of Arts*, the bible of high fashion, noted in 1810 that 'the improved state of the British manufacture of muslin goods, has, for some time, enabled many persons to substitute British for India, and so well have they been imitated, that even many inexperienced vendors themselves have not been able to distinguish them whilst new. From these combined causes, for two or three years past, the Indian goods have sunk in the estimation of the public.'

6. New products

Intimately linked with innovations in materials and technique was a proliferation of new high-design products. Sometimes their novelty amounted to little more than minor variations in established product lines, intended to satisfy the public appetite for novelty or exploit a new fashion. Others, like creamware pottery, transfer-printed ceramics and copper plate-printed fabric, represented genuinely new kinds of decorated artefact. But perhaps the most characteristic form of product innovation in the Georgian period was the multiplication of new varieties of existing artefacts. This process can be observed in furniture, where a whole range of multi-purpose, adjustable designs was developed in the late eighteenth and early nineteenth centuries – dining tables with flap tops and extensions, combined writing and work tables for ladies, dressing tables with a variety of concealed, adjustable mirrors. The same process was visible in coach building.

56

56 *Mule Spinning*, 1835. Drawn by Thomas Allom. Engraved by J. W. Lowry. Plate from *History of the Cotton Manufacture in Great Britain* by Edward Baines, 1835. Engraving. VAM 43.D.88.

57

57 Work and games table, about 1820. This multi-functional table was designed for a woman's use. Below the hinged reading surface is a backgammon board, and embroidery materials could be stored in the hanging bag. Rosewood, with mounts and stringing lines of brass; replacement upholstery. VAM W.60-1931.

SILVERWARES

Helen Clifford

In the Georgian period silver maintained its position at the top of the status-conferring hierarchy of materials, while becoming available to a wider audience as a result of new techniques of manufacture. At the same time it faced a number of challenges. These came from cheaper, imitative materials like Sheffield plate, from new finishes like japanning for cheaper metalwares and from materials like porcelain, which could be substituted for silver in many of its uses.

The introduction of the flatting mill in the 1720s meant that goldsmiths could cut costs by reducing the weight of silver used to make their products. The tea canister known as a 'tub' could, for example, be made from flatted silver using a fraction of the metal employed in its predecessors, whether cast or raised and embossed. Die-stamping, introduced in the 1730s, and fly-pressing were well suited to producing the geometric shapes and repeat architectural motifs associated with neo-classicism. These new hand-operated machines allowed lighter, cheaper wares to be made in the most fashionable styles.

60. Buttons engraved with hunting scenes, about 1750. Probably made in Sheffield. Copper plated with silver (Sheffield plate). Courtesy of Gordon Crosskey.

Although silver substitutes like French plate and paktong had been known since the late seventeenth century, difficulties in manufacture meant that they did not offer much competition to silver. This changed with the invention of Sheffield plate, a sandwich of copper between first one and then two layers of silver, discovered in 1742 by Thomas Boulsover, a Sheffield cutler. The process was first applied to buttons, until Thomas Hancock realized its potential for large objects like candlesticks, which could be stamped with the same dies as were used for silver. In terms of design, weight and surface texture there was no difference between silver and Sheffield plate, save that objects made from the latter might cost as little as one-fifth of the price of the same object made in solid silver.

58. Detail of a dessert basket, with London hallmarks for 1774–5. Mark of Burrage Davenport. Silver, cut out by hand. VAM 756:1-1877.

59. Detail of a dessert basket, with London hallmarks for 1776–7. Mark of Ann Chesterman. Silver, stamped out by means of a fly press. VAM 755:1-1877.

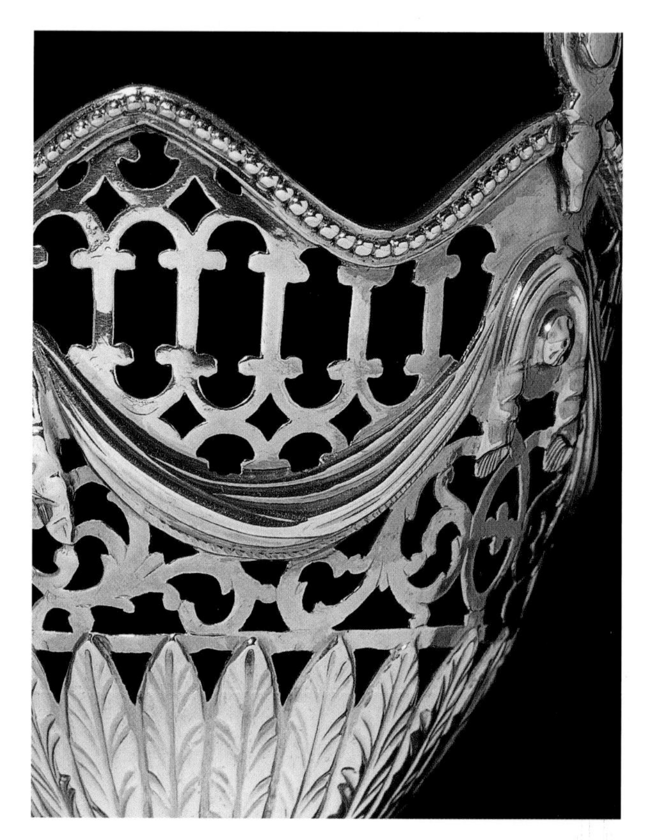

New kinds of silver objects proliferated. The refinement of dining demanded new types of specialized equipment. Tureens, sauce boats and centrepieces, derived from French forms, were introduced from the 1720s; in the 1740s urn-shaped peppers and mustards replaced casters. Smallwares such as funnels, strainers and waiters or trays became more prevalent, and new objects like bottle stands and tickets emerged. Many could be made by means of hand-operated machines. Alongside them were new gadgets, like the cucumber slicer and the tea fountain. John Wadham's patent of 1774 for the tea fountain used an iron to heat the water, thereby liberating the tea kettle from the constraints of a bottom burner and enabling it to adopt the fashionable urn shape.

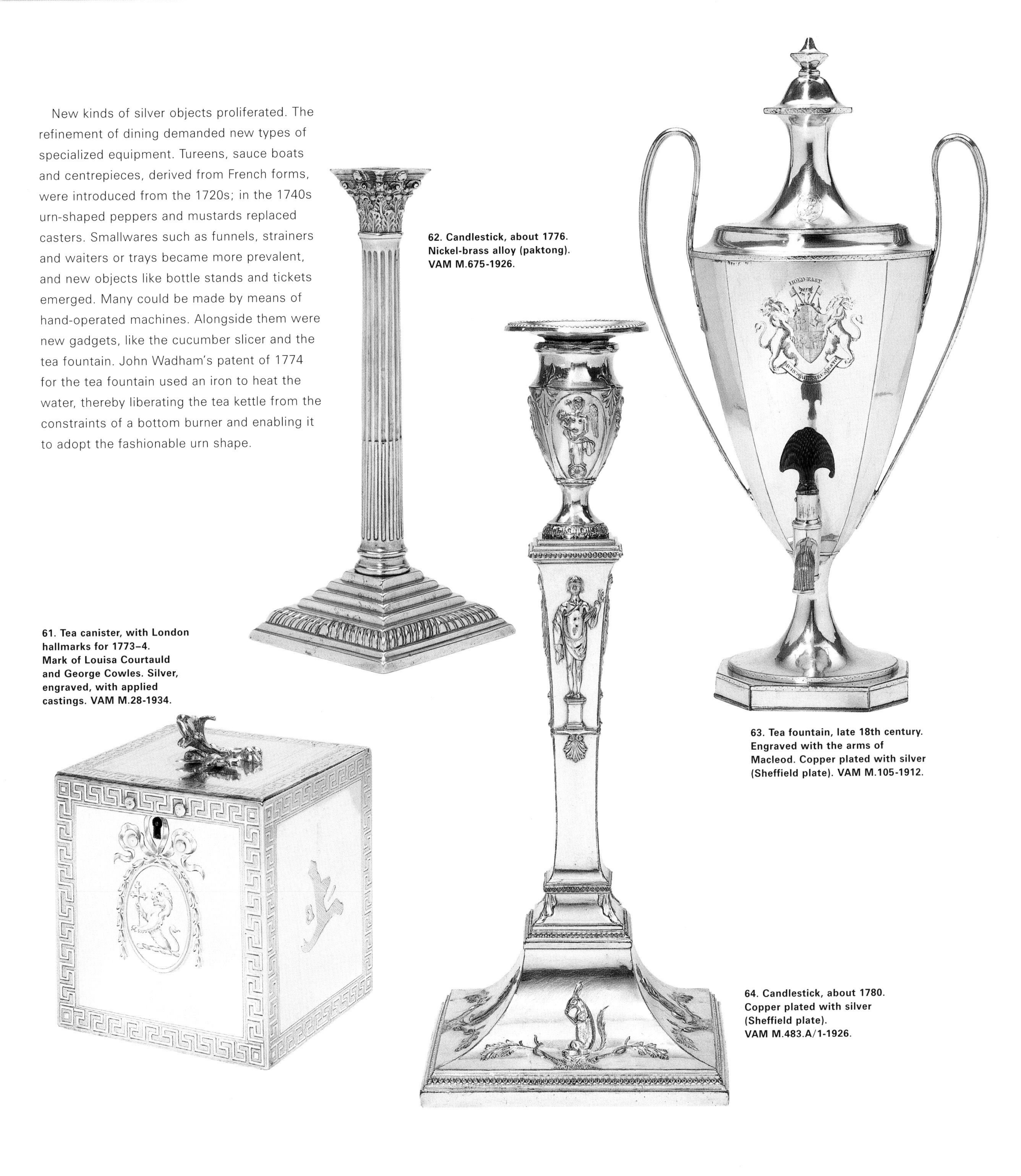

62. Candlestick, about 1776. Nickel-brass alloy (paktong). VAM M.675-1926.

61. Tea canister, with London hallmarks for 1773–4. Mark of Louisa Courtauld and George Cowles. Silver, engraved, with applied castings. VAM M.28-1934.

63. Tea fountain, late 18th century. Engraved with the arms of Macleod. Copper plated with silver (Sheffield plate). VAM M.105-1912.

64. Candlestick, about 1780. Copper plated with silver (Sheffield plate). VAM M.483.A/1-1926.

66

Coaches had been built in London since the sixteenth century, but early in the Georgian period the leading centres of production remained abroad, in Paris and Amsterdam. British coach design was already distinctive at this period, particularly in the use of a body that flared out at the bottom, but this feature was not much copied. By the late eighteenth century all this had changed. The generally held view in continental Europe, expressed in a German magazine in 1799, was that 'the English surpass all other nations in the art of coach-making'. London had become the leading European centre, with a large export trade. British coach design came to be widely copied – particularly technical innovations like the double-bow, crane-neck iron chassis and the S-shaped spring, but also purely aesthetic features like the blacked-out side-window and neo-classical decoration in the Adam style.

Coaches were extremely expensive to purchase and maintain. Their manufacture involved costly materials and highly skilled work, often to exacting aesthetic standards. Even basic models cost between £40 and £300, depending on size, and £40 represented more than a year's wages for a labouring man. The gold state coach built for George III in 1762, 'the most superb and expensive of any ever built in this kingdom', cost over £7,500. A state coach in the most splendid style built in London for the extravagant Irish nobleman Lord Clare in the early 1790s cost nearly £7,000, as much as the annual income of some of his fellow nobles. Ownership was restricted to the well-off, but by 1814 there were 69,200 carriages licensed in England. They were highly visible travelling advertisements for their owners' taste and status, and consequently became fashion items. Late-eighteenth-century newspapers reported frequent changes in the fashions for trim, paintwork, applied ornament and accessories, in just the same way as they reported the latest high-society fashions in dress.

New specialist varieties of coach proliferated – Curricle and Vis-à-Vis, Landau and Berlin – differentiated according to whether the coach was open or closed, heavy or light, driven by a coachman or by the owner. London became an international trend-setter in the development of new types. In 1788 the owner-driven, two-seater Phaeton was the most

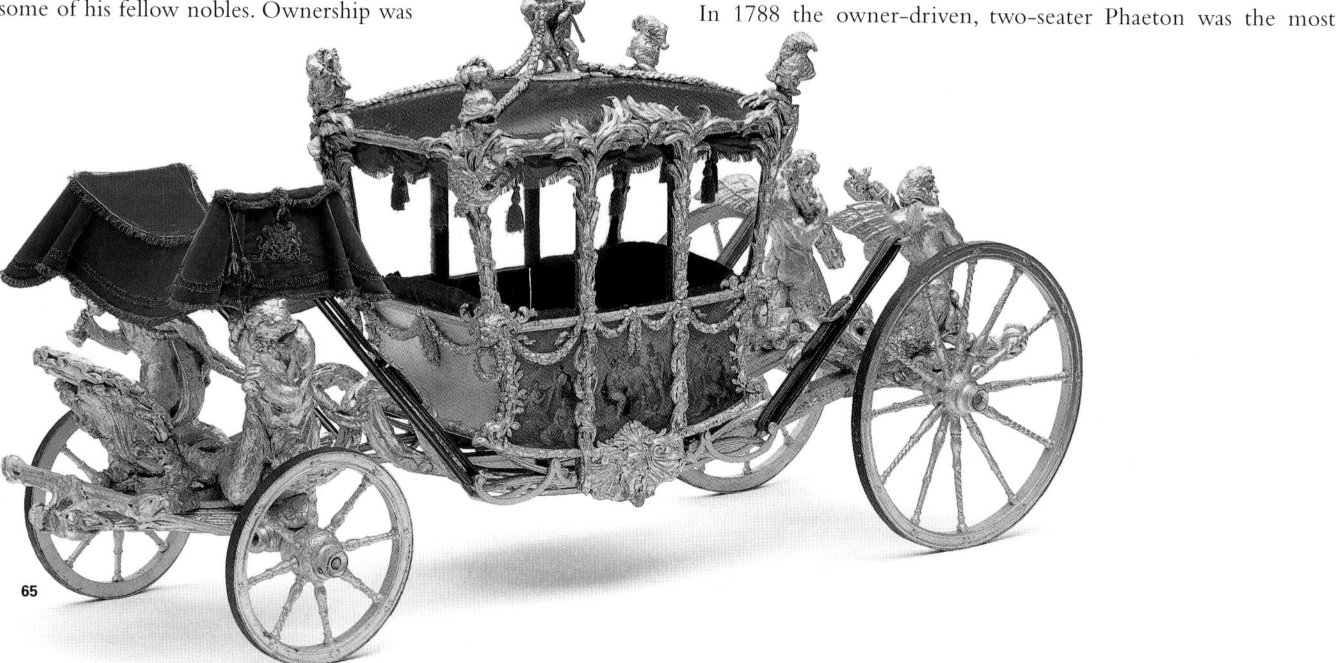

65

65 Presentation model for the state coach of George III, about 1760. Designed by William Chambers. Made by G. B. Capezzuoli and John Voyez. Carving by Joseph Wilton. Painted panels by Giovanni Battista Cipriani. The full-sized coach based on this model was made in London by the coach maker Samuel Butler, with carving by Wilton and painted panels by Cipriani. The slight flaring of the sides of the body towards the base was a typical feature of British coach design in the mid-18th century. Wood, beeswax and metal, gilded and painted. [h. 56cm]. Worshipful Company of Coachmakers.

66 *Design for a town coach*, about 1780–5. Probably by John Hatchett. The design incorporates features that were regarded as characteristically British in the late 18th century, such as the crane-neck chassis, the S-springs and the blacked-out side-windows. Gouache on card. VAM 15595.5.

fashionable summer vehicle, along with the Curricle. The large Phaeton with a crane-neck chassis was described in 1794 'as being a pleasant and easy vehicle to ride in, and, for appearance, has much the superiority over every other kind of open carriages in use'. It enjoyed this reputation for beauty despite the fact that it was a strikingly mechanical object – all wheels, chassis and springs. Mechanical exaggeration was taken to its most extreme in the high-flyer Phaeton, the precariously tall and unstable sports car of its day, which was popularized among dashing young aristocrats by George, Prince of Wales.

Forty years later, at the very end of the Georgian period, the crane-neck Phaeton of the 1790s, far from being the height of fashion, was condemned as 'a monstrous-looking vehicle'. Inevitably reputations rose and fell as new varieties of coach continued to proliferate. What remained constant throughout the later Georgian period was the praise showered on British-made coaches. In 1784 the French guide-book writer François Lacombe had included coaches in his list of 'the objects that no people can furnish in such a range and quality as the English'. In 1837 it remained the received wisdom that 'English carriages, take them altogether, are the most perfect carriages constructed in any part of the world'.

*

By 1837, the year that Queen Victoria ascended the throne, the international esteem enjoyed by British manufactures extended far beyond the construction of coaches and carriages. The opening years of her reign saw Britain acclaimed as the workshop of the world. But early Victorian leadership in manufacturing and technology rested on the innovations of the Georgian era. Global industrial supremacy was Georgian Britain's most valuable legacy to its Victorian successor.

67 Crane-neck Phaeton, 1780–90. Made for Sir George Armytage of Kirklees, near Huddersfield, Yorkshire. Iron, leather and wood, painted; replacement upholstery. Science Museum, London.

Chronology of Events and Publications, 1714–1837

DATES	POLITICAL EVENTS	DESIGN, ART AND SCIENCE	PUBLICATIONS
1714	Death of Queen Anne, accession of George I		Bernard de Mandeville, *The Fable of the Bees*
1715	First Jacobite Rebellion Death of Louis XIV of France	Building of Wanstead House, London, begins	Colen Campbell, *Vitruvius Britannicus* *The Architecture of A. Palladio*, revised by Giacomo Leoni
1717		Thomas Lombe develops his silk-throwing machine	George Frederick Handel, *Water Music*
1720		St Martin's Lane academy of painting and sculpture founded in London	
1722		Building of Houghton Hall, Norfolk, begins Building of St Martin-in-the-Fields, London, begins	Daniel Defoe, *Moll Flanders*
1725		Building of Chiswick House, London, begins	
1727	Death of George I, accession of George II		William Kent (ed.), *Designs of Inigo Jones*
1728		Jonathan Tyers begins to remodel Vauxhall Gardens, London	James Gibbs, *Book of Architecture* Robert Morris, *Essay in Defence of Ancient Architecture*
1729	Methodist Society formed		
1730s		John Kay invents the flying shuttle	
1731		Dublin Society for Improving Husbandry, Manufactures and other Useful Arts established	*Gentleman's Magazine* founded
1732		William Hogarth, *A Harlot's Progress*	
1734		Building of Holkham Hall, Norfolk, begins	
1735		St Martin's Lane Academy, London, established Copyright Act for engraved prints	Bishop George Berkeley, *The Querist*
1738		Herculaneum excavated	Andrea Palladio, *Four Books of Architecture*, English translation by Isaac Ware
1739–48	War of Austrian Succession		
1740s		Benjamin Huntsman invents the crucible steel-making process	
1740		Benjamin Martin introduces the pocket microscope	Samuel Richardson, *Pamela*
1742		Thomas Boulsover discovers Sheffield plate	
1744			Matthias Locke, *Six Sconces*
1745	Second Jacobite Rebellion	Porcelain production begins at the Chelsea factory, London Anti-Gallican Society established William Hogarth, *Marriage à la Mode*	
1748		Building of Strawberry Hill, Twickenham, begins	Samuel Richardson, *Clarissa*
1752	Britain adopts new calendar	Copper plate printing on textiles introduced in Ireland Printed enamel transfers on ceramics introduced	
1753		British Museum founded in London	William Hogarth, *Analysis of Beauty*
1754		Society of Arts established in London	Thomas Chippendale, *The Gentleman and Cabinet Maker's Director* Matthias Darley, *A New Book of Chinese Designs*
1756			Edmund Burke, *A Philosophical Inquiry into the Origin of our Ideas of the Sublime and the Beautiful*
1756–63	Seven Years War		
1757		Building of Kedleston Hall, Derbyshire, begins	William Chambers, *Designs of Chinese Buildings, Furniture, Dresses, Machines, and Utensils*
1759			William Chambers, *Treatise on Civil Architecture* William Ince and John Mayhew, *The Universal System of Household Furniture*
1760	Death of George II, accession of George III	First public exhibition of paintings at the Society of Arts, London	
1761		Bridgewater canal opens in Lancashire	
1762		Building of Syon House, London, begins	James Stuart and Nicholas Revett, *The Antiquities of Athens*
1763			*The Lady's Magazine* founded
1764		James Hargreaves invents the spinning jenny	Robert Adam, *Ruins of the Palace of the Emperor Diocletian, at Spalatro* Horace Walpole, *The Castle of Otranto*
1766	Death of James Stuart, the Old Pretender	Matthew Boulton's Soho works at Birmingham opens	
1766–7			Baron d'Hancarville, *Catalogue of Etruscan, Greek, and Roman Antiquities*
1768		Royal Academy established in London	
1769	Wilkes agitation	Richard Arkwright invents the water frame Royal Crescent at Bath completed Josiah Wedgwood's Etruria works in Staffordshire opens	Sir Joshua Reynolds, first *Discourse*

DATES	POLITICAL EVENTS	DESIGN, ART AND SCIENCE	PUBLICATIONS
1771			*Encyclopaedia Britannica*
1773	Boston Tea Party	Ravenshead plate-glass works opens in Lancashire	
1773–8			Robert and James Adam, *The Works in Architecture of Robert and James Adam*
1775		James Watt invents the rotary steam engine	
1776	American Declaration of Independence		Edward Gibbon, *Decline and Fall of the Roman Empire* Adam Smith, *The Wealth of Nations*
1776–83	American War of Independence		
1779		Samuel Crompton invents the spinning mule First iron bridge at Coalbrookdale, Shropshire, completed	
1780	Gordon riots		
1783		Roller printing on textiles patented Remodelling of Carlton House, London, for the Prince of Wales begins	
1784		Henry Cort's iron-puddling process patented	
1786	Anglo-French trade treaty		
1787		Copyright Act for textile designs	
1788	Death of Charles Edward Stuart, the Young Pretender First British settlement in Australia		George Hepplewhite, *The Cabinet-maker and Upholsterer's Guide*
1789	French Revolution		William Blake, *Songs of Innocence*
1790			Edmund Burke, *Reflections on the French Revolution*
1791			Thomas Paine, *The Rights of Man* Thomas Sheraton, *The Cabinet-maker and Upholsterer's Drawing Book*
1792		John Soane begins to remodel the Bank of England	Mary Wollstonecraft, *Vindication of the Rights of Women*
1792–1815	French Revolutionary and Napoleonic Wars		
1794–1803			Nicolaus von Heideloff's *Gallery of Fashion* published
1795		Building of Fonthill Abbey, Wiltshire, begins	
1798	Battle of the Nile		Robert Malthus, *Essay on the Principal of Population* William Wordsworth and Samuel Taylor Coleridge, *Lyrical Ballads*
1800	Act of Union with Ireland	Robert Owen establishes his model factory at New Lanark, Scotland Henry Maudsley invents the screw-cutting lathe	
1804		Joseph Marie Jacquard patents his punch-card loom in France	
1805	Battle of Trafalgar		
1807	Slave trade abolished in British Territories		Thomas Hope, *Household Furniture and Interior Decoration*
1809–28			Rudolph Ackermann's *Repository of Arts* published
1811	George, Prince of Wales, becomes Prince Regent	Building of Nash's Regent Street, London, begins	
1812	Luddite disturbances	Gas lighting introduced in London streets	
1815	Battle of Waterloo	John Nash's remodelling of Brighton Pavilion begins	
1816			Humphry Repton, *Fragments on the Theory and Practice of Landscape Gardening*
1817			David Ricardo, *Principles of Political Economy* Thomas Rickman, *An Attempt to Discriminate the Styles of English Architecture*
1819	Peterloo Massacre		
1820	Death of George III, accession of George IV	First iron steamship launched	Percy Bysshe Shelley, *Prometheus Unbound*
1821	Queen Caroline Affair		
1822		Charles Macintosh invents the waterproof garment	
1825		Opening of the Stockton–Darlington railway	
1828	Repeal of the Test and Corporation Acts		
1829	Catholic Emancipation		
1830	Death of George IV, accession of William IV	Opening of the Liverpool–Manchester railway	
1831		Charles Darwin begins his voyage on the *Beagle*	
1832	Great Reform Act		Alfred Tennyson, 'The Lady of Shalott'
1833	Slavery abolished in British Territories		
1835		First negative photograph taken by Henry Fox Talbot	
1835–6		Parliamentary Select Committee on the arts and their connection with manufactures	
1836			A. W. N. Pugin, *Contrasts*
1837	Death of William IV, accession of Queen Victoria	Government School of Design, London, founded	

Design and the Decorative Arts: A Select Bibliography

1. Introduction

Barker-Benfield, G. J., *The Culture of Sensibility: Sex and Society in Eighteenth-Century Britain* (Chicago, IL, 1992)

Barrell, J. (ed.), *Painting and the Politics of Culture: New Essays on British Art, 1700–1850* (Oxford, 1992)

Bermingham, A. and Brewer, J. (eds), *The Consumption of Culture, 1600–1800: Image, Object, Text* (1995)

Berry, C., *The Idea of Luxury: A Conceptual and Historical Investigation* (Cambridge, 1994)

Black, J., *The English Press in the Eighteenth Century* (1987)

Black, J., *Natural and Necessary Enemies. Anglo-French Relations in the Eighteenth Century* (1986)

Breen, T. H., 'An Empire of Goods: The Anglicization of Colonial America, 1690–1776', *Journal of British Studies*, 25 (1986)

Brewer, J., *The Pleasures of the Imagination. English Culture in the Eighteenth Century* (1997)

Brewer, J. and Porter, R. (eds), *Consumption and the World of Goods* (1993)

Canon, J., *Aristocratic Century. The Peerage of Eighteenth-Century England* (Cambridge, 1984)

Clunas, C., *Chinese Export Art and Design* (1987)

Colley, L., *Britons. Forging the Nation, 1707–1837* (1992)

Corfield, P. J., 'Class by Name and Class by Number in Eighteenth-Century Britain', *History*, 72 (1987)

Corfield, P. J., *The Impact of English Towns, 1700–1800* (Oxford, 1982)

Daunton, M., *Progress and Poverty: An Economic and Social History of Britain, 1700–1850* (Oxford, 1995)

Davis, R., *The Industrial Revolution and British Overseas Trade* (Leicester, 1979)

De Vries, J., *European Urbanization, 1500–1800* (1984)

Denvir, B., *The Early Nineteenth Century. Art, Design and Society, 1789–1852* (1984)

Denvir B., *The Eighteenth Century. Art, Design and Society, 1689–1789* (1983)

Hont, I. and Ignatieff, M., *Wealth and Virtue: The Shaping of Political Economy in the Scottish Enlightenment* (Cambridge, 1983)

Houston, R. A., *Social Change in the Age of Enlightenment. Edinburgh, 1660–1760* (Oxford, 1994)

Jaffer, A., *Furniture from British India and Ceylon* (2001)

Jenkins, P., *The Making of a Ruling Class. The Glamorgan Gentry, 1640–1790* (Cambridge, 1983)

Klein, L., 'Property and Politeness in the Early Eighteenth-Century Whig Moralists', in Brewer, J. and Staves, S. (eds), *Early Modern Conceptions of Property* (1995)

Klein, L., *Shaftesbury and the Culture of Politeness: Moral Discourse and Cultural Politics in Early Eighteenth-Century England* (Cambridge, 1994)

Langford, P., *A Polite and Commercial People. England 1727–1783* (Oxford, 1989)

Malcolmson, R. W., *Life and Labour in England, 1700–1800* (1981)

Marshall, P. J. (ed.), *The Oxford History of the British Empire. Vol. II. The Eighteenth Century* (1998)

Mingay, G. E., *English Landed Society in the Eighteenth Century* (1963)

Money, J., *Experience and Identity: Birmingham and the West Midlands, 1760–1800* (Manchester, 1977)

Monod, P. K., *Jacobitism and the English People, 1688–1788* (Cambridge, 1989)

Mullan, J., *Sentiment and Sociability: The Language of Feeling in the Eighteenth Century* (Oxford, 1988)

Newman, G., *The Rise of English Nationalism: A Cultural History* (New York, 1987)

Porter, R., *English Society in the Eighteenth Century* (1982)

Porter, R., *Enlightenment: Britain and the Making of the Modern World* (2000)

Price, R., *British Society, 1680–1880. Dynamism, Containment and Change.* (Cambridge, 1999)

Schofield, R. E., *The Lunar Society of Birmingham. A Social History of Provincial Science and Industry in Eighteenth-Century England* (Oxford, 1963)

Sekora, J., *Luxury. The Concept in Western Thought, Eden to Smollet* (Baltimore, MD, 1977)

Smout, T. C., *A History of the Scottish People, 1560–1830* (Glasgow, 1969)

Spadaforda, D., *The Idea of Progress in Eighteenth-Century Britain* (1990)

Szechi, D., *The Jacobites. Britain and Europe, 1688–1788* (Manchester, 1994)

Thompson, E. P., *The Making of the English Working Class* (1963)

Warman, D., *Imagining the Middle Class: The Political Representations of Class* (Cambridge, 1995)

Weatherill, L., *Consumer Behaviour and Material Culture in Britain, 1660–1760* (1988)

Wilson, K., *The Sense of the People. Politics, Culture and Imperialism in England, 1715–1785* (Cambridge, 1995)

Wilson, R. G., *Gentlemen Merchants. The Merchant Community in Leeds, 1700–1830* (Manchester, 1971)

2. Style

Aldrich, M., *Gothic Revival* (1994)

Barnard, T. and Clark, J. (eds), *Lord Burlington. Architecture, Art and Life* (1995)

Copley, S. and Garside, P. (eds), *The Politics of the Picturesque: Literature, Landscape and Aesthetics since 1770* (Cambridge, 1994)

Crook, J. M., *The Greek Revival: Neo-Classical Attitudes in British Architecture, 1760–1870* (1995)

Curl, J. S., *The Egyptian Revival: An Introductory Study of a Recurring Theme in the History of Taste* (1982)

Friedman, T., *James Gibbs* (1984)

Harris, J., *The Palladian Revival. Lord Burlington, his Villa and the Gardens at Chiswick* (1994)

Harris, J. and Snodin, M. (eds), *Sir William Chambers: Architect to George III* (1996)

Honour, H., *Chinoiserie: The Vision of Cathay* (1961)

Jacobson, D., *Chinoiserie* (1993)

McCarthy, M., *The Origins of the Gothic Revival* (1987)

Morley, J., *Regency Design, 1790–1840: Gardens, Buildings, Interiors, Furniture* (1993)

Parissien, S., *Adam Style* (1992)

Parissien, S., *Palladian Style* (1994)

Paulson, R., *Hogarth* (3 vols, 1991–3)

Richardson, M. and Stevens, M., *John Soane, Architect: Master of Space and Light* (1999)

Snodin, M. (ed.), *Rococo: Art and Design in Hogarth's England* (1984)

Stillman, D., *English Neo-Classical Architecture* (1988)

Stroud, D., *Sir John Soane, Architect* (1984)

Summerson, J. N., *Architecture in Britain, 1530–1830* (1991)

Watkin, D., *Thomas Hope, 1769–1831, and the Neo-Classical Idea* (1968)

Wilson, M. I., *William Kent. Architect, Designer, Painter, Gardener, 1685–1748* (1984)

Wittkower, R., *Palladio and English Palladianism* (1974)

Worsley, G., *Classical Architecture in Britain. The Heroic Age* (1995)

3. Who led taste?

Allen, B., *Francis Hayman, 1708–1776* (1987)

Allen, D. G. C., *William Shipley. Founder of the Royal Society of Arts* (1979)

Altick, R. D., *The Shows of London* (1978)

Baker, M., *Figured in Marble. The Making and Viewing of Eighteenth-Century Sculpture* (2001)

Beard, G. W., *Upholsterers and Interior Furnishing in England, 1530–1840* (New Haven, CT, 1997)

Beattie, J. M., *The English Court in the Reign of George I* (Cambridge, 1967)

Black, J., *The British Abroad: The Grand Tour in the Eighteenth Century* (Stroud, 1992)

Bruntgen, S. H. A., *John Boydell, 1719–1804: A Study of Art Patronage and Publishing in Georgian London* (New York, 1985)

Chard, C., *Grand Tour: Travel Writing and Imaginative Geography, 1600–1830* (Manchester, 1999)

Clayton, T., *The English Print, 1688–1802* (1997)

Collard, F., *Regency Furniture* (Woodbridge, 1985)

Dickinson, H. W., *Matthew Boulton* (1937)

Donald, D., *The Age of Caricature. Satirical Prints in the Age of George III* (1996)

Fleming, J., *Robert Adam and his Circle in Edinburgh and Rome* (1962)

Fox, C., *London World City, 1800–1840* (New Haven, CT, 1992)

Gilbert, C., *The Life and Work of Thomas Chippendale* (1978)

Gilbert, C. and Murdoch, T. (eds), *John Channon and Brass Inlaid Furniture, 1730–1760* (1993)

Ginsburg, M., *An Introduction to Fashion Illustration* (1980)

Goodison, N., *Ormoulu. The Work of Matthew Boulton* (1974)

Hallett, M., *The Spectacle of Difference. Graphic Satire in the Age of Hogarth* (1999)

Harris, E., *British Architectural Books and Writers, 1556–1785* (Cambridge, 1990)

Harris, J., *The Artist and the Country House. A History of Country House and Garden View Painting, 1540–1870* (1979)

Hayward, H. and Kirkham, P., *William and John Linnell: Eighteenth-Century London Furniture Makers* (1980)

Ison, W., *Georgian Buildings of Bath, from 1700 to 1830* (1948)

Jervis, S., *The Penguin Dictionary of Design and Designers* (1984)

Lippincott, L., *Selling Art in Georgian London: The Rise of Arthur Pond* (1983)

Moore, A. W., *Norfolk and the Grand Tour: Eighteenth-Century Travellers Abroad and their Souvenirs* (Norwich, 1985)

Myrone, M. and Peltz, L., *Producing the Past: Aspects of Antiquarian Culture and Practice, 1700–1850* (1999)

Pearce, D., *London's Mansions. The Palatial Houses of the Nobility* (1986)

Pears, I., *The Discovery of Painting: The Growth in the Interest in the Arts in England, 1680–1768* (1988)

Pointon, M., *Hanging the Head. Portraiture and Social Formation in Eighteenth-Century England* (1993)

Puetz, A., 'Design Instruction for Artisans in Eighteenth-Century Britain', *Journal of Design History*, 12 (1999)

Reilly, R., *Wedgwood* (1989)

Royal Collections, *Carleton House. The Past Glories of George IV's Palace* (1991)

Sloan, K., *'A Noble Art'. Amateur Artists and Drawing Masters c. 1600–1800* (2000)

Solkin, D. H., *Painting for Money: The Visual Arts and the Public Sphere in Eighteenth-Century England* (1993)

Summerson, J. N., *Georgian London* (1988)

Wainwright, C. (intro.), *George Bullock, Cabinet-Maker* (1988)

Watkin, D., *Athenian Stuart, Pioneer of the Greek Revival* (1982)

White, E., *Pictorial Dictionary of British Eighteenth-Century Furniture Design: The Printed Sources* (Woodbridge, 1990)

Wilton, A. and Bignamini, I., *The Grand Tour: The Lure of Italy in the Eighteenth Century* (1996)

Young, H. (ed.), *The Genius of Wedgwood* (1997)

4. Fashionable living

Andrews, M., *The Search for the Picturesque: Landscape, Aesthetics and Tourism in Britain, 1760–1800* (Aldershot, 1989)

Ashelford, J., *The Art of Dress. Clothes and Society, 1500–1914* (1996)

Ayres, J., *Building the Georgian City* (1998)

Beard, G. W., *Craftsmen and Interior Decoration in England, 1660–1820* (1981)

Borsay, P., *The English Urban Renaissance. Culture and Society in the Provincial Town, 1660–1770* (Oxford, 1989)

Brown, P. B., *In Praise of Hot Liquors: The Study of Chocolate, Coffee and Tea Drinking, 1600–1850* (York, 1995)

Buck, A., *Dress in Eighteenth-Century England* (1980)

Burrows, D. (ed.), *The Cambridge Companion to Handel* (Cambridge, 1997)

Cornforth, J., *English Interiors, 1790–1848: The Quest for Comfort* (1978)

Cruikshank, D. and Burton, N., *Life in the Georgian City* (1990)

Daniels, S., *Fields of Vision: Landscape Imagery and National Identity in England and the United States* (Cambridge, 1993)

Emmerson, R., *British Teapots and Tea Drinking, 1700–1850* (1992)

Fowler, J. and Cornforth, J., *English Decoration in the Eighteenth Century* (1978)

Gere, C., *Nineteenth-Century Decoration: The Art of the Interior* (1989)

Gilbert, C., Lomax, J. and Wells-Cole, A., *Country House Floors, 1660–1850* (Leeds, 1987)

Girouard, M., *Life in the English Country House: A Social and Architectural History* (1978)

Gow, I., *The Scottish Interior. Georgian and Victorian Decor* (Edinburgh, 1992)

Leppert, R., *Music and Image. Domesticity, Ideology and Socio-Cultural Formation in Eighteenth-Century England* (Cambridge, 1988)

McCalman, I. (ed.), *An Oxford Companion to the Romantic Age. British Culture, 1776–1832* (Oxford, 1999)

McKendrick, N., Brewer, J. and Plumb, J. H., *The Birth of a Consumer Society: The Commercialisation of Eighteenth-Century England* (1982)

Mackintosh, I. and Ashton, G. (eds), *The Georgian Playhouse. Actors, Artists, Audiences and Architecture, 1730–1830* (1975)

Moir, E., *The Discovery of Britain: The English Tourists, 1540–1840* (1964)

Oman, C. C. and Hamilton, J., *Wallpapers: A History and Illustrated Catalogue of the Collection of the Victoria and Albert Museum* (1982)

Ousby, I., *The Englishman's England: Taste, Travel and the Rise of Tourism* (Cambridge, 1990)

Rosoman, T., *London Wallpapers. Their Manufacture and Use, 1690–1840* (1992)

Rothstein, N. (ed.), *Barbara Johnson's Album of Fashions and Fabrics* (1987)

Rothstein, N., *Silk Designs of the Eighteenth Century* (1990)

Rutherford, J., *Country House Lighting, 1660–1890* (Leeds, 1992)

Saumarez Smith, C., *Eighteenth-Century Decoration: Design and the Domestic Interior in England* (1993)

Schoeser, M. and Rufey, C., *English and American Textiles from 1790 to the Present* (1989)

Stone, G. W. and Kahrl, G. M., *David Garrick: A Critical Biography* (Carbondale, IL, 1979)

Sykes, C. S., *Private Palaces. Life in the Great London Houses* (1985)

Tinniswood, A., *The Polite Tourist: A History of Country House Visiting* (1998)

Vickery A., *The Gentleman's Daughter. Women's Lives in Georgian England* (1998)

Wainwright, C., *The Romantic Interior. The British Collector at Home, 1750–1850* (1989)

Walsh, C., 'Shop Design and the Display of Goods in Eighteenth-Century London', *Journal of Design History*, 8 (1995)

Wells-Cole, A., *Historic Paper Hangings from Temple Newsam and Other English Houses* (1983)

Williamson, T., *Polite Landscapes: Gardens and Society in Eighteenth-Century England* (1995)

5. What was new?

Archer, M., *Delftware: Tin-Glazed Earthenware of the British Isles* (1997)

Beard, G. W., *Georgian Craftsmen and their Work* (1966)

Berg, M., *The Age of Manufactures, 1700–1820. Industry, Innovation and Work in Britain* (1994)

Berg, M. and Clifford, H., *Consumers and Luxury. Consumer Culture in Europe, 1650–1850* (Manchester, 1999)

Bowatt, A., 'The Commercial Introduction of Mahogany and the Naval Stores Act of 1721', *Furniture History*, 30 (1994)

Chapman, S. D. and Chassagne, S., *European Textile Printers of the Eighteenth Century: A Study of Peel and Oberkampf* (1981)

Charleston, R. J., *English Glass and the Glass used in England, c. 400–1940* (1984)

Craske, M., 'Plan and Control: Design and the Competitive Spirit in Early and Mid-Eighteenth Century England', *Journal of Design History*, 12 (1999)

Edgcumbe, R., *The Art of the Gold Chaser in Eighteenth-Century London* (Oxford, 2000)

Edwards, C., *Eighteenth-Century Furniture* (Manchester, 1996)

Edwards, M. M., *The Growth of the British Cotton Trade, 1780–1815* (Manchester, 1967)

Fores, M., 'The Myth of a British Industrial Revolution', *History*, 66 (1981)

Forty, A., *Objects of Desire. Design and Society, 1750–1980* (1986)

George, M. D., *London Life in the Eighteenth-Century* (1925)

Glanville, P., *Silver in England* (1987)

Hefford, W., *Design for Printed Textiles in England from 1750–1850* (1992)

Hudson, P., *The Industrial Revolution* (1992)

Jones, E. L., 'The Fashion Manipulators: Consumer Tastes and British Industries, 1660–1800', in Cain, L. P. and Uselding, P. J. (eds), *Business Enterprise and Economic Change* (Ohio, 1973)

Kirkham, P., *The London Furniture Trade, 1700–1870* (1988)

Lemire, B., *Fashion's Favourite: The Cotton Trade and the Consumer in Britain, 1660–1800* (Oxford, 1991)

MacLeod, C., *Inventing the Industrial Revolution: The English Patent System, 1660–1800* (Cambridge, 1988)

Marsden, J. and Harris, J., '"O Fair Britannia Hail". The "most superb" State Coach', *Apollo* (February 2001)

Mitchell, D. (ed.), *Goldsmiths, Silversmiths and Bankers. Innovation and the Transfer of Skill, 1550–1750* (1995)

Morton, A. Q. and Wess, J., *Public and Private Science. The George III Collection* (Oxford, 1993)

Rose, M. B. (ed.), *The Lancashire Cotton Industry. A History since 1700* (Preston, 1996)

Rothstein, N., *Woven Textile Design in Britain from 1750–1850* (1995)

Schwarz, L. D., *London in the Age of Industrialisation: Entrepreneurs, Labour Force and Living Conditions, 1700–1850* (Cambridge, 1992)

Smail, J., *Merchants, Markets and Manufacturers. The English Wool Textile Industry in the Eighteenth Century* (Basingstoke, 1999)

Styles, J., 'Manufacturing, Consumption and Design in Eighteenth-Century England', in Brewer, J. and Porter, R. (eds), *Consumption and the World of Goods* (1993)

Tribe, K., *Genealogies of Capitalism* (1981)

Wackernagel, R., 'Carlton House Mews: The State Coach of the Prince of Wales and of the Later Kings of Hanover. A Study in the Late-Eighteenth-Century "Mystery" of Coach Building', *Furniture History*, 31 (1995)

Weatherill, L., *The Pottery Trade and North Staffordshire, 1660–1760* (Manchester, 1971)

Young, H., *English Porcelain, 1745–95: Its Makers, Design, Marketing and Consumption* (1999)

Picture Credits

Albright-Knox Art Gallery, Buffalo, New York. Gift of Seymour H. Knox Jr. 1945 4:15
Courtesy of the Amsterdam Historical Museum 5:20
By courtesy of the Ashmolean Museum 1:40
Birmingham Museums and Art Gallery 1:15
Reproduced by permission of Birmingham City Archives 5:13
Courtesy of H. Blairman and Sons, Ltd. 4:20
Courtesy of the British Library Board 4:18,
© Copyright the British Museum 1:41, 1:44, 3:15, 3:49, 4:24, 4:51, 4:60
Clive House Museum, Shrewsbury, Shropshire, UK/Bridgeman Art Library 1:33
Corning Museum of Glass, Corning, New York 5.9
Corporation of London Libraries and Guildhall Art Library 3:63, 3:65, 5:16
Guildhall Art Library, Corporation of London, UK/Bridgeman Art Library 2:61
The Country Life Picture Library 4:12
Courtauld Institute Gallery, London 3:39
Croome Estate Trustees 2:7
Courtesy of Gordon Crosskey 5:60
Cyfarthfa Castle Museum and Art Gallery 5:42
Derby Museums and Art Gallery 1:32, 5:7
The Alfred Dunhill Museum and Archive 4:61
© English Heritage 2:10, 2:12
© The Worshipful Company of Goldsmiths 1:9
By Courtesy of the Trustees of the Goodwood Collection 1:12
Heritage House Group 2:2
Ironbridge Gorge Museum Trust 1:19
Anthony Kersting 2:42, 2:58, 2:68, 3:1, 3:6
London Borough of Lambeth Archives Department 2:66
© Leeds Museums and Galleries 3:28, 4:4, 4:8
His Grace the Duke of Marlborough and Jarrold Publishing 2:17
© 2003 The Metropolitan Museum of Art, New York 1:26
Courtesy of the Museum of Early Southern Decorative Arts, Winston-Salem 1:24
Courtesy of the Museum of London 1:14, 3:35, 3:58
© National Gallery, London 4:59
National Gallery of Ireland, Dublin/Bridgeman Art Library 4:17
© National Maritime Museum, London 1:21
Courtesy of the National Portrait Gallery, London 3:7, 3:30
National Trust for Scotland 4:43
© The National Trust Photographic Library 2:28, 3:33, 5:54
By kind permission, His Grace the Duke of Northumberland 2:3, 2:4, 2:5
North Yorkshire County Record Office 5:11
Collection of the Duke of Northumberland 3:2, 3:3, 3:4, 3:5
Royal Institute of British Architects 3:31
RIBA Library Drawings Collection 2:11
© Royal Academy of Arts 4:13
© The Royal Collection 2003, Her Majesty Queen Elizabeth II 1:36, 2:39, 3:60, 3:61, 3:64, 3:66
Royal Society of Arts 3:18
Science and Society Picture Library 5:45, 5:67
Sheffield City Libraries 5:27
By courtesy of the Trustees of the Sir John Soane Museum 2:37
Sotheby's 4:22
Stapleton Collection, UK/Bridgeman Art Library 4:23
© Tate, London, 2003 1:38, 1:43, 3:12, 4:14, 4:25
Courtesy of the Lewis Walpole Library, Yale University 2:1, 4:30
Wandsworth Museum 2:46
Image by courtesy of the Trustees of the Wedgwood Museum, Barlaston, Staffordshire 3:45, 5:19, 5:40
In the Collection of Earl of Wemyss 4:40
The Beacon, Whitehaven, and Copeland Borough Council 1:17
Worshipful Company of Clockmakers Collection UK/Bridgeman Art Library 5:26
Worshipful Company of Coachmakers 5:65
Yale Center for British Art, Paul Mellon Collection, USA/Bridgeman Art Library 1:16, 4:50
York City Art Gallery 1:45

Index

Page numbers in *italic* refer both to illustrations and to their captions.